# CHRISTIAN CELEBRATION
## *Understanding the Mass*

CHRISTIAN CELEBRATION:

Understanding the Mass
Understanding the Sacraments
Understanding the Prayer of the Church

# CHRISTIAN CELEBRATION

# *Understanding the Mass*

## J. D. Crichton

GEOFFREY
CHAPMAN

Geoffrey Chapman
An imprint of Cassell Publishers Limited
Villiers House, 41–47 Strand, London WC2N 5JE
387 Park Avenue South, New York, NY 10016-9910

First published 1971 as *Christian Celebration: The Mass*
Second edition first published 1975
Reissued as part of 1-volume *Christian Celebration* 1982
This edition first published 1993

British Library Cataloguing-in-Publication Data
A catalogue record for this book is available from the British Library.

Library of Congress Cataloging-in-Publication Data
Available from the Library of Congress.

ISBN 0-225-66672-3

Typeset by Colset Pte Ltd, Singapore
Printed and bound in Great Britain by
Biddles Ltd, Guildford and King's Lynn

# Contents

~~~~~~

~

*v*

N.R.K.

*velociter scribenti*

# *Preface*

~~~~~~~~

$T$HE FIRST edition of this book (1971) was written at the time of the appearance of the Order of Mass (1969) and the Roman Missal (1970). The book has had a long life and inevitably in some details it is out of date. My publisher has suggested that it should go into a new edition and accordingly I have reviewed the whole text. I have made whatever corrections were necessary, I have rewritten some parts and I have added a new chapter on the Eucharistic Prayers, two of which, on Reconciliation, did not appear until 1975. The other three for Masses with Children are not included in the second edition of the *Missale Romanum* (1975) but they have an interest all their own as possible pointers to the future. Finally, in 1991 yet another Eucharistic Prayer (first issued for Switzerland on the occasion of a synod) was made available in conjunction with 'Masses for Various Needs' (English Missal, nos 1–46).

Within the scope of a book like this it did not seem possible to include any extended treatment of the Lectionary. This too has had a second edition with an important and extended General Introduction. This has suggested a new passage on pp. 199–200. A reviewer of the first edition of my book regretted that I had not given greater space to the Lectionary. I have partly made good the deficiency by my books on the principal part (The Temporal Cycle) of the Liturgical Year in *The Coming of the Lord* (Advent and Christmas, 1990), *Journey through Lent* (1989) and *The Lord is Risen: From Palm Sunday to Pentecost* (1992).

This book on the Mass has been useful, it would seem, to a considerable number of people for now twenty years. I hope this revised edition will continue to be useful. For nearly a generation now most people have known no other rite of the Mass but the one promulgated in 1970 and it is all too easy to take it for granted. If we do, we are in danger of overlooking the deeper meaning of what we celebrate every Sunday. That 'full, conscious and active participation', desired by the Second Vatican Council, can only be acquired by an ever deeper understanding of the rite. It is the hope of the author that this book will continue to help people to that understanding.

J.D.C.

# Abbreviations

~~~~~~

CL = Constitution on the Liturgy.
GI = General Instruction of 1969/70 attached to the *Missale Romanum* of 1970.
OM = *Ordo Missae* (as above).

Other conciliar and post-conciliar documents are given their full title. A number in brackets ( ) after a statement refers, in the case of the conciliar documents, to the section in which it occurs; in the case of GI, to the relevant article. The Instruction is divided into chapters but its articles are numbered throughout from beginning to end (1–341).

For CL I have used the translation of Father Clifford Howell, SJ (Whitegate Publications, Cirencester, 1963) with occasional reference to the Latin as given (with French translation) in *La Maison-Dieu*, no. 76 (1963).

For other Council documents I have used the translations of *The Documents of Vatican II*, ed. Walter M. Abbott, SJ (Geoffrey Chapman, 1966).

Translations of GI are generally my own. I have occasionally referred to that given in *The Order of Mass*, the copyright of the International Commission on English in the Liturgy (ICEL), 1969. The Latin text there translated is that of OM, 1969, and differs from that to be found in the *Missale Romanum* where the revised version is given.

Editions of the Verona (Leonine) and Gelasian Sacramentaries are those of Mohlberg, Rome, 1956 and 1960 respectively.

References to *Liturgy* in notes are to *Liturgy*, now *Music and Liturgy*, organ of the Society of St Gregory.

# Liturgy and
# Contemporary Man

~~~~~~~

A FACT OF OUR time is the mass abandonment of regular Sunday worship. Once, not so long ago, it was remarked upon and deplored. Now it is taken for granted. Yet it is a very extraordinary phenomenon. Throughout recorded history man, in community and publicly, has worshipped in one way or another. Until the nineteenth century the majority of people felt the need to do so and, if not always very regularly, they did in fact join with their fellow human beings in public worship. In this century this practice has ceased. Only a minority in almost every country of the world worship publicly.

To attempt to establish the causes of this phenomenon would require enormous research, the results of which would occupy many volumes. Whether anyone has done so I do not know, but some explanation is required. In the first place, the abandonment of public worship is a function of the abandonment of organized religion. If the 'churches' no longer say anything to you or if you cannot accept their claims, clearly you are not going to join in their worship, except occasionally and for reasons that are not always religious. At a deeper level, it is said that there has been a massive loss of faith in Christianity and this, too, needs careful examination. The faith that some people lost deserved to be lost, for sometimes it was a barrier between them and God, just as the 'image' some people had and have of God is something that ought to be destroyed. On another plane, and without wishing to suggest a reductionist or LCM view of Christian truths, the churches have often been too slow in abandoning impossible positions. One thinks of the Galileo affair in the seventeenth century and the tangled debate over evolution in the nineteenth century and indeed later. The cosmology churchmen have simply assumed and the notions of divine providence they have put about have proved to be incompatible with the scientific world-picture of contemporary man. This is not to say that all he holds is necessarily true or that the church has to adapt her faith (as opposed to her theology). As the Second Vatican Council made plain, the church wishes to enter into dialogue with the modern world, and it is to be supposed that there will be some modification of ideas on both sides. In brief, the credibility gap between the modern man and the church has become too great for him to give his allegiance to it.

Where liturgy is concerned, the difficulties are different and in some ways greater. The Christian liturgy exists in a realm that is hardly open to the intellectualist and sometimes highly rationalistic mind of modern man. If he works in the physical sciences he is concerned with measurement and the exact application of tested principles to a problem, and if he is engaged in technological processes he knows that the *correct* application of scientific principles is vital to the success of his project. His reasoning mind is at work all the time, he is dealing with what he believes to be solid reality (though the picture physicists give of its solidity, in normal terms, hardly justifies such notions), and even if he does not do so, he knows that everything he is concerned with can be tested and proved. The world of liturgy is, on the other hand, a world of poetry, of symbol, a world where one thing often means another. In the eucharist the church says that the bread is not bread but the Body of Christ and then goes on to act in a certain way towards it, bowing to it or kneeling to it or holding it aloft. Water, oil and other elements are used in a quite non-utilitarian fashion, men are invested with mysterious powers and wear strange clothes as a sign that they have such powers. It all looks very much like magic or, more respectably, primitive religious practices that he has read about at one time or another.

Is this world closed to modern man? Or need it be? If the writing of verse has declined in our time, it is perhaps the only art that has. Music, the plastic arts, drama, to mention no others, are in a flourishing condition and there are many with a wholly scientific training who take a keen interest in them. They are aware, too, that the considerable powers of science and technology are at the service of highly sophisticated forms of entertainment on television and radio. Like all of us, they are daily confronted with various art-forms which communicate to them over the whole range of mind, will and the senses. What is in question at the moment is not the quality of the communication but the style of it. If it does not engage the *whole* of the personality it is useless. With a little reflection we realize that we are not just reasoning beings, that there are values that cannot be scientifically analysed or accounted for and that there is a world beyond the pedestrian necessities of everyday life.

We become aware that we have *needs* that cannot be satisfied by a multiplicity of material goods or economic prosperity or political power and it is at least a fair guess that much of the emotional and psychological disorders of our age is to be attributed to the fact that man *is* trying to live on bread alone. There seems to be a wide measure of agreement that the protests and demonstrations of our time and the feverish searchings for something other *in kind* than the materialistic system in which we live are the symptoms of a spiritual malaise. It is distressing to older people to hear that the young who are demonstrating all over the world are doing so because they are rejecting the materialistic way of life that so many have assumed was a good thing in itself. Even the scourge of drug-taking witnesses to a desire for the Good Life, although the means to achieve it are and must be totally unacceptable. Drugs may be mere escapism of the crudest and most destructive kind, there are indeed many, too many, unscrupulous characters who are concerned simply to make money by 'pushing' the stuff, there are many of the young who are moved by fashion or the social pressure of their contemporaries, but the whole phenomenon cannot be explained by simply saying that the young are more vicious than their forefathers.

All this does not add up to saying that religion in general and worship in particular, if adopted, will settle all these troubles. On these terms religion would become simply another drug, the opium of the people indeed. What is necessary is an attempt on the part of Christian thinkers of various competences to show that there are values in religion which are authentic, which accord with the deepest needs of man. If people today can be brought to see this, they will be delivered from the narrow world of materialism and begin to realize what is their situation *vis-à-vis* that world and from this self-realization will come a confrontation with Reality. Such a confrontation may not lead to God or to worship, but it will inevitably pose ultimate questions.

Part of this work has already been done, and while it would be absurd to suggest that existentialist philosophies are going to be the bedside reading of the ordinary man, they do offer a way into reality which theologians, whether orthodox or unorthodox, have been exploring for some years. The great virtue of the existentialists is that they do not start with large and abstract notions but with man in the concrete predicament of his historical situation. Modern people are aware more or less clearly that they are involved in a world of 'things' over which they seek to gain the mastery, but when they have done so they become conscious of the absurdity of everything: what is it all for? This situation may be experienced with greater or less anxiety, with greater or less concern, and a man may feel hemmed in, limited, frustrated. There seems to be a good deal of evidence that this is so among modern people. This is to experience what Heidegger calls the 'thrownness' of man: he is thrown into a world to exist there in his situation, but his whence or his whither is concealed from him and, to lose his anxiety, he can take flight *into* things, into the 'instrumental' world which he constructs for himself, only finally to lose his identity in them. Or, having experienced the void of *things*, he can open himself out to being, and this 'unconcealedness' is for Heidegger simply truth. But before this happens he will have to experience 'nothingness', the absurd, or the great void that the world of things seems to be when he has turned from it. There is one further stage: he now becomes open to being and then the way lies open to him to feel the need for the Being Christians call God. This is not exactly Heidegger's conclusion, but it is where certain theologians have seen his argument to lead, and since he seems to be describing what is the predicament of so many people today we may suppose that this is the way they will find to God.[1]

But there are one or two more things to be added. If a man underwent this experience and found God, it is true, I think, that he would find him in encounter and not through a process of reasoning or abstraction. This might well come later. It is this element of encounter that we find in another, more specifically religious philosopher, Martin Buber. As is well known, he holds that man can have a twofold attitude, the first an 'I–Thou' one and the second an 'I–It' one. Only the first can be a truly personal relationship, involving the whole being. The second is concerned with the world of experience, the world of objects about which man reasons or thinks, or which he imagines or investigates. It is Heidegger's 'instrumental' world. With this, man cannot have a relationship which involves his whole being. On the other hand, the 'I–Thou' attitude is precisely a relationship that is total and complete, a relationship that is expressed and maintained by the exchange that is called dialogue.

This relationship Buber describes as 'meeting' or 'encounter' and is expressed and maintained by the exchange that is called dialogue and represents a true reciprocity. 'Such a relation is direct, and it is also

~
4

mutual, as involving a response which is absent in the detached objective attitude which may be taken up in experience. It is, furthermore, a relation of the whole person.'[2] This is the relationship we must look for and strive after, a relationship that for Gabriel Marcel involves commitment, and as with Heidegger, so with Buber, every 'I–Thou' relationship can degenerate into an 'I–It' relationship. Buber's thought then is intensely personal and it is not surprising that for him 'every particular "Thou" is but a glimpse through to the eternal "Thou" ' who enters into a direct relation with us men in creative, revealing and redeeming acts, and thus makes it possible for us to enter into direct relation with him.[3] Martin Buber writes as a Jew and his sense of the co-inherence of human and divine relationships, the glimpse *through* the particular 'thou' to the eternal 'Thou', strongly reminds one of the gospel: 'In so far as you did it to them, you did it to me'. Buber's thought was no doubt born of a prolonged meditation on the Bible and it is the same source that has produced the 'encounter' theology of Catholic theologians since. As we shall see, this is a necessary basis for thinking about liturgy.

So far, we note that these thinkers (and, in fact, many others) provide an approach to God that is at once intensely personal and concrete. It is an approach that involves the *whole* personality in all his sheer human-ness and over the whole range of his possibilities. It is the con-crete 'I' in his here and now situation who, out of the meaninglessness of his world, looks for meaning and who, whether he is fully conscious of the fact or no, is seeking God with whom he would enter into a living personal encounter. This, it seems to me, is exactly what Christ was saying in all that teaching about the presence of the kingdom or in the Johannine vocabulary about the 'judgement' that is *now*, the *crisis*, the challenge that involves a decision and possibly a division. But in thinking about Christian worship it is on the wholeness of the personality, body, mind and spirit, in its approach to God that I would wish to insist. Man goes to God or seeks to go to God with all that he has. It is not just an intellectual or rational process. You can produce all the arguments from reason in the world, but if a man is not aware of his concrete situation both in what he himself is and where he finds himself, unless he realizes the ultimate absurdity of that situation *in itself*, he will not be moved by reasons. It is not that way that *in fact* he goes to God.

We are the heirs of a long tradition that owes more to Descartes than to St Thomas Aquinas. For Descartes, man was 'an angel in a machine', made up of two constituents of which the mind or soul was all-but a foreign body in the composite. Aquinas's simple teaching that the human soul is not a disembodied angel, was never intended to be such and will never be such, seems to have gone mostly unregarded if one examines the reams of pious literature that have been written in the last four centuries. The notion that a human being is a body–soul composite in which it is impossible to discern the 'seams', whose soul is precisely *human* and whose mode of operation is totally conditioned by the body, seems to be largely unknown to this day. Aquinas's thought may have been 'essentialist' or, rather incautiously, has usually been represented as if it were, but he was in fact fully 'humanist' and saw the importance of the body in every department of human living. It is because this teaching, too simply sketched here, has been disregarded that the body in recent centuries has been virtually excluded from worship. The thought that we can worship God with our bodies has hardly occurred to anyone. Worship in particular and religion in general has been regarded as something mental, interior and private and the more interior, the more genuine. The Mass-liturgy of the last eight or nine centuries has, of course, driven the laity to this attitude, for it was a liturgy that they could only see (though not always) and hear (though again not always) and in which their own activity was reduced to walking to the altar rails for communion. The devout occupied themselves with books of devotion and later, under the influence of the first phase of the liturgical movement, with their missals, and the undevout spent the time as best they could. This situation, I believe, more than anything else, is responsible for the resistance to the 'new' liturgy which is in fact very old.

From what we have said so far, it might seem that this existentialist approach to God is purely personal. In a way it must be. Everyone has to discover God for himself and if he discovers him out of his own experience God will be real for him in a way that no argument can make him real. But does the 'I–Thou' relationship involve *nothing* but God? As we have seen, Martin Buber already suggests that this is not so and Gabriel Marcel carries the matter a stage further. He distinguishes between *Having* and *Being*. *Having* is 'an external egocentric relationship' which gives us power over objects, including our own ideas. This is the 'instrumental' world of Heidegger. We cannot, of course, obliterate it or, in the last analysis, do without it. So *Having* has to be transformed into *Being* 'which brings us into different kinds of relationships, in which the sharp distinction of the self and its objects gives way to reciprocity and existence transcends any narrow egocentricity'.[4] For Marcel *Being* involves not only commitment but community: 'In Marcel's view what is typical of a person is that he is continually engaging himself–for instance, he says "I'll see you tomorrow at three o'clock". But in doing this, he is already existing in community. Like Buber, Marcel finds the *locus* of human existence not in the isolated "I" but in the "we".'[5] Perhaps it could be put in this way: it is only in encounter, between two persons with all the reciprocity that goes with it, with dialogue and mutual giving, that they realize the being or existence that is theirs, that they *are*. Man is not naturally an isolated being, and a sane view of things must reject Sartre's despairing 'Hell is others'. We need to recall the conventional teaching that individualism is not personalism, that, as Gerald Vann said somewhere many years ago, individualism is a kind of materialization of the person, emphasizing what is particular and turning the person into a being who exists only for himself. Two persons find themselves in each other, become persons, and what is true of interpersonal relationships is true in its measure of the relationships that are set up by community. A community is not a miscellaneous collection of individuals but an assembly of those who have relationships between them and who through community come to achieve not merely in measurable output what individually they could not achieve, but an enhancement of personality. They become fuller, richer beings with a firmer grasp on existence and a deeper realization of what they are. This, too, is part of the human situation and through reflection on it in communion with others they will come to a realization of God. It may be that one of the reasons why Godlessness, whether willed or not, has become endemic in modern industrialized civilization is that society has been atomized, people do feel desperately alone, cannot solve their problems because they are isolated from any real and really personal relationships with their fellows.

One of the inferences that may be drawn from the above view of reality is that man discovers God from out of the depths of his personality as it exists in the concrete situation of his life and if, by reflection on this situation, he does in fact go to God, he does so with his whole being and with all its potentialities. You can distinguish in him, if you like, body and soul, but in *fact* he exists in the wholeness of his being and it is with this that he approaches God and it is with his whole being that eventually he will embrace God. But this is as far as he can get. His whole being can cry out for God, but is there a possibility of real encounter with him of the person-to-person kind? Can he enter into communion with God? Will he in fact be able to commit himself to God without at the same time fearing that he is ultimately committing himself to himself and no more? If man needs to approach God with the whole of his being, there must be an answer that transcends the limits of human-ness.

The Christian answer is that since man needs to go to God in this way, God has approached him in a way that meets the deepest needs of his nature. The transcendent God became a man, involved in the whole human predicament, and far from this being a 'condescension' to the lowliness of humankind, it is, in the mind of Aquinas, the *highest manner* that God could communicate himself, give himself to man.[6] The purest religion therefore is not the solitary contemplation of The Other, it does not consist of lonely musings on the Divine nor yet of an effort to slough off the materiality of the person. The self-communication of God resulted in an 'enfleshment', the Word became flesh, and it is those who receive him who become sons of God: 'no one can come to the Father except by me'. And the 'religion' that Jesus inaugurated in the world was an 'enfleshed' religion; it is, by the very exigencies of the case, a *sacramental* religion through which man can go to God because he is that sort of being.

Even our knowing of God is 'sacramental'. Christ is the 'sacrament' of God, what St Paul calls 'the mystery' of God: 'the mystery *is* Christ among you' (Colossians 1:27) and, as he shows, the purpose of the mystery is to *reveal*, to manifest the richness of God's love that has been at work among the old people of God from the beginning, though that love is so great and so rich that in the last analysis it must remain a mystery. We come to know God in and through Jesus Christ: 'Philip, he that has seen me has seen the Father' and, as we have seen, there is no other way. We may read and study and theologize – and all these things are necessary at one time or another – but if we are to know God existentially we can only know him in and through Christ.

But we do not merely *know* God through Christ, we are able to make an encounter with God through Christ. He is not only the revelation of the Father, he in himself is the communication of the Father's love.

Christ makes God present to men with all his redeeming power and love and this he did in his life, passion, death and resurrection. His passion and death were a self-giving, both to his Father and to us, a *total* giving of himself to his Father and to us, and through that self-giving he makes available to us and to men of all time the love of his Father. To this self-giving we are called, invited, urged to respond with a self-giving of faith and love, and in that exchange we meet God, we come to 'know' him in St John's sense, to enter into a communion with him that makes dialogue possible, the dialogue of prayer in which, for St Paul, the Spirit of God is present. The whole life of the Godhead indeed can be seen as a dialogue, but a dialogue at the infinite depth of divine life in which there is a perpetual giving and receiving of love, without loss or diminution, and it is through the encounter we make in Christ with God that we are drawn into the vital dialogue of Father, Son and Holy Spirit that is the life of the Trinity itself. This is the end-purpose of all worship and we see that it occurs 'in community' and through the total response of the human person, body, soul and all.

From a slightly different viewpoint, we also see that the *manner* of salvation was through community. God called a people and made them a holy and priestly people (Exodus 19:5–6; and cf. 1 Peter 2:4–9 and Revelation 1:6) to whom he could communicate his love. Jesus came as the head of a people, the whole human race; he summed up in himself the experience of the old people of God and identified himself with the human predicament, feeling in himself the impact of sin (Mark 14:32–42; 15:34 and parallels; cf. 2 Corinthians 5:21) and from within the human race lifting it up to a new life (John 3:13–15), so that man could enter into union with his Father. In this way he brought into existence a new people of God whose purpose would be to show to the world the redeeming love of God and whose function would be to make Christ present to every succeeding generation of man. The people now became the 'sacrament', totally dependent on Christ, but *sent* with his word and his redeeming love to all mankind (Matthew 28:18–20). In language that has long been traditional and adopted by the Constitution on the Liturgy (6), 'it was from the side of Christ as he slept the sleep of death on the cross that there came forth "the wondrous sacrament of the church" '.

Clearly, it is this sheer visibility that is the sacrament of Christ, revealing that he, with the Holy Spirit, is active in the world; and visibility means institution, structures, among other things liturgy. And here we encounter all the scandal of particularity. Man's large aspirations, the most spiritual of his desires, his longing to be in contact with Being, these, he now realizes, are to be satisfied in and through the materiality of institution and rite. Not only that, but the institution and the rite can become opaque. The one can become complicated, weighed down with legalism, appearing to be an end in itself and, since the institution is a people, it can be defaced by all the sins and follies of humankind. The rite can become encrusted with non-functional elements, it can degenerate into the meaningless performance that is called ritualism, it too can appear to be an end in itself. All this is not only possible but has happened and then Christ is not proclaimed, Christ is not made visible to the world and the institution and the rite become barriers to the encounter with Christ. The church becomes a 'scandal', a stumbling block.

But what is the alternative? Even the purest religion of the word can degenerate into formalism, the freest form of prayer can petrify and large aspirations can vanish in clouds of unrealism. Either way, the seeds of human imperfection can mar the vaunting idealism of man. He, too, is part of the scandal of particularity. It is part of the human condition and he has got to come to terms with it. If he does, he should find that the material, the particular, the humble element can become for him a theophany. Without, for the moment, going into the nature of the liturgical mystery, there is a St Francis to bear witness that the sun and the moon, fire and water and even the humble body can in Christian eyes be the images, the far-off echoes, of divine Beauty. This, it seems to me, is as genuine an intuition of Being as is that born of the anguish that seems to have been the *point de départ* of the existentialists.

Of course the church must always be purifying herself—*semper reformanda*—of course there must be a constant moral effort within the church to seek Christ and to make him visible to the world. But not even the church can abolish the concrete, the symbolic, the sacramental. These are of the stuff of the Christian way of life and, one may think, are, whatever the danger of corruption, the singular means by which man can make religion real to himself, by which he can grasp it so that in effect he can live by it. It is possible, I suppose, for a man and woman to agree wordlessly that they are married, but throughout history, if they have not declared this publicly and if the community has not borne witness to it, not only do they hardly realize that they are man and wife but the community is not willing to accept them as such. We can go to God directly in repentance and we must, but unless that repentance is 'sacramentalized', until we are faced with God and ourselves in the process of confession, we have a weakened realization of sin that can eventually disappear. We can, as the Lord commanded us, seek God in private prayer, but if we never join with a community in praying, if even in private prayer we regularly shut out the community to which we belong, then our prayer will become a self-regarding activity, a species of what a former Bishop of Oxford called 'a self-regarding soul culture'.[7] It, too, will deteriorate and may disappear altogether.

Can man then come to an *experience* of God in community? To suggest that he can and does seems to run counter to so much that has been held, by both non-Christians and even some Christians, in recent centuries. Religion has appeared to be mental, interior and solitary and worship to be private if it is to be true and genuine. In the Catholic church even the Mass was turned into a kind of meditation, the occasion when people thought holy thoughts and silently made their prayer to God. But if man is the concrete personal being we have seen he is, if *by his very nature* he needs 'I – Thou' relationships if he is to come to self-realization and if, as is suggested, these inter-personal relationships inevitably involve community, it would seem that it will be normal for him to find God in community worship.

*How* this may happen is indeed a little difficult to describe and where Christian worship is concerned it can be regarded as no more than an indication that it is possible. For in Christian worship man is presented with realities, with the reality of the human condition which is a fallen condition, but also with the reality that he has been lifted out of it or can be if he accepts in living, dynamic faith the divine reality that is present in worship. All these realities, however, are matters of faith, of the self-communication of God to his creatures, a self-communication that invites and makes possible a response and a commitment. If, then, man realizes his personal existence, comes to know what and who he is, in inter-personal relationships with other human beings, it would seem to follow that he is going to come to a knowledge of God that is deeper and more embracing than purely intellectual knowledge through his dialogue with God in worship.

But there is another sense that goes much deeper in which we can say that man comes to God in worship and here we have to do with the deepest things of Christian reality. We move out of the world of psychological experience into the world of being, of reality, the reality of the intimate life of God. It is only through the relationships we have with the *persons* of the Holy Trinity, says Dom Alban Stolz, that we enter into the life of God: 'It is in fact of the essence of these relations that we are incorporated into the Son by the Holy Spirit and led to the Father by the Son.' But all this occurs within the church that is the body of Christ, union with whom is the very basis of mysticism. Because we are made members of Christ, because we have to be conformed to him, because there has to be an *imitatio Christi* in the depths of our being, we have to undergo a transformation. We have to make the passover of the Lord from death to life our own:

> In the eucharist our insertion into Christ, that is, the passage of our whole sinful being into the transfigured being of Christ, becomes a *sacramental* reality. Our union with Christ delivers us from our sinful condition. Christ disentangles those who have become like him from the restrictions of this world and leads them before the face of God, as he himself preceded them at the ascension. By sharing in the eucharist the Christian is snatched out of himself and out of the world and is led by the Son to the Father. . . . The assimilation to Christ and the union with him that are effected sacramentally in the eucharist set the Christian (in Christ) in the presence of God.[8]

At this level of Christian faith, then, the eucharist is a transforming process. As St Leo says somewhere, we are transformed into what we receive. This is what happens, though it is only faith that can perceive it. Whether and in what circumstances Christians can experience this process are questions that would take us very far but *that* it is possible can hardly be doubted. There are the experiences of the saints recorded sufficiently often, and particularly those of the Benedictine St Gertrude whose whole spiritual and mystical life was centred on and sustained by the liturgy. Mystical experience and liturgical celebration were for her almost one thing and, apart from a single occasion, there were no outward manifestations. Yet *what* she experienced she was able to express in the (dictated) writings of hers that survive.[9] There can hardly be any

~

doubt that she achieved the highest mystical union.

There were, of course, several co-efficients at play here. Gertrude was a Benedictine nun, the whole framework of her life was the liturgy and she lived at the time of a 'mystical invasion' which in itself is so difficult to understand. But she brought to her worship an unusual spirit of self-giving and openness and it was this, humanly speaking, that made it possible for her to know God in and through the liturgy experientially. But the fact that, apart from that one occasion, there were no outward manifestations puts us on the right track. A recent writer usefully distinguishes the 'empirical' and the 'experiential' and he says that to look for the former in worship (or in the spiritual life in general) is to put the secondary for the primary. Empirical experience, something that is tangible and almost palpable and much sought after today, is 'an overflow and a bonus if it is genuine'. Since he summarizes much of what we have been trying to say, the whole passage is worth quoting:

> The stress on the experiential provides a new insight into the primacy of the inner, contemplative, transcendent dimension of life and thus supplies the impetus to move out of a pedestrian, lifeless, 'ho-hum' style of religion that bores people to death. The christian life is a thrilling adventure, a call out of the living death many people endure into the exuberant life of freedom and love that is thoroughly personal. *The christian life is God's answer to man's search for transcendence*; it responds to man's desire and hope to live for something bigger than himself, to move out of and beyond the limitations and imprisonment of his own body and psyche. Every man is embarked on that search; most take the road of experiences. This is the road of the empirical rather than the experiential. The two are by no means the same. The empirical is the observable, the tangible and measurable aspect of human life. It is prayers as opposed to prayer, feeling sorry rather than being sorry, kind acts compared to charity, experiences rather than experience. The first member of these doublets ideally contains and is a manifestation of the second. But it is not always so. And to confuse the two can be disastrous in religious thinking. For those who fail to make the distinction, a 'meaningful liturgy' has to be a 'happening' every time, deeply moving, imaginatively enriching and emotionally rewarding. This is too much to ask

from a daily liturgy. It is to want something approaching a mystical experience wherein there is an immediate touching and sensing of transcendent realities. Empirical experience of this kind is an overflow and a bonus if it is genuine. When it occurs, it is an integral and rewarding part of a religious experience, *which is a depth reality and consists in insight and personal commitment.* The experience may be present in the worshipper without any observable sign other than the peace and desire of the person to be there in the presence of the Lord.[10]

This is a very balanced statement and the writer does not scorn, as some Catholic writers have, the incidence of 'empirical experience' but, like St Thomas in fact, sees it as the overflow, the *redundantia*, of something much deeper. However the process may be described (and it may be indescribable), the worshipper receives an insight into the faith, into the will of God for himself or into the ways of God with man and through this understanding (*intus-legere*) he realizes that he is making an encounter with the living God. He is drawn into closer union with him and this may produce *ex redundantia* an experience of which he is conscious. *But even if it does not,* it remains true that worship can and does have effects in the order of experience: it deepens faith and kindles love, and though these effects are often not immediately perceived by the worshippers, they are observable in their lives. It is a matter of pastoral experience (and a subject for grateful wonder) that Christians who have no intellectual pretensions frequently acquire a depth of insight into the faith and what St Thomas called a 'connaturality' with the things of God through their faithful worship Sunday by Sunday. Oddly enough, this we should expect, and it is even odder that we should be surprised when we see it happening. Even under the old order of things this was observable, but now that the word of God is so much more adequately laid before the people, it is reasonable to expect that that deepening of faith will become an ever more important result of worship. For it is, I believe, the deepening of faith that provides the basis for the sort of 'experience' which we have been considering. More will be said about the relationship of word to sacrament later in this book, but immediately it is clear that the movement of the worshipper in faith and through faith in the first part of the Mass leads to an encounter in love in the second.

There is another aspect of the matter. Modern people have been

*Service.*

saying for some time that they cannot, or cannot easily, find God in silent prayer or even perhaps in vocal prayer. The whole business of 'meditation' is repugnant to them. There have even been those who have said that prayer was a waste of time, that instead of praying for people we should get out and help them. It is of course always possible to make prayer a surrogate for the active service, in love, of others, but to abandon prayer in the interests of action is to fall into the heresy of activism, which means 'good works' without 'faith'. As I have written elsewhere, 'unless we are "in communication" with God by prayer, we shall have no true love to offer'.[11] Love needs constant purification if it is not to become either possessive or dominating, a *self* seeking (however disguised) instead of 'other' seeking. And that Other is both God and man. Modern people are quick to say that they can find God in others, and philosophers and some theologians have been suggesting that God's transcendence is meaningless. They, too, have perhaps been the victims of spatial images, for transcendence as Christians have understood it means the complete otherness of God and not that he is *somewhere else*, absent from the universe he has made and occasionally visiting it, as it were, to see how it is getting on. There is a co-inherence of God in creation and of created things in God which respects his complete otherness yet at the same time affirms that he is present. If we do in fact find God in other people, we find *God*, because he is here, and not just people. But it is not at all as easy as people think. *opportunity Greetings!*

Worship, it seems to me, is the privileged moment (*kairos*) where we can meet both God and man. *In community* we become aware of the divine realities that are present first in the word and then in the sacrament but also in the hearts of our fellow-worshippers. They with us have heard God's call, they with us have received God's word into their hearts, they with us receive the one Bread that makes us, though many, one body in Christ and all establish the horizontal relationship that ties man to man. In the service that various members of the worshipping community do for each other, whether it be reading or serving or singing or even the humble task of welcoming people at the door, they are acknowledging the presence of God in each other. This is brought to its clearest expression in the sign of peace that is exchanged before communion and in the act of communion itself when by gesture and song the community recognizes that all share one faith in the one Spirit through Jesus Christ. No doubt we need to be more keenly aware of our relationship one with another, no doubt individualistic attitudes can atomize the community and no doubt there are still people who regard their Christian brethren almost with hostility as they kneel alongside them. But the realities are there and it remains true that we can find God in others at a deeper level in our worship than anywhere else.

Of course the faith and love we find in worship has to be carried into the world we live in where in hard fact our service of others begins, but it may be thought that if modern man is looking for what I might call a credible God, if he is looking for a personal encounter with God, if he wants to come to a God who is not the conclusion of a metaphysical argument, he should not discount worship as the place where he will find him. It goes without saying that the style of worship he encounters will have much to do with whether he does meet God or not, but every human institution is weighed down with imperfection, with the sheer materiality of human existence, and while Christians must seek constantly to purify themselves and their institutions, the God-seeker (hypothetically a non-Christian) must learn to be patient and tolerant not merely of the shortcomings of Christians but of the limitations of his own human nature when he is approaching God. If it is true, as we have suggested, that man goes to God humanwise, through people and symbols, there will be times when both people and symbols become opaque, but that does not invalidate the way. It merely means that it is fraught with all the limitations of human existence as we know it.

For those who have experienced in faith the divine realities that are expressed in the liturgy, a further step is possible. However improbable it may seem, this earthly, indeed earthy, liturgy is but the sacrament of the heavenly liturgy, a reflection of the heavenly liturgy of the 'city of the living God', the new Jerusalem where Jesus is the supreme *leitourgos*, celebrating in festival with the angels and with 'the whole church in which everyone is a "first-born son" '. There is a continual come-and-go between heaven and earth but it is through the concrete community and the symbols of its worship that we are able to penetrate into the new and better temple not made with hands, where Jesus is ever living to make intercession for us.[12] The vision of the writer of the Letter to the Hebrews is very remarkable, for in it the earthly church and the heavenly are hardly distinguishable: through the one he sees the reality that is present in the other. This is what the earthly assembly meant for him, this is what he *saw* in it. We may suppose, too, that the John of

Revelation who had his visions on the Day of the Lord (1:10), the day of Christian worship, had a similar insight into the co-inherence of the earthly and the heavenly liturgy (4 and 5). It is an aspect of worship that is very strongly marked in the Orthodox and Eastern traditions generally[13] and although it is less marked in the Roman tradition, there are the typical Roman prefaces to remind us that always we celebrate with the *whole* church in heaven and on earth. Nor are these, at least for men of faith, idle dreams or merely poetical expressions. That the earthly church inheres in Christ who not only suffered and died but also rose and is now enthroned in glory with his Father is an elementary truth that Western theology has never wholly forgotten, though the *theologia crucis* of both Catholic and Lutheran traditions has not always given sufficient emphasis to the theology of the Risen Christ. As sober a theologian as St Thomas Aquinas could see the church as the sacrament of our communion with God. One of the finest commentators on his ecclesiology can sum up the matter like this:

> (For St Thomas) the church is concerned with communion in the mystery of God. The deepest reality of the church, by which she achieves her greatest extension, the element that will remain eternally when all else is gone, is divinizing communion with *God*. But in our earthly, physical and historical situation, this can only be achieved through Christ, the incarnate Word, and through what he has given to us: faith, sacraments, institutions. . . . The church is fundamentally and supremely union with God in his godhead. In heaven, glory and vision; here below, grace and faith. But grace is the seed of glory and faith of vision so that in principle there is on the one hand a unity of existence between the angels and the *comprehensores*,[14] that is the heavenly church, and on the other, the faithful or the earthly church.[15]

*Yves Congar*

Whether and how far we experience these realities in worship is another matter, but there they are and perhaps the mere fact that we are aware of them may help us gradually to pierce the envelope of symbol and sacrament to God whom they convey to us but whom (because they are inevitably opaque) they also obscure.

# *Notes*

1 The above summary is based on John Macquarrie's account in **Twentieth Century Religious Thought** (London, 1963), pp. 353–5.

2 **Ibid.**, p. 196.

3 **Ibid.**, p. 197.

4 **Ibid.**, p. 360.

5 **Ibid.**

6 ST III, q.l., a.i. His argument is that since God is the **summum bonum** it is congruous with his nature that he should communicate himself to man in the best way possible: this happened in the incarnation because he united a human creature to himself and 'personalized' that nature: 'one person was made out of three things, the Word, the soul and the flesh'.

7 K. E. Kirk, somewhere in his vast study called **The Vision of God**. This, of course, does not mean that mystical prayer is invalidated but, as Dom Alban Stolz insisted, Christian mysticism is always ecclesial (**Théologie de la Mystique**, French trans., 2nd ed., 1947), and he was not afraid to say that it was basically liturgical, sacramental and eucharistic, pp. 249–52.

8 A. Stolz, **op. cit.**, pp. 249–50.

9 J. Leclercq, F. Vandenbroucke, **Histoire de la Spiritualité**, 2 (Paris, 1961), p. 539, and C. Vagaggini, **Il Senso Theologico della Liturgia** (2nd ed., 1958), pp. 578–627. The single occasion was at Mass, at the introit, when she was so moved that she found she was not following the movements of the choir and she besought the Lord to let her do so!

10 Ernest E. Larkin, 'The Search for Experience', **The Way**, vol. 11, no. 2 (April 1971), p. 102.

11 **Liturgy** (April 1968), p. 35.

12 Hebrews 12:22–5; 8:2; 9:11; and cf. CL 8.

13 Cf. Erik Peterson, **The Angels and the Liturgy** (Eng. trans., London, 1964).

14 In Aquinas's language, these are all those who now **see** God.

15 Yves Congar, **L'Eglise de Saint Augustin à l'époque moderne** (Paris, 1970), pp. 232–3.

# *The World of Symbols*[1]

~~~~~~

I N THE PREVIOUS CHAPTER I have attempted to show that
liturgy is fundamentally in accord with the nature of man. The matter
can be stated in Christian terms: God has approached man in
Christ who is the embodiment of the divine love, and this God did because
if man is to have something more than a merely mental apprehension of
God, he must be approached in this way. On the other hand, man needs
to approach God in the wholeness of his personality a.1d if he is able to
do this the relationship that he desires and needs to establish with God
can in its turn become embodied, made concrete. It is in this area of
reality that liturgy exists and it would not be too much to say that it is
an embodied relationship if always we see that relationship as based on
faith and love. That is, there is nothing automatic about it. It follows from
this that liturgy exists in a world that is neither that of pure speculation
or meditation, nor yet on the other hand of mere feeling. The realities it
contains and conveys are embodied in certain gestures and in certain
things that are used in a special way. We have, in other words, to understand the world of symbol if we are to understand liturgy.

As we have seen, modern man by the conditions of his culture is not
adjusted to this world—or at least he may think he is not. In fact, he is
living in a world of images which, it is true, are not always symbols—
though unwittingly they may refer to hidden values, such as the making
of money—and a great part of his life is controlled by signs. He has only
to take out his car to be confronted with a forest of signs that condition
and control his driving. Something, then, must be said about symbol
and sign, though it is important that symbol should come first. There is
a danger of intellectualizing signs that has not always been avoided
by Catholic sacramental theology. The sign-value, the sheer power of
significance, of the sacraments has been diminished by casuistry (how
*little* water must flow for a 'valid' baptism) and by a faulty liturgical
practice. The very liturgy in the books, the wealth of signs to be found
there, was often disregarded and the minimum done to secure a basic

validity. Even under the old order, it was impossible to understand what the church was saying about baptism unless one took into account both the whole ritual to be found in the book and the basic context that was (and, of course, still is) to be found in the Easter Vigil.[2]

In opposition to the Reformers' views of sacraments, Catholics emphasized the *efficiency* of the sign, they were causes of grace and sometimes the metaphors used to enforce this teaching gave the impression that they were utensils, tools. St Thomas's simple teaching that *sacramenta significando causant*, their very efficiency is by way of signification, was too little known. Attention then concentrated on 'matter' and 'form', both no more than analogical notions where the Christian sacraments are concerned, and *all* that was required was the proper 'application' of the latter to the former. The wider and deeper significance of the gestures done and things used just did not enter into the picture. That was possibly piety or, worse still, poetry, and you can't let poetry into the liturgy! Bread no longer looked like bread, oil was dabbed on only to be wiped off, the supplicatory attitude of the *orante* who held his hands palms upturned to beseech God's mercy was reduced to a hugging of the ribs, an attitude that was fiercely insisted on by 'Roman' rubricists. As a modern Thomist has said,[3] analyses of the sacraments along the lines of cause and validity led to a sort of rationalism. The sacrament looked very much like a machine; you could take it to pieces and (almost) evacuate the mystery.

The case with symbols is even worse. If you say 'symbol' it is immediately assumed that you mean 'empty symbol', that it has no content. It is reduced to rather less than a metaphor. If you say that the bread and wine are symbols of the eucharist, people immediately think you are saying that they are *no more* than symbols and that you are endorsing a receptionist and subjective theology of the eucharist. The usual view is that the bread and wine with the words are *efficient causes* of the Real Presence, and so you get a eucharistic theology that concentrates on the words of institution to the exclusion of almost all else. Yet there are those disturbing expressions of the Fathers of the Church, of Origen and Ambrose, to mention no others, who speak of the bread as being the *homoioma* (likeness), the *figura*, of the body of Christ.[4] But the Fathers were right. The bread *is* a symbol of the body of Christ who is 'the bread of life' and who said 'Take and *eat*'. There is nothing abstruse here and the answer to the question why Christ took bread and wine at the Last Supper is simply that they are symbols, which everyone can understand, of nourishment. As Masure wrote long enough ago now:

> Thus it is through the enactment of a sacramental sacrifice of *bread and wine* that the Mass becomes the symbolic and moreover the *veridical* affirmation of the sacrifice of the cross. The bread and wine were admirably chosen by Christ to *show forth* to us not only that he died but that in dying he has given us life, and that by his resurrection he imparts it to us for ever. For the eucharist is both his flesh delivered up to the cross for the salvation of the world and *the bread of life come down from heaven.* . . .[5]

These matters are now becoming clearer. The terminology has been changing for some time, the eucharist is referred to as a 'meal', a term to be found in the General Introduction to the Order of the Mass (e.g. 48, 56), and 'meal' indicates eating and drinking, whatever else may need to be added for a full statement of Catholic doctrine. The restoration of communion from the cup for the laity and, in many countries, of communion in the hand, all emphasize in liturgical, that is, symbolic language that the eucharist is a meal of which the chief symbols are the bread and wine. For an Origen, for an Ambrose and a host of other Fathers, the bread *was* the symbol of the body of Christ. *Of its very nature* it led the communicant to think of eating and drinking. Thus it was, and is, something much more than a sign of the Real Presence; it indicates, as far as it can, the real meaning of the eucharist, namely that it is an eating of the Lord's body and the drinking of his blood. But even that is not the whole truth. The symbols of bread and wine are, in a certain context, that of the *paschale convivium*, to use the term of the General Introduction, and this again has a special framework: as at the Last Supper the eucharist was instituted in the context of the paschal *berakah*, the prayer of blessing and thanksgiving, so the bread and wine are in the same context. They are elements of a whole action which is comprised of gestures (the taking and breaking of the bread) and of words which give their ultimate significance to the bread and wine as symbols: they no longer signify natural life, they are transformed so that they may become the means by which Christians enter into the death and life of Christ. They become what the Roman Canon says they are, the Bread of Life and the Cup of Everlasting Salvation. But they need to undergo this 'transignification' if they are to achieve their purpose as *sacramental* symbols.[6]

Symbolism, then, is an integral part of the liturgy, but if we are to understand it more fully it is necessary to put the matter in a wider context. Symbolism is not a quality of the Christian liturgy merely. As scholars have revealed for some long time now, it is part of all religious worship as they have investigated it in its origins or in its more primitive state.

It will be best to begin at the beginning. Here we meet the ambiguous word 'myth' which, as used by the phenomenologists, does not prejudge the question whether its content is true or not. Myth is concerned with primordial events, in particular creation, when primitive man believed that the gods or hero figures were reducing chaos to cosmos (the organized universe) which was the *real* world, the world in fact of the sacred. But the activity of the gods represented for him an abundance of life and energy. It was his desire to make contact with the primordial event so that he could lay hold of its life and energy not simply for himself as an individual, for a sense of individuality was weak, but for the whole community of which he was a member or, rather, with which he was con-corporate. It was vital to the survival of the community that it should be in contact with that power and so he was led to *mimesis*, the imitation in ritual of the primordial events. *Mimesis* involved the re-enactment of the primordial events in gesture, dance, song and the use of objects that were necessary for the 'drama'. It is at this point that symbolism, gestures and objects became part of worship. Both gestures and objects referred away from themselves to the events they were recalling but *at the same time* arrested the attention of the participants in such a way that they knew they were being put in touch with those events. This is the first function of symbol. As opposed to sign (which is 'thin') the symbol is solid, even opaque, something on which the senses can rest and which, because as yet undetermined by word, can suggest a whole range of meaning that the sign cannot. As I have written elsewhere, symbol is more apt to convey the breadth of the liturgical mystery. Its very opacity makes it possible for it to suggest mystery; it contains within itself echoes of the infinite. It arouses our interest, gives the mind something to work on, but it also stimulates the whole affective side of the personality.[7]

Yet the use of symbols has its dangers. Just as the sign can become so 'thin', concerned with merely intellectual processes, giving no more than information, the symbol, because it is concrete and opaque, can draw all the attention to itself, making impossible the passage from itself to the thing symbolized. This is what happens, has happened, when ritual is seen as an end in itself, when it is not reflected on, when its meaning and purpose are not discerned, when it becomes divorced from the reality it is meant to convey. For it is of the essence of the symbol to be different from that which is symbolized as well as having a certain likeness to it. This 'difference from' has been called 'the symbolic hiatus'; you have to make a leap from the symbol to the reality symbolized. Anointing in the New Testament signifies the giving of the Holy Spirit and yet how vast is the distance between the symbol and the reality! Yet it is in this hiatus precisely that the power of symbols lies, as can be seen when we look at the Mass:

> We no longer know it simply in the nakedness of its essence (as if we knew the doctrine of the Mass as defined by the Council of Trent), but we know it as something radiating relationships with other elements of the world, clothed in analogies and likenesses with other things. It is thus that the 'symbolic hiatus' constitutes the power and richness of the symbol: to knowledge pure and simple (given by the sign) it adds an impression of life and mystery, a value of delight and sentiment. These the thing alone or merely signified could not give. The symbol which is concrete, more immediate to us—we might say coarser—evokes them and transfers them to the thing that is symbolized.[8]

Symbols, then, belong to this concrete world and enable man to concretize his relationship with his origins, to get in touch with the events that lie at the origin of his world and to bring their power into the present so that he can lay hold of it. Symbols are concerned with reality (not with unreality), but in worship they transcend themselves and lead man to a world that would otherwise be beyond his grasp. They are related to the world of poetry and indeed metaphor which is unreal only to those for whom all things can be measured, analysed and weighed. The poet, the lover, says 'My love is a consuming fire'. That does not mean that his love is unreal but that it is so real that he can only express it by what might seem an extravagant metaphor. Likewise, we say not that God's word is *like* a seed but that it *is* a seed: 'Is there here simply a literary artifice? In a sense, yes, but it expresses by a metaphor the leap of the mind and heart. Hence the realism of the symbol, particularly of the symbolic gesture for which no explanation is adequate even if (later) it becomes necessary. . . . It is indeed true that according to the condition of man mystery finds in the symbol its homogeneous expression', that is, an expression that is in accord with the nature of man.[9]

It is in this world of symbol that the liturgy exists, a world that is other than the world of science and reason, and yet that is real. Wholly in accord with man's nature, it enables him to communicate, first with his fellows (the kiss, the handshake) and then with another world where he has glimpsed the *mysterium tremendum et fascinans* that for him is God.[10] When we come to the Christian liturgy, the symbolism achieves a density of reality that is based on God's action and on the symbols chosen by Christ that become efficacious by his power. If the Christian is able to make contact with the events by which the Christian community was brought into being, it is because God has made this possible. He has approached man in Christ who is 'the mystery of God among us' (Colossians 1:27).

We find, then, that there are three terms now in play, sign, symbol and mystery, and each needs to be understood if we are to understand what liturgy is. The Constitution says that 'in the liturgy man's sanctification is signified by signs perceptible to the senses' but 'signs' here need to be taken in all their density and not in the somewhat etiolated sense of recent sacramental theology. These signs are not just 'indicators' like a road sign, nor simply efficient causes; they are pregnant with reality, they are 'solid', addressing man in the wholeness of his personality, inviting him to make the leap from their humble materiality to the transcendent realities they show forth and convey. In other words, they are symbols that express a whole range of meaning and through that very expression effectively lead men to an encounter with God. They are efficacious, yes, but efficacious because they are full of reality which of their nature they can convey. This traditionally is called their 'causality', but even the causality is reduced if it is thought of as the efficiency of a tool. Human beings are not raw matter on which God carves his purpose, but free, willing, believing people who concretize their faith in the sacraments and who through this concrete, *human* approach to God come to meet him.

What, then, is the importance of 'sign' as such? It is here that 'word' becomes of crucial importance. Symbols remain vague in the sense that they can signify several things. Water symbolizes both life and death, for it is necessary if man is to live and it can suffocate him to death. How, then, does it symbolize life in baptism if not through the sign that makes of it the sacrament of life? But, further, how can it become the symbol-sacrament of death and life *in Christ* unless it is used in the Christian context? The meaning of water in baptism is part of the proclamation of the Gospel. Its meaning is only known to the believer, as St John Chrysostom said so long ago:

> Here the believer judges differently from the unbeliever (who) learns about baptism and thinks it is nothing but water. *But I do not think merely of what I see* (it is a symbol). I think of the purification of the soul which has been effected by the Holy Spirit. The unbeliever thinks that baptism is no more than a simple washing of the body, but I believe that it makes the soul pure, and holy, and I think of the tomb, of the resurrection, of sanctification and redemption and the adoption of sons, of our heavenly inheritance, of the kingdom of heaven and the gift of the Holy Spirit (it is a Christian symbol).[11]

So the believer must have the gospel preached to him, the word must be communicated, but that word has the task of making clear to him also what exactly is the meaning of this symbol here and now:

> Precisely because the supernatural saving reality, veiled in historical events, and surrounded by the darkness of mystery, is present to us only in earthly form (*sacramentum*), it demands the revealing word (*verbum*) as the interior aspect of its earthly appearance. Only in and through the prophetic word is the divine dimension of saving history brought to light. 'Word' and 'sacrament' are therefore constituents for revelation in the Old Testament as well as in the New, and, after this revelation has been brought to an end, for the life of the Church which grows out of it.[12]

But we need to go a step further. What is the exact significance of this action that is being performed? Oil is used in the ordination of bishops and priests, in baptism and confirmation, for the consecration of objects as remote from these as churches and chalices. Sign is not opposed to symbol, it is 'the illuminating point of the symbol'[13] but is still one with it. The symbol does not lose its density and yet it achieves the significance that is necessary if it is to play its part in liturgy. It is only when symbol is dismissed and sign is left in all its thinness that it begins to be less than adequate in suggesting the range of the mystery that it is its function to express and convey. Object-symbols are indeed used in the Christian liturgy and the burning paschal candle during the Masses of Easter-time or during baptism carries its own message as a symbol of the Risen Christ, the light of the world. But this is only because it has formed part of a rite that proclaims the message of salvation of which the passion and resurrection of Christ is the climax. It is true, too, that simple gestures and actions like a genuflexion can and do convey worship, but this again only in the context of Christian faith in the eucharist. However, normally and especially for the heart of the liturgy which is made up of the eucharist and the other sacraments, it is the *word that is the illuminating point of the symbol*. If the meaning of the different uses of oil is to be apparent it is only through the word that this can be so. Anointing with chrism at baptism signifies, as the prayer accompanying it makes clear, incorporation into Christ who is priest, prophet and king. But neither does the word remain separate from the symbol; it is indeed in a fashion incarnated in it and nowhere does human word operate at so high a potential as when it is combined with the objects and gestures of the eucharist where the Word who is proclaimed in the scriptures becomes bodily present in the bread and wine. These in turn become luminous through the word so that their *sacramental* significance can be grasped.

From another point of view, word is of the greatest importance in the liturgy. It saves it, as nothing else can, from the automatism that is always ready to overtake it. In the traditional phrase, now brought back to Catholic consciousness, we are saved by faith and the sacraments of faith (CL 59) and the word first expresses the faith of the church of which the whole sacramental action is the embodiment and, secondly, enables the Christian to express his faith in response to that declared by the liturgical action. It is the word that makes the celebration of the liturgy an encounter with God through which we enter into the redeeming work of Christ. Perhaps it is not necessary to repeat that through the sign-symbol this encounter is an embodied one and, as we have seen at the beginning of this chapter, the relationship that man desires with God is an embodied one so that we can say that liturgy is the 'incarnation' of the union of man with God.

The word is pre-eminently revelatory of the meaning of the symbol and so points to the reality it symbolizes. In more conventional language, the liturgy (the sacraments) declares the faith of the church but this faith is not declared in propositions or in an intellectualized manner. It is a faith that points to Christ and to his saving acts, the whole Christ whom the Christian embraces in the liturgical action. St Paul saw baptism as the 'revelation' in action of the death and resurrection of Christ and the New Testament accounts see the eucharist as the showing forth (and making present) of the Christ who first under the signs of bread and wine gave himself to his apostles, a giving that was the sacrament of his complete and total self-giving on the cross. That is why St Paul could say that when we celebrate the eucharist we are proclaiming the Lord's death until he comes again.

It should not be surprising (or offensive) that primitive man found something very similar in his worship. Dom Odo Casel, who pondered the meaning of the Christian mystery for years, writing on 'The Notion of Festival',[14] singles out the element of epiphany, manifestation, in celebration:

> What is characteristic is that the divine life comes down, in some fashion effectively, among those who are taking part in the solemnity. This is not a simple recalling; it implies a presence. The divinity is present in the festival procession,[15] visible or recognizable by his efficacious action. For all this, the rich terminology of Hellenism has the word 'Epiphany'. God has appeared among those who serve in the liturgical worship. He has been summoned: listen, come, show yourself – and he has come, he is present: *advenit, epephanē, adest*. His presence is in no way passive: he has come to act, to rescue, to conquer through suffering, as at his first epiphany he suffered, fought and overcame. But his followers act with him in the liturgy because he is with them and their action becomes a sacred imitation (*mimesis, imitatio*) of the divine events which ensure the life of the community. It is a sacred action, a religious drama. Through it his followers appropriate to themselves divine life and so are renewed. . . . Here, then, there is play but play of a life incomparably richer and deeper than anything we have found hitherto.

The play becomes mystery because in symbol it makes God present. Celebration of the religious feast ends in a liturgy in which is to be found its climax.

It may be thought that Dom Casel has unconsciously christianized hellenistic worship, but in fact his description is in accord with the findings of much later experts, such as G. van der Leeuw and Mircea Eliade who relate myth, mystery, symbol and 'epiphany' to worship. Thus 'the myth relates a *sacred history*, that is, a primordial event that took place at the beginning of time, *ab initio*. But to relate a sacred history is equivalent to *revealing a mystery*. . . . The myth, then, is the history of what took place *in illo tempore*, the recital of what the gods . . . did at the beginning.'[16] The myth contains the 'mystery' that is revealed in the recounting of it and this narrative 'is the attempt of primitive man to express *in a symbolic way*, namely, in a symbolic story [and we could add through gesture, dance and song], a fundamental experience of his existence, that is, an aspect of his connection with the world or his relationship to the mystery of being'.[17]

We may note in passing that this view is closely related to the existentialist approach of man to God that we have sketched out in the previous chapter and also to the 'encounter' theology that has come in recent years from a deeper consideration of the Bible. This, too, is found to be the basis of a theology of the liturgy. What is of more immediate interest is that this analysis of worship shows that mystery is at once something hidden and yet also revelatory of the divine action that it is re-enacting. The 'epiphanic' aspect of the liturgy has been too little regarded in recent centuries but it is a matter of immense importance. How do we know that God is present among us, active among us? The liturgy is the concrete sign of the divine presence enabling us to grasp existentially the reality of that presence and, in the case of the Christian liturgy, actually conveying to us the richness of redemption. If man's mind can be opened by faith to all this, he has an evidence of the reality of God and of his presence in the world. In the Christian liturgy, too, the 'epiphany' of God is spelt out in the recounting of the saving events in the word of the scriptures which in its own mode is a revelation of God, for there is never any liturgy without the proclamation of the word, even if it is very brief. We may say, then, that liturgy is a symbolic action that re-enacts the sacred events of saving history and makes God present with his redeeming power. Liturgy lives in the world of symbol and it is in this sense that we should interpret the words of the Constitution that 'the sanctification of man is signified by signs perceptible to the senses and *is effected* in a way which corresponds with each of these signs' (7). We may add, as the Constitution does in many places, that at the same time man gives glory to God, *in the same way* he goes to God through signs and symbols and he goes to him in the wholeness of his being. As Irenaeus said, *Gloria Dei, vivens homo*: it is the whole, living man who has encountered God in the concreteness of the liturgy and in the concrete situation of his being who can give him the glory. The Christian is a sign of God's presence.

We are now in a position to consider 'mystery', which lies at the heart and origin of liturgical celebration. As we have seen, for Eliade myth is practically to be identified with mystery, the sacred events, real or imaginary, that were recounted in a sacred history which was acted out in various ways. There are differences of opinion as to whether myth or ritual came first and also as to what content primitive man found in the rituals that he performed. This is of no importance for our purposes here, for with Judaism and, above all, with Christianity we move into a different world which is characterized by historical time. Events really did happen and we can tie them to specific times, persons and places. Eliade, who more than anyone else has emphasized the importance of the elements of primitive worship we have considered, is equally emphatic about the difference between the Judaic-Christian *Weltanschauung* and all others. He speaks first of Judaism where he finds historical time as the mark of the religious outlook and actions that are the actions of a Personal God: 'His gestures are *personal* interventions in history and reveal their deep meaning *only for his people*, the people that Yahweh had chosen. Hence the historical event acquires a new dimension: it becomes a theophany.' God reveals himself in these particular, never-to-be-repeated events and it is here that the Hebrews found him. But

Christianity goes even further in valorizing *historical time*. Since God was *incarnated*, that is, since he took on a *historically conditioned human existence*, historical time acquires the possibility of being sanctified. The *illud tempus* evoked by the Gospels is a clearly defined historical time—the time in which Pontius Pilate was Governor of Judaea—but it was *sanctified by the presence of Christ*. When a Christian of our day participates in liturgical time, he recovers the *illud tempus* in which Christ lived, suffered, and rose again—but it is no longer a mythical time. . . .[18]

This shows the great difference there is between primitive, non-Christian (and non-Jewish) worship and our own, but the manner in which we 'recover the *illud tempus*' remains the same. When we make the memorial of what the Lord did at the Last Supper, when we recount the sacred history and perform the same gestures, when in short we do once again in symbol what he did long ago, we come into his presence or he makes himself present to us with all his power and love. There is 'epiphany', *adest*, he is present.

It is into this thought-world that the theology of the Christian mystery can without difficulty be fitted. The Constitution may be thought to be somewhat sparing in its use of the phrase and no doubt the Council Fathers had no intention of committing themselves to any particular theory of 'mystery-presence'. But it does see the mystery of Christ as mediated through the liturgy to the lives of men (CL 2) and says that the mysteries of Christ's redemption are 'in some way' made present to the people who are put in contact with them and are filled with the grace of salvation (CL 102).[19] If the differences between the pagan mystery-celebration and the Christian mystery-presence must be emphasized, the likenesses between the two cannot be overlooked. But mystery, fundamentally, is what the Constitution says the liturgy is and it goes on to make the necessary concrete applications. The climax of the history of salvation (sacred history) was the paschal mystery (Christ's passion, death and resurrection) and it is this that is the centre of the church's liturgy (CL 5).

So we have the historical mystery, rooted in time, and we have its liturgical celebration in which the original events by which the Christian community is established (CL 5) are recalled and made present. But since we are dealing with the Christian mystery the whole matter needs to be set in a wider context.

The history of salvation does not begin with the New Testament. Throughout the ages God by event and word had been revealing himself and offering his love to mankind represented by the people of Israel. This self-revealing was brought to its culmination in the sending of the Son, the Word, the very utterance of God, made flesh, who made God's love present to men in this world by his passion, death and resurrection. It is this same redeeming love that the liturgy conveys to us by its celebration in sign, symbol and sacrament. So we have three levels on which the mystery of Christ exists:

1. The Mystery is God, 'dwelling in light inaccessible' (1 Timothy 6:16) and in the plenitude of a love that is always giving itself, always being communicated from Father to Son and Holy Spirit and back again. This love God freely communicated outside himself first in creation and then in redemption so that all could share that love.

2. The mystery exists in the historical order. As we read in 1 Timothy 3:16, Christ is the mystery of God, showing him forth:

> Great indeed, we confess, is the mystery of our religion:
>> He was *manifested* in the flesh,
>> vindicated in the Spirit,
>> seen by angels
>> preached among the nations
>> believed on in the world,
>> taken up in glory (RSV translation).

The mystery of God was made visible in Christ, the only-begotten of the Father, whose glory John and the other disciples had seen (in his risen state and in his ascension). He came in 'the fullness of time' and not only summed up in himself the whole history of salvation but gave that history meaning. It was God's plan to unite all men and all things in himself through Christ who 'in his body of flesh, by his death, reconciled' mankind to his Father so that we could be holy and blameless and irreproachable before him. In him is revealed the mystery of God's saving love and through his passion, death and resurrection he made that love present among men and available for their salvation.[20]

Here mystery is essentially *event*, in the terms of Eliade, the primordial event, Christ's redeeming work by which the church came into existence. But it, too, looked back to the past which it interpreted and on to the future, the emergence of the church through which the saving power would be mediated to the world, which would be indeed the sign to the world that God is present to it and at work in it. It looked on further into an undetermined future when God's plan would have been fully worked out and all things would be renewed and restored in Christ.

3. But the event has to be experienced in the present. Christ, as Dom Odo Casel liked to say (and apparently Kierkegaard before him), has to become man's contemporary. This is achieved by the liturgy which so many of the older prayers of the Roman sacramentaries called the *mysterium.* Christ's passion, death and resurrection are present to us *in mysterio* and are active among us through the mystery:

> The religious experience of the Christian is based upon an imitation of Christ as *exemplary pattern*, upon the liturgical repetition of the life, death and resurrection of the Lord and upon the *contemporaneity* of the Christian with *illud tempus* which begins with the Nativity at Bethlehem and ends, provisionally, with the Ascension . . . the liturgical time in which the Christian *lives* during the divine service is no longer profane duration but is essentially sacred time, the time in which the Word is made flesh, the *illud tempus* of the Gospels. A Christian is not taking part in a commemoration of the Passion of Christ, as he might be joining in the annual celebration of the Fourth of July. . . . He is not commemorating an event but *re-actualizing a mystery*. For the Christian, Jesus dies and resurrects before him *hic et nunc*.[21]

Apart from the last sentence, which offers a number of theological difficulties,[22] this passage by the most famous scholar of religion in our time is a very clear description of what is meant by the liturgical mystery. It looks to the past to recover the power of the primordial event, it makes this power present in the here and now and enables the worshipper to come into contact with the Person and the power that were active and present in the beginning. Through the sign-symbols it uses it manifests the presence of Christ's action and because these are sacraments to which Christ committed himself, they convey the saving power of his passion and resurrection.

In more conventional language, the liturgy is the sacrament of Christ showing him forth as present and conveying the power of his redeeming work to Christians who are living here and now and who through the liturgical action (which involves faith) are taken up in his saving activity. Although the terminology of mystery may seem strange and perhaps 'pagan' to some, it is not new. St Leo the Great was constantly using *sacramentum* in this pregnant and comprehensive sense and a phrase of his has had considerable currency in recent years: *Quod nostri redemptoris conspicuum fuit, in sacramenta transivit* (what our Redeemer did visibly, has passed over into the sacraments).[23] The sacraments (meaning here in particular the eucharist, I think, though not exclusively) contain what Christ did and the fact that in Leo's mind it was (saving) actions that were in question is clear from the context. The above phrase is the conclusion of a passage in which he says that Christ, after the forty days of his resurrection-life, in the presence of his apostles was lifted up to remain at the right hand of his Father until the number of the sons of the church should be fulfilled. *Now* all that he did in his earthly life is to be found in the *sacraments*, the liturgy that he and his hearers were celebrating.[24]

The purpose of the mystery-theology of the liturgy is to preserve the realism of the liturgical action and to deliver it from the narrowness of mere efficient causality (which is never denied) and to show that it has a richer and broader range and significance that meets the human condition. Man, in the whole richness of his own being, wishes to meet God, desires that God should be real and present to him. He achieves this in the first instance by faith but it is in the symbolic-liturgical action that faith is concretized. The church in the use and celebration of the liturgy is declaring that Christ the Redeemer is present and active and man through involvement in the celebration can make encounter in the whole of his being with the living God who comes to him in signs and symbols and mysteries. Perhaps the whole matter of the liturgical mystery can best be expressed by saying that it is the concrete (symbolic) and manifold expression of God's presence and action among his people now.

It has a further advantage. Not being restricted by the theory of efficient causality, the liturgy is thereby given a range of reference that would otherwise be impossible. The Catholic liturgy does not consist just of the eucharist and the sacraments. Nor does the eucharist itself consist simply of the words of consecration and the reception of the elements. Christ is present in the proclamation of the word, he is present in the prayer of Christians when they gather for it and all the rites and gestures of the liturgy show him forth and in one way or another make him present. The numerous aspects of his life, teaching, death and resurrection can be shown, brought to the attention of worshippers, through the very various actions of the liturgy. The paschal candle moving into the darkened church is visibly Christ, the Light who has overcome the darkness of death, the ashes placed on the head on Ash Wednesday are a symbol of repentance, the oil of chrism signifies either the entrance into the Christian community or consecration for its service. The instances could be multiplied; what is important is that all these are efficacious of Christ's redeeming love and power at different levels and in different ways. They are addressed to the different needs of the human person and have the power totally to penetrate his life. Thus spelt out, it may be thought somewhat laboriously, this is what the Constitution is saying when it teaches that man is sanctified by (a variety of) signs in ways that correspond to each of them (7).

If the Constitution speaks only sparingly of mystery as such, it has no hesitation about taking for the foundation of almost the whole of its first, and most important, chapter the paschal mystery. It is the climax of Jesus' life as it is the culmination of the history of salvation. It is the 'primordial event' that brought the sacrament-church into existence and it was the heart of the apostolic preaching. By baptism men 'are plunged into the paschal mystery of Christ, they die with him, are buried with him and rise with him'. When they eat the supper of the Lord they proclaim his death until he comes again and in celebrating the eucharist in which '*the victory and triumph of his death are again made present*' they are able to 'give thanks to God through him to the praise of his glory' (CL 6 (2 Corinthians 9:15; Ephesians 1:12)). Through the liturgical, symbolic re-enactment of the primordial events by which it was brought into being, the Christian community throughout the ages can transcend time and space and make encounter with the living, Risen Christ who is the same yesterday, today and for ever. It is by this that the community exists and it is because of this that the liturgy is the summit of the church's activity and the source of all her power (CL 10).

Ineluctably the church is concerned with the paschal mystery. It is not only the centre of her life but the pattern of her existence. Because she is the body of Christ extended in space and time she will be 'in agony until the end of time' and her resurrection will only be seen in those who through the enactment of the paschal mystery are themselves able to undergo resurrection. It will not be until the Christian community is able to celebrate the heavenly liturgy, of which the earthly is but a foretaste, that the power of the Christ's resurrection will be finally and completely effective and all will be able to share the glory that is his now. Meanwhile, we journey as pilgrims towards the heavenly Jerusalem

~

where Christ is in glory, the *leitourgos* of the temple not made with hands, and we through the earthly liturgy are able to join in his in which eternally he intercedes for us (CL 8; cf. Hebrews 8:2, 7:25).

# *Notes*
~

[1] The bibliography on the subject is enormous. See Mircea Eliade, **Myths, Dreams and Mysteries** (Fontana, London, 1968). In *La Liturgie après Vatican II*, ed. Yves Congar (Paris, 1967): M. D. Chenu, 'L'Homme de la Liturgie' and P. Colin, 'Phénoménologie et herméneutique du symbolisme liturgique'. L. Bouyer, **Rite and Man** (Eng. trans., London, 1963), which summarizes much that has been written on the subject. I. H. Dalmais, **Introduction to the Liturgy** (Eng. trans., London, 1961), which is, in fact, a very good introduction to the matter.

[2] In speaking in various places some years ago about the new baptismal Order, I was at first puzzled by the constant questioning about original sin: doesn't the new Order then say that baptism takes away original sin? One had to reply that it has very little to say about it (e.g. the prayer of exorcism). Then I realized that for a great number of people baptism simply meant 'the taking away of original sin', just like that. It apparently had no further or other consequences and any question of delaying the baptism was regarded as improper. The giving of the Holy Spirit, the incorporation into Christ and all the rest about which the Order has so much to say seem to have been widely unknown in any real sense of knowing.

[3] A. M. Roguet, OP, **Somme Théologique, Les Sacrements** (Paris, 1945), pp. 255–379.

[4] The English translator of Jungmann's **Missarum Solemnia** was indeed so disturbed by the introduction of **homoioma** into a paragraph quoting Origen on the eucharist that he purposely mistranslated it. Or perhaps it was the Censor librorum who insisted on a 'modification'.

[5] E. Masure, **The Sacrifice of the Mystical Body** (London, 1954), p. 63. My italics.

[6] To this extent and irrespectively of what conclusions theologians draw or do not draw, the 'new' theology seems to me to have emphasized an element in the eucharist that is important. As far as I can see, too, they are to this extent traditional. Unless I am mistaken, they are saying that whereas in the first instance bread and wine signify simply ordinary food and drink, if they are to signify what the eucharist intends, the body and blood of Christ, they must be 'transignified' so that they become signs of the everlasting life that comes from Christ.

[7] 'Signs, Symbols and Mysteries' in **Worship** (USA), vol. 39, no. 8 (October–November 1965), which summarizes much of what A. M. Roguet has to say in Appendix II of his trans. and commentary, **Somme Théologique, Les Sacrements** (Paris, 1945).

[8] A. M. Roguet, **loc.** and **art. cit.**

[9] M. D. Chenu, 'Anthropologie de la Liturgie' in **La Liturgie après Vatican II**, ed, Y. Congar (Paris, 1967), p. 173.

[10] R. Otto, **The Idea of the Holy** (Eng. trans., OUP, 1923, and Penguin Books, 1959).

[11] Quotation in J. D. Crichton, 'Signs, Symbols and Mysteries', **art. cit.** I regret that I have misplaced the reference.

[12] E. Schillebeeckx, 'The Sacraments: An Encounter with God' in **Christianity Divided** (London and New York, 1961), p. 246.

[13] J. D. Crichton, 'Signs, Symbols and Mysteries', **art. cit.**

[14] **La Maison-Dieu**, no. 1 (1945), pp. 25–6.

[15] **Panèguris**, the same word that is used in Hebrews 12:22, quoted in the previous chapter.

[16] Mircea Eliade, **The Sacred and the Profane** (New York, 1959), cited in **Phenomenology of Religion**, ed. Joseph D. Bettis (London, 1969), p. 209.

[17] Albert Dondeyne, **Faith and the World** (Eng. trans., Dublin, 1963), p. 103.

[18] J. D. Bettis, **op. cit.**, p. 217. Italics Eliade's.

[19] I follow here the French translation, which seems to do full justice to the Latin, which is not without its difficulties. Cf. **La Maison-Dieu**, no. 76 (1964), pp. 118–19.

[20] Ephesians 1:9; Colossians 1:22; 2:2 and cf. **ibid.**, 1:27.

[21] Mircea Eliade, **Myths, Dreams and Mysteries** (Eng. trans., Collins, Fontana ed., 1968), pp. 30–1.

[22] Christ cannot die again, and his self-offering was once-for-all.

[23] **Serm.** LXXIV, **De Ascens.** II, PL 54, c. 398.

[24] It is well known, of course, that Leo constantly used the word **mysterium** also, whether in the singular or the plural, and it is a nice question exactly what he meant on each occasion. But that he used it in the active–symbolic sense cannot be doubted. For a study of the whole matter see Dom Maria B. de Soos, **Le Mystère Liturgique d'après Saint Léon le Grand** (LQF, Heft 34; Münster, 1958).

# THREE

~

# The Worshipping Community [1]

~~~~~~

F EW AREAS OF theology have seen such considerable and rapid development in recent years as ecclesiology. When Pius XII's encyclical on the liturgy (1947) spoke of the 'church' it meant almost exclusively the hierarchical church. The Constitution on the Liturgy (1963) emphasized the community aspect of the church and during the Council itself there was a development of thought. The Constitution on the Church (1964) saw the church as above all the ministerial, the servant church. This in turn affected the redaction of the documents on the bishops' pastoral charge and that on the ministry of priests. All this and the course of events since the Council have considerably affected the way in which Catholics are now thinking and speaking of the Christian community whether inside or outside worship. In writing of the liturgy this may not seem to be a matter of primary concern, but the Constitution on the Liturgy has the germinal and, as one is inclined to think, prophetic statement right at the beginning: 'the liturgy is the outstanding means whereby the faithful may express in their lives, and manifest to others, the mystery of Christ and the real nature of the true Church' (2). The liturgy is the *sign* and, according to the same document (41), 'the pre-eminent manifestation of the Church'. If this is so, then all that is going on in the church, the movement towards the change or modification of structures or different ways of doing things that remain fundamentally the same, is of interest for both the celebration and formation of the liturgy. No doubt the liturgy cannot and should not reflect every detail of the church's changing life but the Council delivered the church from a form of worship that had become immobilized and that for four centuries had been incapable of manifesting its life.

Already the teaching of the Council on the status of lay-people is changing practice. In various parts of the church they and religious women are now performing liturgical functions–giving communion whether inside church or outside it, presiding over services of the

~

37

word – that a few years ago would have been regarded as inalienably the right and duty of the ordained minister. Somewhat reluctantly, women have been allowed first to read at eucharistic celebrations and then in the same place as lay*men* or the clergy![2] The Constitution itself recognized that a wide variety of lay-people exercise a liturgical function in celebration and, if that document is to be consistent with itself, that means a priestly function. The style of liturgy has changed beyond recognition and it is not surprising that Père Congar can say that the 'subject' of celebration was changed by the Council. The celebrants of the liturgy are the people even if we must add, with the Constitution, that it is an ordered people who celebrate with bishop or priest. It is, in fact, this change that makes it possible for the assembly to be the liturgical sign and manifestation of the church.

The journey to this point – and it has been a return journey – has been a long one, and practice still limps behind theory. Priests still need to realize that in celebration they are the servants of a community (GI 60) and the people still need to make efforts to establish the bonds that will make it a living community. Both need to realize that the liturgical assembly is as much 'a reality of the order of salvation'[3] as the rite they are celebrating. It is part of the mystery, for it is, as we have said, the sign of Christ who is the head of the body with whose members he celebrates the liturgy.

But, as we have tried to show in previous chapters, liturgy is human, though transcending human categories, and the same is true of community. Much has been written about community from a sociological as well as a theological point of view and the matter is very complex. We cannot go into it here. We must confine our attention to those aspects of it that are relevant to worship.

Everyone is aware that people gather together for various purposes from the simplest domestic celebration to elaborate assemblies through which it is hoped to achieve some common purpose. This is a sign that people need each other both for the fulfilment of their personalities and to promote a cause they all believe in. Community is a fundamental human phenomenon, so well known that it hardly seems necessary to mention it. Yet in worship there is still strong resistance to the notion and people still come to church thinking that they are isolated individuals who cannot possibly have any relationship with their fellow-worshippers, except those who have been carefully inspected and approved of. Yet normally people do reach out to each other, do feel the need of contact and intercourse with their fellow-human beings and express that need through gestures. This is (very summarily) the basis of community as it exists in worship. But it has this to tell us, that community is basically what has been called a face-to-face relationship. People need to *know* each other and as modern life becomes more and more impersonal, and as church life in so many places suffers from the same disease, it is ever more difficult to establish and maintain community in worship. This means that we have to make efforts to do so. Such efforts bring an air of artificiality to the whole business and it may be that it is this sense of strain and unnaturalness that some find offensive. Yet this again is but another sign that modern life *has* become unnatural–inhuman–and it must be the church's task to re-establish a human value that is of enormous importance.

In any case, the way of salvation has been communal and was and is to be found in community.

> If we turn to the history of salvation we find that God enshrined his promises of redemption in a people. It was to a people that he gave the law, a people who responded to his love with obedience to that law and with sacrifice by which they sealed the covenant with him . . . when the fulness of time came, it was with the establishment of the new Israel of God that salvation became possible for the individual. If the New Testament is radically personalist it is as radically communal. . . .[4]

In the Old Testament, God made the Israelites the *qahal*, the assembly, by covenant, law and sacrifice. This became *ecclesia* in the New Testament but only through Christ,

> for all that had happened in the past was recapitulated in him and, to adapt a statement from St Paul (Romans 9:4–5), the Israelites, adopted as God's sons, are now Christ. He is the presence of God made visible to men; he is the covenant; he is the law; he is the promise fulfilled; he the temple; he first the new holy people who came into existence on the cross. If we have inherited the promises it is through Christ we have done so. If we are a covenanted people, it is because we are united to him. If we are a holy people, it was he first who was holy, the Holy One of God.

~

If we are a priestly people, it was because he first was the high priest. If we are body, if we are bride, it is because he is head and because he, the bridegroom, has united us to himself as bride. What lies behind Ephesians 5:25–27 is that the Christian people are Christ's body, his bride, a consecrated people, holy, the temple of God.[5]

The Christian people are a community and Christ's salvation is mediated through it, though each has to appropriate it to himself. But, as the New Testament makes clear, it is a community that is constantly in the making. As it was called, convoked, by God in the beginning, so it has to be called again and again in the present. Every time the Christian community gathers for worship, it is called by God – that is the purpose of the entrance rite and the word that accompanies it. It is at this point that it begins to be the sign of Christ and of the church (*ecclesia*) scattered throughout the world. By the proclamation of the word (and the reception of the word in faith) and by the celebration of the eucharist, which according to St Augustine is the 'sacrament of the sacrifice' of Christ, the community becomes existentially the body of Christ offering itself to God.[6] Indeed, we can say that in celebration the church becomes a *Christian* community or, better, communion (*koinonia*): the church makes the eucharist and the eucharist makes the church.

But if the church is, through its worship, an organic union, it has to become a union of *persons*. There can be nothing mechanical about it. The faith and love that are generated in worship have to be appropriated, the worshipper must respond to the word of faith that is proclaimed and take to himself the love that is made present. Since it is the Holy Spirit who distributes the gifts in the body, it is through him that the worshipper will be able to appropriate the faith and love that is offered to him and it is in the Spirit that he is able to respond. This is why worship is dialogue and this is the sort of dialogue it is. It is not a mere saying of prescribed words or the singing of hymns, it is a dialogue at the level of life, the life of the Spirit, in him it is a dialogue with God.

Emphasis on the work of the Holy Spirit in the church and in worship has not been common in the West and even in the Constitution on the Liturgy it is not marked. The balance was partly corrected by the Constitution on the Church (12) where it is said that the laity, too, possess the gifts (*charismata*) of the Holy Spirit. Although the expression has not been familiar, it is none the less true that the church is to be described as a charismatic church and the people exercise their *charismata* in the general life of the church but also in worship. The *charismata* are extraordinary (1 Corinthians 14) and ordinary (Romans 12:4–8). The former gave St Paul a good deal of trouble, though he did not deny their validity, but it is the latter that are exercised in worship. All the services, 'ministries' that various people do are exercises of the gifts of the Holy Spirit for the building up of the community and its worship.[7] Such gifts will often be conspicuous in music, singing, organ-playing and so on, and it should be realized that they *are charismata* and are to be encouraged. Further, the contributions the people can make to the celebration will also be the fruits of their *charismata* and means must be provided for them to exercise them.[8]

*music*

But this community is also by its nature a liturgical, that is, a priestly community. It came into existence by the sacrifice of its head who as priest of the whole human race offered himself in a total self-giving to his Father. It inherited the priesthood of the Old Testament, though only through Christ, who transcended and transformed that priesthood.[9] In a passage that is filled with liturgical overtones, the community-church is described as being a house of the Spirit of which the 'living stones' are a holy priesthood who have to offer 'spiritual sacrifices' (*pneumatikas thusias*) to God through Jesus Christ (1 Peter 2:1–6). The house, the priesthood and the sacrifices all correspond to each other. They are 'pneumatic', not merely 'spiritual' in the weak modern sense, but 'of (the Holy) Spirit'. All the materialistic worship of the old Israel has gone, all the old sacrifices of bulls and goats, the old sacral priesthood and with them all the exclusiveness and the taboos that made Israel a *separate* people.[10] Nor is the Christian priesthood in any way comparable with the pagan priesthoods that filled the ancient world. It lies not so much between them as beyond them. It is a 'spiritual' priesthood that is at the service of a worship 'in spirit and in truth', not tied to Jerusalem or to any earthly location. The priesthood is indeed visible (in the first instance the church itself) but it has no sacrifice of its own. Its sacrifice is that of Jesus Christ who is the Priest that now offers it, the 'minister in the sanctuary . . . which is not set up by man but by the Lord' (Hebrews 8:2). The church's sacrifice is the 'memorial' of that sacrifice and makes it present. It does so by the operation of the Holy Spirit 'who is the principle in virtue of which the faithful become the church (*ecclesia*) and (thus) in their organic unity as body of Christ, the subject of liturgical actions'.[11]

The church is the Spirit-filled (pneumatic) body of Christ and in this sense its worship is and must be 'spiritual', of the Spirit. One is inclined to say that the nearest we can get to the 'spiritual' of the New Testament is 'sacramental', for it is through the symbolic-sacramental liturgy that the Spirit is communicated to the church and through which the church is able to establish contact with the Spirit. This may not be the only way the Spirit is communicated. There is faith and love, there are the *charismata*, the special gifts, but faith is 'sacramentalized' in baptism, love in the eucharist (*signum amoris*) and ordinary *charismata* are exercised in the celebration of the liturgy. The repentance of the sinner is actualized in the sacrament of penance and filled with the love of God that forgives sins. This last is the most striking example of how the free movement of the Spirit, who is, of course, not confined to either the liturgy or the church, can be concretized in the liturgy. And this is why the liturgy is the mystery-sacrament of Christ and the Holy Spirit who are present among men invisibly but whose presence becomes in a sense visible in the celebration of the liturgy.

The people of God, then, are a priestly people, or simply, as the New Testament says, a priesthood,[12] and on the other hand there is the ordained priesthood. The two are not opposed but complementary. The ordained priesthood is *ministry*, a *diakonia*, a service of the people, that is, of the whole body of Christ. There is but one priesthood, that of Christ in which both people and ordained priests share in different ways. Massively the church is at the service of Christ's priesthood which consisted of word and saving work and it is this word and this work that the priestly church exists to prolong in space and time until the consummation. But because the ordained minister has a special relationship to the whole people, he is appointed and constituted by a special sacramental act for the service of the people. His relationship is, if you like, sacramentalized. But he is also specially related to Christ and shares in his teaching, priestly and ruling office. As the Council documents proclaim tirelessly, the ministry of God's word is a primary obligation of the ordained ministry. This has a priority not so much of time but of importance, for the ordained minister, by his participation in Christ's priesthood, has to continue the work of proclaiming the Good News of salvation to those who have not yet heard it and to those who have,

~
42

in the name of God summoning them at the beginning of worship to assemble as the Christian community and evoking their faith and love during its course. It is his function, too, to form the people so that they may be fitted for their task of carrying the gospel to the world in which they live and work. Finally, he presides at liturgical services and especially at the eucharist where his role is irreplaceable.

As we have seen, the whole people have as their vocation the offering of 'spiritual sacrifices', their lives and work (and so has the priest), and this offering, which is basically self-offering, is realized and expressed in the liturgical offering of the eucharist where they offer not merely through the priest-celebrant but with him (GI 62). They have a real, active part in that offering, for both 'priesthoods' are necessary for the building up of the church and both *together* make the sign, the eucharist, that in a pre-eminent way manifests the church. But the ordained minister has a special, a representative function, not of the people, but of Christ, the head, and it is through this that he is able to perfect the spiritual-sacramental offering of the people:

> While the priesthood presupposes the sacraments of initiation [which he, as well as the people, has received, making him one of them], the sacerdotal office of priests is conferred by that special sacrament through which priests, by the anointing of the Holy Spirit, are marked with a special character and are so configured to Christ that they can act in the person of Christ the Head.

But his participation in the priesthood of Christ must not be interpreted in any narrow, exclusive sense, as if he were only a eucharistic offerer. It is through his preaching of the gospel as well as through his purely eucharistic role that he is able to perfect the people's offering:

> They (priests) shoulder the sacred task of the gospel, *so that* the offering of the people can be made acceptable through the sanctifying power of the Holy Spirit.[13] For, through the proclamation of the gospel, the People of God is called together and assembled so that when all who belong to this People have been sanctified by the Holy Spirit, *they can offer themselves* as 'a sacrifice, living, holy, pleasing to God' (Romans 12:1). Through the ministry of priests, the spiritual sacrifice of the faithful is made perfect in union with the sacrifice of Christ, the sole Mediator.[14]

We need not go into the theological complexities that are connected with the relationship of the two 'priesthoods'. The documents of the church state that they exist and that they differ in kind and not in degree.[15] But it will be useful to pursue the question of 'active participation' which is often misunderstood. At one level participation is simply the means by which it is achieved, the recitation of prayers, responses, the singing of chants of various kinds and the making of gestures. But at a deeper level these are all symbols of the active *offering* of the people through which, and with the priest-celebrant, they may enter into the sacrifice of Christ. The means can vary, they can be richer in symbolic expression or weaker. There *is*, at the level of means, a difference between a eucharist celebrated in a house and one celebrated in a large church with choir and servers. But the end remains the same.

Some of the difficulty has, I think, come from regarding 'sacrifice' as a *thing* (the-thing-that-has-become-sacred-by-immolation). As St Augustine said long ago, it is first an attitude and then an action that externalizes the attitude.[16] In the eucharist the attitude is that of self-offering. This is not a 'pious' extra nor of course is it only the people who have to offer themselves. The priest must do likewise. It is of the very stuff of the eucharist, for it is the very condition of the insertion of Christ's sacrifice into the church's offering. When this is achieved, as it is through the sacramental-liturgical re-enactment of the eucharist, Christ's sacrifice can become hers and *then* she is in a position to offer herself, to be united with Christ's sacrifice and so come to union with the Father. It is only on account of the identity of the church's offering with Christ's sacrifice that she can 'offer' and in this offering become herself.[17] The whole body of the people is lifted up into the sacrifice of Christ and in this the priest has *his* sacramental role to play because of his special relationship with Christ. This relationship is a sacramental one (by Holy Orders) and through it he enables the people to bring to sacramental expression their self-offering and so to enter into the sacrifice of Christ.

All this expresses the vertical relationship of the people of God in the community. But a horizontal relationship is of the very essence of community. People are related to one another and give service to one another. This is pre-eminently true of the liturgical assembly, and one of the less noticed features of the reformed rite of the Mass, not to mention other sacraments, is that this horizontal relationship is built into its very structure. In the Constitution (CL 26–31) it is the first principle of the reform of the liturgy and is expressed in three principal ways:

1. *All* liturgical services are celebrations of the community and, among other things, this must include the sacrament of penance, which offers peculiar problems for its reformation.

2. Within the community there are different services which are necessary for the proper celebration of a liturgical service and which are liturgical, i.e. priestly functions.[18] Each must be allowed to perform his or her function which may not be absorbed by anyone else, least of all the priest-celebrant.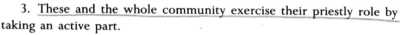

3. These and the whole community exercise their priestly role by taking an active part.

This last is again not an optional extra but is necessary if the local community is to construct the liturgical sign that is a manifestation of the church itself. The sign that the liturgical service requires is a great deal wider (and richer) than the 'matter' and 'form' that used to be regarded as the sign of the sacraments. The sign is people, the worshipping community, and it is only they that can construct the sign that is going to manifest the real nature of the church. You may *say*, if you will, that the eucharist is the sign of the unity of the mystical body, but it remains mere theology if the people do not speak, act and sing and if the various ministers of the rite do not perform their services. This is why 'active participation' is in an entirely different order from secular participation. *That* goes no deeper than the psychological needs that a gathering has or is conceived to have and it may be that because some think active participation is of that order they resist it. They do not wish to be associated with a football crowd.

Yet there is an interior aspect of active participation that is not always given its due. Although it has always been denied, Catholic liturgical worship has often in the past *looked* mechanical. It was a thing to be done, it was done and that was the beginning and end of it. The Constitution demands that the participation shall not only be active, exteriorized, but conscious and devout (CL 14, 41); the people are to come to worship 'with proper dispositions' and 'their minds should be attuned to their voices'. A whole programme of spiritual formation is in the background here, and at the lowest level people should be brought to realize that worship is not just the performance of pieces of ritual.

But what we are concerned with is something deeper than psychological dispositions of a merely human kind. Now it is realized once more [19] that we are saved by faith and by the sacraments of faith and that *this faith is in play in the celebration of the liturgy*. Everyone knows that we need faith if we are to receive the sacraments fruitfully, but what is perhaps not always realized is that the liturgy declares in concrete fashion the faith of the whole church and conversely the people express their faith in the liturgy. It is a declaration *in sacramento*, in the celebration itself, of their faith in Christ. Here the proclamation of the word, as we shall see, has a peculiarly important role to play, for it evokes faith and strengthens it. It is out of faith that we are able to respond to the message of faith that is proclaimed and it is through faith thus enriched that we are able to meet Christ at a deeper level, more wholeheartedly and with a greater sincerity.

The liturgical assembly is a community of faith, shared by all and professed by all. The recitation of the creed is the most obvious expression of this. But the assembly is also a community of love because the eucharist itself is the 'sacrament of love, a sign of unity and a bond of charity'.[20] This love, and the union that comes from it, is expressed in the common reception of the body of Christ in holy communion and in the signs that accompany it, the sign of peace, the communion procession and the singing of the communion chant. But the service the various ministers of the assembly perform is also a sign of love, the manifestation of the *charismata* that are distributed in the community by the Holy Spirit for its 'edification'. Of this the most striking liturgical expression is the Washing of the Feet on Maundy Thursday when the priest as the president of the community does a service which is the symbol of his whole relationship to the people who are represented by certain members of the congregation. As the texts indicate, this is all done in the spirit of the service of love of the Last Supper (John 13:4–16, 34, 35).

As far as eucharistic celebrations are concerned, all this is summed up in the General Introduction to the new Order of the Mass (62–64). The people are the royal priesthood who give thanks to the Father, who offer themselves and the victim not only through the priest but with him. Their union is expressed in the hearing of God's word, in common prayer and song, in the common offering of the sacrifice and in the sharing of the Lord's table. Even the bodily attitudes they adopt and the gestures they make are signs of their unity. But the unity is not a uniformity and the different groups (the choir who are at the service of the congregation and individuals, cantors, readers, servers and the rest) all in different ways express different aspects of the community and together build up the 'sacrament of the church'.

*How* all this is to be done in practice is a matter of local judgement and organization (GI 5, 6), but one of the more striking features of the conciliar and indeed post-conciliar documents is their emphasis on the local church and, within the broad limits laid down, the principle of adaptation (CL 39–40). This has, of course, a practical value: not everything can be done everywhere in the same fashion. The General Instruction, which is remarkably flexible in its directives, has made it possible to organize a truly community Mass even where the resources are of the most limited. To have a celebration that is full of life it is not necessary (or desirable) to do a sort of mock-up of cathedral worship. Indeed, it is being found that in the circumstances of the smaller group, whether at home or elsewhere, it is possible to achieve a sense of community and intimacy that is often wanting in the celebration of the eucharist in a large parish church.

The emphasis on the local church, then, is not only leading to different styles of celebration but is revealing the need so many Christians feel for a genuine experience of community. As has been remarked, the sociologists think of community as that assembly of people where there is a face-to-face relationship. People *know* each other. As everyone is aware, it is very difficult if not impossible to establish such a relationship in a large city parish. Hence the felt need for decentralization even within the parish, with the consequence that eucharistic and other celebrations in people's houses are desired. Such celebrations, it is felt, are necessary to express at a deeper level than mere good fellowship the sense of unity in the community thus gathered.

There are those who fear the separatist tendencies that such assemblies might set up. But all will depend on the spirit in which they meet and the guidance (and instruction) they receive from their clergy. Separatist tendencies can be avoided if the house-groups realize that the celebration of the Mass among them is the sign of their missionary work for the neighbourhood. No mission, no Mass. That is to say, they must be groups that in various ways are reaching out to the people among whom they live. They are trying to serve them in whatever way is open to them and they are willing to gather people into their houses where questions of religious faith can be discussed. On these terms, they will be the most dynamic places within the parish community which, in fact, though often invisible, they will be building up. Finally, if they bring to parish worship on Sundays the experience they have had in their smaller communities, they will do much to turn the parish worship into a genuine expression of the whole parish community.

We naturally think of the parish as 'the local church' but it is not autonomous. It belongs to a wider grouping, the diocese, and is dependent for the sources of its Christian life on the bishop. In the documents 'the local church' seems to mean primarily the diocese and some have described, perhaps not too happily, the parish as 'the particular church'. Certainly, the Constitution on the Liturgy (41) sees the diocese as the key grouping. It is the liturgy of the bishop when celebrated with his priests, ministers and people that is 'the pre-eminent sign' of the whole church. But on the one hand, the picture suggested by this statement is that of a diocese that is a credible community and not merely a jurisdictional area 'ruled' by an ecclesiastical official called a bishop. For a liturgy that is going to be the sign of the church as community, smaller dioceses would seem to be a necessity. On the other hand, the picture leaves out of account the ever-increasing part the parish plays and has played for a very long time in the lives of the people. Some may not be very closely attached to it, but it is here normally that people come to know what the Catholic church is and it is here that they 'experience' church. Regrettably, the bishop is an occasional, if welcome, visitor.

There is, too, something of a theological problem about the relationship between the bishop and the priest.[21] One Council document speaks of him as making the bishop present but it is agreed that he is no mere delegate. He depends on the bishop in various ways, but what is more important is that the basis of his union with him is a sacramental one. *Both* share in the one priesthood of Christ and both have the common task of proclaiming the gospel and bringing people to God through the celebration of the liturgy. None the less, the parish liturgy makes the sign of the church: 'Parishes, set up locally under a pastor *who takes the place of the bishop* . . . in some manner . . . represent the visible church constituted throughout the world' (CL 42). This is sufficient to point up the importance of parish liturgy. It may well be that it cannot construct as full a sign of the church as the episcopal liturgy, but it *is* such a sign and everything should be done to show that it is.

There are various ways in which the sacramental union that exists between bishop, clergy and people can be demonstrated. In some dioceses the Holy Oils, consecrated in a typical episcopal liturgy on Maundy Thursday (or earlier in Holy Week), are carried to the parish church and placed before the altar at the evening Mass. This shows the link between the parish clergy and the bishop because the oils the former use in baptism (exceptionally in confirmation) and in the anointing of the sick are consecrated by the bishop. This is an ancient tradition and even where, as in the Eastern churches, priests regularly confirm, the chrism must always be consecrated by the bishop. In the new regulations concerning confirmation and baptism – they may be conferred during the Mass – it is possible for the bishop to preside at the parish eucharist and to show by the celebration of these sacraments that he is indeed the president of the whole diocesan liturgy. Where the adult catechumenate is established, he is able to celebrate the sacraments of initiation in the order in which they are intended to be given. Again, it has become an established custom to confer the sacrament of Holy Orders in parish churches and here the sign of the church is very plainly made. Not only are there the necessary ministers of various ranks but it is a truly community occasion when the parish gathers together to celebrate what is realized to be an important event. The bishop is the source in some sense of the Christian life of the whole diocese (CL 41) and it is in ways like this that he can bring home to the people that this is so.

The eucharistic liturgy is the sign of a church that is a community and this is to be achieved by allotting to the laity those roles or ministries that belong to them. These ministries are listed in the General Instruction 66–71 (and for the choir 63). We are familiar with some but the list includes others that do not seem to be common in most churches in this country. Choirs exist, though it is becoming ever more difficult to maintain them. For the General Instruction they exercise a truly liturgical function – as we have suggested above, a *charisma* – and it is for them to undertake those parts of the liturgy that are proper to them and to serve the people by assisting their active participation in song. There are altar servers, too, of course, but there are also other officers who serve the community in different ways and help to construct the sign of community. Even at parish level the liturgy is 'hierarchical'. Among these we may note the cantor or what the Instruction (GI 67) calls the *psalmista* whose special task is to intone the psalms or other biblical canticles of

~

the liturgy but who, as experience shows, can animate and carry with him a whole congregation if he has the necessary *charisma* (a combination of nature, art and grace!). There is a strong case for training such people since the difficulties in the way of training and maintaining choirs are becoming so great.

There are also humbler officers, those who take up the collection and those who welcome people to the church. These last are to be found all too rarely and yet their role, given the impersonality of modern life, is all the more important. Such officers can welcome people, indicate or show them to their places, and hand them whatever literature they may need for the celebration of the Mass. It is in these humble ways that a crowd begins to be a community, a community of people sharing a common faith and engaged on the common task of making Christ present in the here and now. It remains for the president to realize that he, too, is the servant of the community and to do his all-important part in bringing this local gathering of people to a realization that they are the people of God.

As we have seen, there is no doubt about the church's teaching that liturgical services are celebrations of the Christian community, ordered under its bishop and clergy. There is no doubt about the church's desire that all should take their proper part in the celebrations and the different roles have been generously allotted. But have the laity any other contribution to make to the liturgy? The complaint has been heard often enough in recent years that the new liturgy has been imposed on the people without their advice or consent. If formal consultation is meant, there is a degree of truth in the complaint. But it also implies that the priests, bishops and a considerable number of lay-people who have been involved in the shaping of the new liturgy are in no way representative of the church. In fact, opinion had been forming for a great number of years on what our worship required and if some bishops, priests and laity chose to ignore what was being said and done in the church until the Vatican Council, they are not in a very strong position now to complain of what has happened. However, the decentralization of the church in recent years has made it possible for the local church, and that includes everyone, to make its contribution to the formation of the liturgy. This is not only possible, but is in certain circumstances required. Thus the General Introduction to the new Order of the Mass (GI 73) says that in the preparation of the liturgy, the rector of the parish should consult with his choir, his servers, his other helpers and also the people, at least for those matters that directly concern them. And this consultation is to concern itself not merely with liturgical matters in the stricter sense but also with pastoral matters. This means that the whole circumstances of the parish and its people must be taken into account when shaping the liturgy for the needs of the local church. This will cover a very wide range of matters indeed and could have a decisive effect on the worship of a particular parish.

In detail, the people are to be invited to contribute to the General Intercessions of the Mass by proposing petitions and by reciting them before the congregation. According to the Order of Holy Week, there may be several such persons among whom are to be included those recently baptized (49). When smaller groups come together for the Mass they may choose (from the Lectionary) texts that are appropriate to the occasion (e.g. anniversaries of weddings). *Before* baptism the parish clergy are required to consult with the families concerned, who will choose from the ritual the texts they prefer. The same is true of the marriage rite.

But there will be those who think that is insufficient. In the present situation little more is possible, but in the future that is opening out to us there remains the possibility of creative liturgy. Not in the sense of liturgical free-lancing (people deserve to be protected from that awful fate) but in the sense of consultation with bishop and clergy who will in discussion discover what are the needs of the people, will be willing to accept from them various suggestions (the people, too, have their charism) and finally will be able to shape the forms of the liturgy so that they will be truly expressive of the people's needs and desires. All somewhat utopian, some may think, but it would seem to be the condition of a living liturgy that continues to speak to the people and through which they will be able to give themselves in worship to God.[22]

# *Notes*

[1] Summary bibliography: Yves Congar, ' ''L'Ecclesia'' ou Communauté Chrétienne, sujet intégral de l'action liturgique' in *La Liturgie après Vatican II* (Paris, 1967), pp. 241–82. Yves Congar, *Lay People in the Church* (Eng. trans., 2nd ed., London, 1965). J. D. Crichton, 'The Worshipping Community' in *The People of God*, ed. L. Bright (London, 1965), pp. 75–97. A. G. Martimort, 'The Assembly'

in **The Church at Prayer** (Eng. trans., new ed.), I: **Principles of the Liturgy** (Liturgical Press/Geoffrey Chapman, 1987), pp. 89–112. J. Gelineau, ed., **Nelle Vostre Assemblee** (Brescia, 1970), pp. 45–192.

[2] Third Instruction, 7 (**Notitiae**, 60 (January 1971), p. 19).

[3] J. Gelineau, **op. cit.**, p. 54.

[4] J. D. Crichton, 'The Worshipping Community', **art. cit.**, p. 84.

[5] **Ibid.**, p. 85.

[6] **De Civ. Dei**, X, 20.

[7] Cf. Gelineau, **op. cit.**, p. 98.

[8] See pp. 44–51.

[9] See in **The Christian Priesthood**, ed. Nicholas Lash and Joseph Rhymer (London, 1970): John A. T. Robinson, 'Christianity's "No" to Priesthood' and Robert Murray, SJ, 'Christianity's "Yes" to Priesthood'.

[10] See Gelineau, **op. cit.**, p. 58. Christianity 'pure and undefiled' is without taboos though some apparently have turned Christian practices into taboos or tribal customs and would like to retain them. Hence a certain falling away from religion. Cf. Mary Douglas, **Natural Symbols** (London, 1970).

[11] Y. Congar, ' "L'Ecclesia" ou Communauté Chrétienne', **art. cit.**, p. 259.

[12] **Hierateuma** (1 Peter 2:5); **hiereis kai basileian** ('priests and a kingdom') (Revelation 1:6; 5:10).

[13] Romans 15:16. This reference to St Paul here is very remarkable. He sees the preaching of the gospel and its consequences in the life of the people as a **liturgy**. The Council took this up and applied it to the priest's ministry of the word which it relates to the people's eucharistic offering.

[14] Decree on the Ministry and Life of Priests 2 (**Documents of Vatican II**, ed. Abbott (London, 1966), p. 535).

[15] See A. Grillmeier in **Commentary on the Documents of Vatican II** (London, 1967), p. 158; David Power, **Ministers of Christ and His Church** (London, 1969), chapters VIII and IX.

[16] 'Sacrifice is the visible sign of the invisible offering (**sacrificii**)', **De Civ. Dei**, X, c. 5; and cf. St Thomas, ST II-II, 85, 2.

[17] Cf. St Augustine: 'Of his self-offering (**oblatio**) Christ willed that the church's sacrifice should be the daily **sacramentum** and since she is his body, she learns to offer through him' (**De Civ. Dei**, X, 20). Or again: 'In that which she offers, she herself is offered' (**ibid.**, X, 6).

[18] This means that women can (and do) in this sense perform priestly functions.

[19] Once more, for even St Thomas was merely summing up the tradition when he said that we are saved by faith and the sacraments of faith (cf. ST III, 62, 6; 64, 2, ad 3; and cf. CL 59).

[20] CL 47, quoting St Augustine.

[21] See David Power, **op. cit.**, chapters VII, VIII, IX.

[22] See J. D. Crichton, 'Liturgical Forms', **The Way**, Supplement 11 (London, 1970), pp. 35–7. For a condemnation of unauthorized experimentation see the Third Instruction from the Congregation for Worship in **Notitiae** 60 (January 1971), pp. 12–25. However, the same document says that it is for bishops 'to control, direct, and **stimulate** the liturgical life of the diocese, as well as rebuking if necessary'.

# FOUR

~

# The New Order of
# the Mass

~~~~~

THE ORDER OF the Mass that was promulgated in 1969 was the fruit of several years' work of the *Consilium* set up shortly after the promulgation on 4 December 1963, by the Second Vatican Council, of the Constitution on the Liturgy. The terms of reference of the *Consilium* were the principles of reform laid down in the Constitution, 21–40, and in particular for the eucharist, 49–55. The *Consilium* as such had no independent authority. It was answerable to the Congregation of Rites and to other congregations, to the bishops of the world who had voted the Constitution into existence and, of course, finally to the Pope. At all stages there was widespread consultation and among the members and consultors of the *Consilium* there were not only liturgical and other scholars but a considerable number of diocesan bishops and priests engaged in pastoral work. In addition, through the process of experimentation promoted by the *Consilium* itself, various rites were tested in actual pastoral situations and the results were collated for the final redaction of the texts. In this way the laity, too, have been able to make their needs known.

In view of certain misunderstandings of the procedures of liturgical reform it is necessary to give this summary account of them. The new rites that have been issued in recent years are not the work of a few liturgical bureaucrats who by unscrupulous intrigue have managed to impose dubious liturgies on an unsuspecting and unwilling church. At every stage the *Consilium*'s work has been scrutinized, sometimes over prolonged periods of time, and, among other things, documents have to be sent to the Congregation for Doctrine as well as, of course, to the Pope for his final approval. This is by no means a formality. The church has committed herself to these liturgies and they thus become authentic expressions of her faith. To complete the recent story, the *Consilium* became the Congregation for Worship in April 1970, and as a recent writer has said: 'The new Congregation for Worship is a more permanent version of the post-conciliar *Consilium*'. But the work is not yet

~

finished and will not be finished for some years to come. Not only are there further liturgical texts to be issued but the liturgy is now in a state of change. There is the adaptation now going ahead in Africa, India and elsewhere, and although the main lines of the rites have been fixed, it is very likely that even in Europe and North America there will be considerable adaptation over the years. As the same writer observes: 'The liturgy can never be regarded as static, fixed and complete. An awareness is visible [in the Congregation for Worship] that liturgy is alive, evolving, adapting like any living organism to its environment. Like all living things, it adapts to a continually evolving world or it dies.'[1] The role of the Congregation will be to control the procedures of adaptation but also, no doubt, to stimulate them as and when necessary.

Another feature of the current liturgical reform is that more and more discretionary power is being given to local conferences of bishops. They, too, must work within the limits of the Council and post-conciliar documents, but they have a certain power of initiation even if their projects and *desideranda* must be submitted to the Congregation. As the nature of the case demands, translation is almost entirely in their hands. Each of the great language zones of the world have their episcopal committees and a working committee under them whose texts they either accept or reject. Each local conference of bishops must give their approval for their own areas and this by a two-thirds majority vote. In judging new rites it is necessary to make a distinction between the Latin texts that come from the Congregation and the vernacular versions that come from the episcopal conferences. Liturgical translation is a very hazardous business and, incidentally, inevitably involves some adaptation, but all this is controlled both at the local level and at the Roman level and it is unlikely that anything unorthodox will get through.

It may be questioned, and has been questioned, whether the policy of having uniform versions for given language zones is a wise one. The differences in idiom and mental association in the English-speaking world are certainly very great and impose difficulties, but with the flexibility that Rome itself recognizes these can be largely overcome. Only those texts that are common to the *people* must be uniform. The rest, scripture versions and the like, can differ. In any case, all texts are subject to revision after a period of time laid down by the respective episcopal conferences.[2]

It may be said that liturgical reform has been done by way of authority while on the other hand liturgy is said to be a living, growing thing. In the circumstances of the modern church it is difficult to see how the reform could have been done in any other way. Either it would not have been done at all or we should have been the victims of individual caprice. There are those, of course, who say there was no need of reform, but they must recognize that the general sense of the church is against them.

For nearly fifty years before the Council the Liturgical Movement, eventually involving a vast number of bishops, priests, scholars and lay-people, had been working to bring the liturgy to the people and to encourage the people to take an active part in it. At first there was no question of liturgical reform, but experience showed that if the people were to take that active part in the liturgy that its nature demands, some change was necessary . The very shape of the liturgy and perhaps as much as anything the current style of celebration made it impossible for ordinary people to *use* it. More often than not they were just present at it. The language, Latin, was a barrier to true prayer and in the liturgy itself there were obscurities, obsolete rites and duplications that made it impossible for the ordinary Christian to appreciate its true significance. As is well known, the draft on the liturgy was the first presented to the fathers and was the only one they accepted as a basis for discussion without radical re-shaping.[3] After a strenuous and lengthy debate that took up nearly the whole of the first session and part of the second, the Council finally decreed that, as far as the eucharist was concerned, its liturgy should be reformed, certain rites simplified and the whole to be of such sort that all could easily understand it. Above all, 'the aim to be considered before all else' in the reform of the liturgy was 'the full and active participation' of *all* the people in its celebration. Active participation, even if not the happiest of expressions, is no mere psychological or 'popular' gimmick but in the words of Pius X in 1903 (so long ago!) 'the primary and indispensable source from which the faithful are to derive the true Christian spirit'.[4] If the new Order of the Mass has done nothing else, it has provided the means to make this possible.

In the *Missale Romanum* of 1970 there are three introductory documents: the Apostolic Constitution of Paul VI, the Proemium and the General Instruction, first issued with the *Ordo Missae* of 1969 and now appearing in a revised version.[5] It may seem strange that a new rite should need such a barrage of introductory material. Obviously, a papal document was needed to promulgate the new Order and the missal to the church and the General Instruction, which, as we shall see, is a document of the greatest interest and importance, was necessary to convey to both priests and people the deeper significance of the new rite. But it is to be regretted that the Proemium, a controversial statement, intended to rebut the criticisms of the new Order and in the nature of the case a very ephemeral document, should have a place between the other two. We may regret, too, that for the same reason the Order itself had to undergo revision. After due consideration I have decided that since the Proemium does not add to a liturgical understanding of the new Order, there was no need for me to treat of it in this book. I have, of course, had to take into account the revision of the General Instruction which it occasioned and the principal modifications that have been introduced are considered in the next chapter.

## *The Apostolic Constitution*
~

Apostolic Constitutions are legal instruments, well known in Roman practice, by which important decisions of the Holy See are promulgated. At times, they may seem to be no more than a formality, but the one that is to be found in the *Missale Romanum* of 1970 is no formal piece of writing. It breathes an air of personal conviction and concern, and if those who had objected to the new Order had read it, they would have found many of their objections answered. The suggestion heard, for instance, in certain quarters that Paul VI had no right to undo what Pius V had done, or, more bizarrely, that he had sold the church out to the Protestants, would never have been made.

After mentioning the fruitful results that had come from the missal of Pius V, the Pope recalls the words of Pius XII that the liturgical movement was a sign of God's providence and of the work of the Holy Spirit in the church, and points out that his predecessor had in fact initiated the revision of the Roman Missal by his reforms of the liturgy of Holy Week. Further, the revision of the missal was not the result of a sudden decision. Liturgical study, a better knowledge of the ancient liturgical texts (many of which have only been edited in modern times) and, above all, the decisions of the Second Vatican Council had made possible and necessary the revision of the eucharistic liturgy. He patiently lists the main principles of the reform (the texts and rites must express more clearly the realities they convey, the proper relation of part to part must be set out, the active participation of the people must be facilitated, a more generous provision of holy scripture must be made and facilities for concelebration provided), points out that the addition of three new eucharistic prayers is an innovation which is justified as an enrichment of our appreciation of the mystery of the eucharist, that the simplification of the offertory was necessary to eliminate useless 'repetitions' and that the importance of the homily and the restoration of the prayer of the faithful are examples of a return to an older tradition. A long passage is devoted to the importance of the new lectionary and urges in moving tones upon clergy and laity alike a serious study of God's word which is a source of the spiritual life, the main theme of doctrine and the heart (*medulla*) of all theology. As far as the eucharist is concerned such a study will ensure that the people will come to it properly prepared.

After drawing attention to certain other features of the missal (e.g. new Masses for modern needs) he recommends it to the church:

> When our predecessor St Pius V promulgated the editio princeps of the Roman Missal he presented it to the Christian people as an instrument of liturgical unity and as a monument of sincere worship in the church. We do the same and although we have admitted into the new missal legitimate variations and adaptations, according to the prescriptions of the Second Vatican Council,[6] it is our confident hope that it will be received by the Christian people as a means by which they will be able to bear witness to and strengthen the unity existing among them. In this way, and though uttered in a great variety of languages, one and same prayer will ascend from all to the heavenly Father through our high priest, Jesus Christ in the Holy Spirit. . . .

The document concludes as usual in the *stylus curiae*, but it is important to realize that it enshrines a legal decision formally abrogating the missal of Pius V. What Pius could do, Paul can undo. If the primacy of the Pope does not mean that, it means nothing.[7]

# *Notes*

[1] P. Coughlan, 'Consilium to Congregation', **Life and Worship** (April 1971), p. 25.

[2] ICEL, the International Commission on English in the Liturgy, has come in for a good deal of criticism in the course of years. Some of their work earlier on perhaps deserved it, but it remains to be proved that there is any other body in the English-speaking world that can do as good a job of work as, on the whole, they have done.

[3] See P. Coughlan, **art. cit.**, p. 26.

[4] CL 14. Psychological and popular needs are not to be despised and one wonders how much longer ordinary people would have gone on tolerating the sort of liturgy they had. There were signs of restiveness **before** the Council. But, as we have tried to show, active participation goes a great deal deeper than the satisfaction of psychological needs.

[5] The Calendar is considered in Chapter 8 below, the General Instruction in Chapter 5.

[6] CL 38-40, where the above phrase is to be found.

[7] It may, however, be questioned whether this legal language and the rubric that heads both Pius V's Constitution and that of Paul VI **Ad perpetuam rei memoriam** does not overdo it a bit. Paul XXVI could abrogate what Paul VI has done. When does 'perpetual' mean 'perpetual'?

*F I V E*

~

# The General Instruction

~~~~~

P UBLISHED TOGETHER WITH the new Order of Mass is a document called *Institutio Generalis*, or General Instruction, which takes the place of the old *Ritus Servandus* of the 1570 missal and of the other rubrical injunctions that were added to it from time to time. The difference in spirit and character between the two is startling. Whereas the old rubrics were concerned with the minutiae of ritual and, with two exceptions,[1] with what the priest did at the altar, the new Instruction must be described as a liturgical document of the first importance. It goes far beyond rubrical direction and is concerned with the nature of eucharistic celebration. Each major section of it is prefaced by a theological statement about the Mass or about that part of it for which it is giving directives. True, these statements are for the most part summaries of Council documents, but they are very skilful and sometimes clarify the statements of the documents. Their great value is that they make the Mass appear as a totally meaningful action and those who are being trained for the ministry and laity who have to teach, or, indeed, would know what the Mass is, will find here a theology they can assimilate without difficulty. As far as seminarists are concerned, it is one that will form them for celebration. It will be impossible in the future to train people for the celebration of the Mass without at the same time teaching them what the Mass in general and particular is. With one blow this document kills rubricism stone dead.

Since the Instruction is a long document consisting of 341 articles, divided into eight chapters covering a vast amount of detail, it will be as well to give a summary of it. Experience shows that since it is not as yet indexed, it is often necessary to spend a considerable amount of time tracking down a single item.

*Chapter I, 'On the Importance and Dignity of the Eucharistic Celebration'*, is the principal though not the exclusive liturgico-theological statement of the Order.

*Chapter II, 'On the Structure of the Mass, its Elements and Parts'*, is a *rationale*

~
59

of the new rite (though so very different from that of a Durandus!), giving the meaning of each part. It is the most important chapter in the whole Instruction and to it we shall return.

*Chapter III, 'On the Functions and Ministries'*, deals with all those engaged in the celebration of the eucharist from the priest through deacon to readers, cantors, commentators, people and choir (the people being placed immediately after the deacon in order and before the lesser ministers).

*Chapter IV, 'On the Different Forms of Celebrating the Mass'*, covers Mass with the people in its typical form together with the directives on the functions of deacon and subdeacon, concelebrated Masses, Mass in the absence of a congregation and 'Certain more general rules' about ceremonial (veneration of the altar and gospel book, genuflexions and bows, incensations, the cleansing of the hands and vessels and the various ways of administering communion in both kinds).

*Chapter V* deals with the arrangement and furnishing of the church for eucharistic celebration, largely repeating the directives of the Instruction of 1964.

*Chapter VI* gives directives about the bread and wine, the vessels to be used in celebration and the vestments.

*Chapter VII* sets out the principles on which liturgical texts are to be chosen for different Masses, and

*Chapter VIII* those concerning Ritual Masses, Votive Masses and Masses for the Dead.

## *The eucharistic theology of the* Ordo Missae

The form of the Mass that is given in the Order itself expresses the theology of the eucharist that is set out more formally in the Instruction, but for practical purposes it will be best to examine first what the Instruction has to say and then go on to see how its theology is reflected in the Order.

The three main features of this theology are that it is firmly anchored in what the Lord said and did at the Last Supper, that it speaks a language that goes back beyond the Council of Trent and belongs to the Fathers and liturgies of the early Christian centuries, and that it is set in a community context.

This teaching is found principally in articles 7 and 48 of the Instruction, both of which have undergone some re-writing, occasioned by the objections of its critics (see above, pp. 55, 56). It will be instructive to set out article 7 in both versions:

1. The Lord's Supper or the Mass is the sacred synaxis or gathering[2] of the people of God who come together to celebrate the memorial of the Lord under the presidency of the priest. The saying of Christ that 'where two or three are gathered together in my name, I am in the midst of you' (Matthew 18:20) is thus eminently verified in the local gathering of holy church (1969).

2. *In the Mass, that is the Lord's Supper, the people of God* are *called together* to celebrate the memorial of the Lord, *that is the eucharistic sacrifice*, under the presidency of the priest *who acts in the person of Christ*. The saying of Christ that 'where two or three are gathered together in my name, I am in the midst of you' is thus eminently verified in the local gathering together (*coadunatione*) of holy church. *For in the celebration of the Mass, in which the sacrifice of the cross is perpetuated, Christ is made really present in the congregation gathered in his name, in the person of the minister, in his word and indeed substantially and continually in the sacramental species* (1970).[3]

The procedure is obvious: every time there is an incriminated expression, what may be called for short a 'Tridentine' phrase is put beside it. Thus 'memorial' is 'corrected' by 'eucharistic sacrifice', the 'presidency of the priest' by 'who acts in the person of Christ' and it is not safe/acceptable to say that 'the Lord's Supper or the Mass *is* the sacred synaxis of the people of God'. This, it may have been thought, looks like some sort of Congregationalism, though I do not know that any Congregationalists have ever held anything of the sort.

Although the commentators on the new version of the Instruction say that nothing new has been added,[4] the picture is subtly changed. They indeed say elsewhere that the *teaching* is the same.[5] If this is so, we can take the changes as simply so many warning signs that should be borne in mind but which do not affect the teaching of the Instruction.

But before we do, it will be as well to look at some of the other emendations in the above paragraph.

We may speculate on the reasons why the description of the Mass as 'the sacred synaxis of the people of God under the presidency of the priest' was objected to and the commentators indeed say that the revised version is more accurate, though, they also say, it was never the intention of the Order to give a doctrinal definition of the Mass (*loc. cit.*, 178). They point out that it gives a description of the general liturgico-ritual structure of the Mass and state that the structure of the eucharistic celebration is drawn from the community Mass (*Missa communitaria*), that is, one celebrated with the people in which is fully verified the principle (to be found also in CL 7) that the eucharist is the 'action of Christ and the Church', namely of 'the hierarchically ordered people of God'. Here is but one example of what the commentators mean when they say that nothing new was added to the Instruction. Patiently, and one does not know with what irony, they are spelling out its meaning and, in fact, giving nothing away. What in fact is in conflict is two totally opposed theological worlds, what E. Schillebeeckx called the essentialist theology as opposed to the existentialist theology at Vatican II. The objectors want to cling to a static essentialist theology of the Mass which cheerfully abstracts from its liturgical forms and celebration. On the contrary, the Instruction sees it as something in action, a celebration, and it is perfectly legitimate to describe it as the 'sacred synaxis of the people of God who come together to celebrate the memorial of the Lord under the presidency of the priest'.[6] This is what it in fact is, this is what you can discern and, as the liturgical documents affirm, it is from the Mass-in-action that you can see what it is and indeed what it is saying about the church.[7] The people gathered by God and acting with and under the presidency of the priest are the sign of the church, explicitating its meaning. They are part of the total sacramental sign of the eucharist itself and that is why it can be said that 'the structure of celebration is drawn from the community nature of the Mass'. It is this 'hierarchically ordered people' who celebrate the eucharist, bring it into existence in the here and now and who consequently should not be excluded from any comprehensive definition of the Mass. The eucharist, like the other sacraments, is the legitimate object of theological reflection but it, like them, is an existent thing and its nature will only be known in celebration.

Along with their concern over the sacrificial nature of the Mass, the objectors show a certain fussiness about the role of the priest in the eucharist. Perhaps they have been used to defining the priesthood in the terms of cult and 'powers'; the unique 'power' of the priest is to celebrate the sacrifice of the Mass, to be a 'sacrificer' in fact, although the whole analogous nature of the terms fails to impress them. No doubt they are not much concerned with modern theological reflection on the ministry, but there are the documents of the Vatican Council (on the church, on bishops and on the life and ministry of priests, to mention no others) that give a rather different emphasis.

The objectors are concerned to emphasize that in 'sacrificing', the priest acts in the person of Christ but they nowhere state that he is acting in the same way when he is preaching God's word, when he is visiting the sick or consoling the bereaved. And yet in one way or another the Council documents do say this. Thus the Decree on the Ministry and Life of Priests (4) can say 'that the *primary* duty (of priests) is the proclamation of the gospel of God to all'. This they have to do both by word and by their life, but their preaching in the liturgy is of special importance:

> Such is especially true of the Liturgy of the Word during the celebration of Mass. In this celebration, the proclamation of the death and resurrection of the Lord is inseparably joined to the response of the people who hear, and *to the very offering* whereby Christ ratified the New Testament in his Blood. The faithful share in this offering both by their prayers and by their recognition of the sacrament for what it is.

In prayer, especially that of the Divine Office, they pray *in the name of the church* (5), they have the task of forming Christian communities, leading them *through Christ* and in the Spirit to God the Father (6) and, not to prolong the list, they have to care for the poor and lowly, an apostolate that is 'a sign of Messianic activity' in which they are following Christ (6). A comprehensive paragraph sums up the whole life of the priest, and if it does not say that in all his priestly tasks he is acting in the person of Christ, it says much the same thing when it says that they 'result from Christ's Passover':

> The purpose, therefore, which priests pursue by their ministry and life is the glory of God the Father as it is to be achieved in Christ. That glory consists in this: that men knowingly, freely, and gratefully accept what God has achieved perfectly through Christ, and manifest it in their whole lives. Hence, whether engaged in prayer and adoration, preaching the Word, offering

the eucharistic sacrifice, ministering the other sacraments, or performing any of the works of the ministry for men, priests are contributing to the extension of God's glory as well as to the development of divine life in men. Since all these activities result from Christ's Passover, they will be crowned in the glorious return of the same Lord when he himself hands over the kingdom to his God and Father (2).

We need not delay over the last part of this article. The concern for the Real Presence in or 'under the eucharistic species' is hardly necessary within the confines of the Roman Catholic Church and, in fact, the Proemium simply points to the *practices* of the liturgy, the elevation and the feast of Corpus Christi, as sufficient proof of the church's unwavering faith. We merely remark that the revisers have strengthened the statement of the Constitution on the Liturgy about the presence of Christ in different parts of the liturgy (CL 7): 'Christ is *really* present in the assembly, in the celebrant, in the word . . .'. As we know, the Council's teaching here startled some people, so used had we become to thinking of only one kind of presence of Christ. The reason for its inclusion here is obvious but again it is unnecessary.

The second place where there is some change is in article 48 which introduces 'The liturgy of the Eucharist'. It is slight, though showing the same concern: 'Christ, at the Last Supper, *instituted the sacrifice and paschal banquet by which the sacrifice of the cross* is continually made present in the church . . .'. The words italicized are the ones added to the original article that read: 'The Last Supper, at which Christ instituted the memorial of his death and resurrection, is made continually present in the church when the priest, representing Christ, does what the Lord himself did and gave to his disciples to do in memory of him thus instituting the paschal sacrifice and banquet'. The addition, which is not much more than a re-arrangement of the words, was hardly worth making and the need for the change is found in the inability or unwillingness of the objectors to accept the ancient and wholly traditional language of 'memorial'. The memorial of the death and resurrection of Christ is the memorial of the paschal mystery by which he redeemed the world and when the church makes the memorial, it is making present in the here and now the effects of the redeeming work of Christ.

What picture of the eucharist, then, emerges from a study of the

Instruction and of the rite itself? It will be convenient to take the Instruction first and then the rite.

## *The Mass in the Instruction*
~

The first thing emphasized is that the Mass is a community celebration. Especially since the Constitution on the Liturgy, this is a theological platitude.[8] It is, however, worth pointing out that it is a complete change from the picture given by the rubrics of the Pius V missal. These were concerned almost wholly with the actions of the priest who is envisaged as concentrated on what he must do and say almost regardless of the people. Although the term is harsh, he appeared as the minister of a mysterious cult of which he alone had the secret. Even the gestures he was required to make were regarded as a clerical secret, and when in the seventeenth century the first translations of the missal and breviary were made, they were condemned as profanations.[9] Even educated people would read a book of devotions, one of the many *Manières d'entendre la Sainte Messe* or the Hours of Our Lady, during Mass and all were thought to be devoutly kneeling looking in wonder at the mystic rite (if they could see it) as it unrolled before them. The rubrics instructed the celebrant to 'show' the Host to the people after the consecration (by raising it over his head) and likewise the chalice, but frequently this was so badly done that they could not be seen. The people are spoken of in the *Ritus Servandus* once again, at the time of communion, and in spite of the strong recommendations of the Council of Trent to frequent communion, the rubric assumes that it is going to be rare: '*If* there are any to be communicated' (*si qui sunt communicandi . . .* ). If to this we add that the custom grew up that people were communicated either before or after Mass (a custom that remained until about fifty years ago), it will be seen that the part of the people in the Mass was visibly non-existent.

How different the picture of the Mass as given by the *Ordo Missae* of 1969: the celebration of the Mass is the action of Christ and of the hierarchically ordered people of God, or in the words of the Constitution, the action of Christ in his church (CL 7). The celebration must be so ordered that all, ministers and people, in their various roles, may be able to take their part so that they may receive as copiously as possible the fruits of the Mass. It was to this end that Christ the Lord instituted the sacrifice of his body and blood and entrusted it as the memorial of his passion and resurrection to his beloved Bride, the church. Nor is this left in the realm of exhortation: since the eucharist requires and uses visible signs for its celebration, the greatest care must be taken to select those forms and elements that in local circumstances are best adapted to secure the full and active participation of the people (GI 3, 5). Celebration must be the visible sign of the worshipping eucharistic community and this community is the sign or sacrament of the church. It reveals its nature, it shows and teaches that the church is the union of those who love one another in Christ and who through him are lifted up to the Father in praise and thanksgiving. As article 1 of the Order says, the eucharist is the centre of the whole Christian life both for the church as a whole, for the local church and for the individual, and is the culminating point of its existence. By it God in Christ sanctifies the world and men give their worship to the Father through him.

The teaching that the local church in its eucharistic celebrations is the sign of the great church is repeated at the opening of the long chapter on the structure of the Mass and the revised version does nothing to minimize it (GI 7). The people are *called together* to celebrate the memorial of the Lord and the whole body, under the presidency of the priest who represents Christ, is a conspicuous manifestation of the truth that 'where two or three are gathered together in my name, there I am in the midst of them' (Matthew 18:20). As we shall see, this, which has always been true, is made plain in the rite itself.

This teaching about the local church, whether the diocese or, less perfectly, the parish, is of both theological and practical importance. Theologically it suggests that the church, the *Una sancta*, is made up of innumerable communities throughout the world, each related to the other because they are parts of the body of Christ in which the Spirit dwells and is active. Each has a different function and each casts a different light on the church as a whole. More important still, it is here in these local communities that the church really exists.[10] Until the modern renewal of the church and of its theology, we tended to look on it as a vast institution or organization, spread indeed throughout the world, propagating, in ways that were not very particularly examined, Catholic truth and getting (some) people into heaven. There was some temptation to see the church as a vast propaganda machine and many of those outside it in fact saw it as that. Rome and the Pope dominated the scene. What it came to, in fact, was an ecclesiastical institution that made itself present in different parts of the world largely juridically. The renewed theology of the church, the Second Vatican Council and now the *Ordo Missae*, make it clear that the great church exists and acts in and through the local church and principally through the celebration of the liturgy. It is here that God's word comes alive and is proclaimed, it is here that through Christ glory is given to God, it is here that men are sanctified and ultimately saved.

Practically, the teaching is important for it means that those in charge of the liturgy in a local community have to consider their own situation, have to decide what, within the limits of the Order, is right and possible. They have to construct a local liturgy that is adapted to the capacities and needs of the local church. This might seem too obvious to mention and everyone is more or less aware that it has always been necessary to adapt the liturgy to circumstances. No one can be unaware of the difference between a cathedral and a small parish church, though this awareness has not always been sufficiently vivid to prevent priests and choirmasters from emulating those they have thought were their betters. Nor was adaptation (lawfully) easy under the old regime. It was a case of all or nothing. You either had a low Mass or a 'pompous' high Mass. The principle of adaptation has been built into the new Order. Incense may or may not be used at any kind of Mass and its use within the Mass may be varied from one kind to another (GI 235). The suggestions (they are nearer to this than to rules) about singing are even more flexible (GI 19). This or that rite may be done 'if convenient'. For instance, there should normally be an offertory procession but there are circumstances in which this is impossible. So you need not have one – but it would be against the spirit of the Order to decide that *nothing* can be done. What is required is that *some* gesture of offering on the part of the people (collectors or others can bring the elements to the altar) should be made. The mind of the Order is that the Mass should be a community action. Like the Constitution on the Liturgy, it says again and again that the *purpose* of the new rite is that the full, conscious and devout participation of the people should be made possible, a participation to which they have a right by baptism (GI 3, 5). Through this kind of celebration 'in which those elements of the rite are chosen to secure the active participation of the people' (GI 5) the 'real nature of the true church' will be manifested (CL 2) and the work of Christ's redemption will be effected (*ibid*.). The image of the church, the community of Christ, will be reflected in such a celebration and will be truly discernible. It will not be distorted.

What, then, does this community come together to do? The answer falls under three heads: (1) to celebrate the memorial of the Lord; (2) to meet Christ in his word; (3) to receive him in holy communion.

The phrase 'to celebrate the memorial of the Lord' is at once the simplest and most profound way of describing what the Christian community does at Mass. It is to say no more, but *no less*, than what Christ said at the Last Supper: 'Do this in memory of me' (*touto poieite eis tēn emēn anamnēsin*).[11] When the Christian community *makes* the eucharist, it is making the memorial of the Lord and of all he did from the Supper to the resurrection to redeem mankind. It should not be necessary to re-affirm, but apparently it is, that 'making the memorial', *anamnesis*, in fact, is not to be understood in the weak modern sense of just recalling to the mind a past event. All scripture scholars[12] and liturgists[13] are agreed that it is to be understood in the active sense: by 'making the memorial' we are 'in some way', as both the Constitution and the Order say (CL 102 and GI 1), making present the redeeming work of Christ. When celebrating the eucharist, the church is put in possession of the power of Christ's redeeming actions from the Supper to the resurrection (what the documents call 'the paschal mystery'). Or, you can put it another way round, Christ, faithful to his promise, comes to his church once again, makes himself present to it and communicates to it his saving life. It is then, and only then, that we are able to give that worship to the Father through Christ of which the Order speaks (GI 1) and which alone is acceptable to God.

Needless to say, if the people have or are given a sense of the active, redeeming Christ in the Mass, their appreciation of it as 'sacrifice' will in no way be weakened. They will realize that sacrifice is not an inert object immolated and offered to God but that it is in its very essence Christ's act of self-giving[14] that continues in heaven where he is ever-living to make intercession for us (Hebrews 7:25). This same teaching, too, will evoke from them that other important New Testament teaching that our response to Christ's self-giving is a giving of ourselves to him and through him to the Father: 'offer your living bodies as a holy sacrifice truly pleasing to God' (Romans 12:1).[15]

Emphasis on 'memorial' also makes the pattern of the whole eucharistic action more comprehensible. There is the age-old problem of the relation of the 'once-for-all' sacrifice of the cross and the sacrifice of the Mass. Various words have been used, 'renewal', 're-enactment' and so on, all of which give the impression (at least) that the Mass is in some way a *separate* sacrifice. This will not do, as it at least seems to derogate from the uniqueness of the cross. Then again, the Mass has often and perhaps usually been called 'the renewal or re-presentation of the *cross*', but this over-simplifies things. This direct relationship of the Mass to the cross was not without its influence on the unhappy practice of looking for events of the passion and death of Christ in the Mass. Christ did not say on the cross 'Do *this* in memory of me'. It was after the Supper, in which he declared the meaning of what he was to do next day, that he said 'Do this in memory of me' and as the Council of Trent carefully said, by so doing he left a *memorial* of his sacrifice to the church. What we are doing in the Mass is to make the memorial of what Christ did at the Last Supper and through the making of that memorial we are able to make encounter with the sacrifice of Christ, which, as St Thomas said, is perpetual.[16] The church was put in possession of the means by which the men and women of all time could enter into the redeeming work of Christ. These means remain within the initiative of the church which, in obedience to Christ's command, inaugurates in the here and now the rite of the Mass. These successive 'inaugurations' can obviously be numbered, these can be called 'Masses' and the Proemium (2) can call the Mass a '*sacramental* renewal' where full weight must be given to the word 'sacramental'. It is the sacramental, ritual, liturgical action that remains within the competence of the church and through which, to repeat, it makes the memorial of the Supper, which in turn makes the sacrifice of the cross present to people here and now.

Even to narrow the memorial of the Mass to the cross is to say less than the truth of the matter. As the documents of the church affirm again and again, the Mass is the memorial of the Lord's death and resurrection, what the Constitution calls the paschal mystery (CL 5), by which he brought his 'worshipping' church into existence, redeemed mankind and gave glory to the Father. Because it is this kind of memorial, the church *now* can enter into the redeeming work, can make its own the effects of the redemption. In the Mass we encounter the Risen Christ, who has suffered and died. It is he who enfolds our self-offering in his, unites it to his own and offers us to his Father. Once this is achieved the whole community through the operation of the Holy Spirit (as the *epicleses* of the new eucharistic prayers make clear) is able to offer that sacrifice of praise, thanksgiving and propitiation of which both the Council of Trent and the Proemium speak. When the church speaks of 'active participation' it is all this it has in mind, not merely a voicing of certain formulas. These and actions and gestures and a dozen other things are merely the means by which the community may enter into union with God.

This is a rather different picture of the Mass from one that sees it as an offering of some object 'out there' to which people can attach themselves by pious thoughts or devout desires. This view of the Mass, which is not new but very old, means that the community must be involved in its action 'as the very nature of the celebration demands', to quote the Instruction (GI 3). It is an action not an object to be contemplated, it is by definition a community action and normally the effects of Christ's redeeming work upon the participants will be in proportion to their active involvement. The church documents say this over and over again, but not all as yet realize that this is what they mean.

## The role of the priest

The worshipping community is a 'hierarchically ordered' people made up of many 'ministries' united under the presidency of the priest. Thus the Constitution and other documents.[17] This means that in the celebration he is *visibly* head of the assembly, occupying the chief place and pronouncing certain texts, above all the eucharistic prayer, that belong to him alone.[18] But that is to describe no more than his material function. During celebration it is for him to *animate* the community, to set the tone for the act of worship and throughout to maintain the action of the people and of all the other 'ministries' that collaborate in the celebration of the eucharist. His mentality, attitude and general bearing are of crucial importance. He must be concerned not for himself but for the community he is leading. In his presidency he is above all the *servant* of the people, helping them not merely to say prayers and sing chants, but to move towards God and be united with him, which is the purpose of the whole action. The various ways by which he may do this will be considered later.

But if he is to achieve this presidency *in worship* he will also have to exercise it before worship in preparing all those people and things that are necessary for celebration, combining and harmonizing the work of choir, servers and readers especially. Of diocesan bishops the Decree on the Bishops' Pastoral Office in the Church (15) says that they are the principal dispensers of the mysteries of God and the '*governors, promoters* and *guardians* of the entire liturgical life in the church committed to them'. What is true of the bishop is true also of the pastoral priest within the limits of his own sphere and in dependence on his bishop and the regulations of the church. He is not just the performer of certain rites that can be found in the official books. Nor does he exercise this leadership-service without the collaboration of his people. They have their various functions to perform which may not be taken away from them (CL 28, 29) and they must be 'trained to perform their functions in a correct and *orderly* manner' (*ibid.*).

But the presidency of the priest goes much further. He is very much more than the organizer of ceremonial or the reciter of words. He is the *minister* of Christ 'who in the liturgy exercises his priestly office on our behalf by the action of the Holy Spirit' (Decree on Priests 5). He is first the minister of God's word both outside the liturgical sphere and especially inside it: 'In the Christian community itself, especially among those who seem to understand or believe little of what they practise, the preaching of the Word is needed for the very administration of the sacraments. *For these sacraments are sacraments of faith, and faith is born of the Word and nourished by it*' (*ibid.*, 4). Thus through his ministry of the word he is the minister of faith which leads men and women to Christ, and exercises his priestly office in their regard in the celebration of the sacraments.

In the eucharist there is the closest possible connection between the word and the sacrament. The priest leads the people into the sacrament by his ministry of the word: 'In this celebration, the proclamation of the death and resurrection of Christ is inseparably joined to the response of the people who hear, and to the very offering whereby Christ ratified the New Testament in his blood. The faithful share in this offering both by their prayers and by the recognition of the sacrament for what it is.' As we have seen (in Chapter 3) by his total ministry the priest leads the people in the offering of the eucharist and makes it possible for them to unite themselves and their whole lives to the sacrifice of Christ.

*All* of this is comprised in 'the presidency of the priest' at the eucharist and it will be seen that the other phrase used in the Council documents and in the Order of the Mass 'the priest acts in the person of Christ' is merely a more concrete, and shorter, way of putting the matter. The priest is indeed 'configured to Christ' so that he can act 'in the person of Christ' (Decree on Priests 3), but he is so acting both when he is proclaiming the word and when he is leading the people into the offering that includes the offering of themselves. His action is indispensable but it does not obliterate that of the people. The whole community celebrates, the whole community offers, the whole community receives into itself the self-offering of Christ and the whole community is made one by communion in the body and blood of Christ. The 'presidency of the priest' is a leadership of service, making it possible for the whole community, of which he is a member, to be enfolded in the eternal sacrifice of Jesus Christ. Such collaboration may indeed be regarded as the model of that relationship between priest and people which the Council has called for and it irresistibly reminds one of St Paul's teaching of the need that one member of the body has of the others (1 Corinthians 12: 12–26).

## The eucharistic action
~

The first feature of the theology of the Order we mentioned above, namely that it remains firmly rooted in what Christ did and said at the Last Supper, can best be seen in GI 48 which summarizes much that has gone before and expresses it with great succinctness:

> Christ instituted the memorial of his death and resurrection at the Last Supper. This is continually made present in the church when the priest, representing Christ, carries out what the Lord did. When he instituted the paschal sacrifice and meal (*convivium*), he handed it over (*tradidit*) to his disciples for them to do it in his memory.

Simply, the memorial, paschal meal that Jesus instituted at the Last Supper is the recalling (in the full sense) or the 'making the memory' of the Lord's death and resurrection. Through it his sacrifice is made present to us. This is the ancient and traditional way of speaking of the Mass, and the Order goes on to draw out the consequences as they are shown in the liturgy itself:

Christ took bread and the cup and, giving thanks, broke and gave to his disciples, saying: 'Take and eat, this is my body. Take and drink, this is the cup of my blood. Do this in memory of me'. The church has arranged the celebration of the eucharistic liturgy *to correspond to these words and actions of Christ:*

1. In the preparation of the gifts, bread, wine and water are brought to the altar, the same elements which Christ used.

2. The eucharistic prayer is the hymn of thanksgiving to the Father for the whole work of salvation, and in it the offerings become the body and blood of Christ.

3. The breaking of the one bread is a sign of the unity of the faithful, and in communion they receive the body and blood of Christ as the Apostles did from his hands.[19]

This apparently simple description of the eucharistic action in fact isolates its main features: the presentation of the gifts, the recitation of the eucharistic prayer, the breaking of the bread and the communion. These are the basic structural elements on which any liturgy of the eucharist must be built and while faithful to the New Testament data, they do not slavishly repeat them. The description in the Order closely follows the pattern discerned by the late Dom Gregory Dix, now some long time ago. He observed that with absolute unanimity the liturgical tradition reduced the 'seven-action scheme' of the New Testament to the four-action scheme with which we are familiar:

1) The offertory; the bread and wine are 'taken' and placed on the table together. 2) The prayer; the president gives thanks to God over the bread and wine together. 3) The fraction; the bread is broken. 4) The communion; the bread and wine are distributed together.[20]

The first example of this 'absolute unanimity' is to be found in the earliest description of the eucharist we possess, written by St Justin the Martyr about the middle of the second century:

(a) bread, wine and water are brought to the table at which the president (*proestōs*) is standing;

(b) he 'sends up' the prayer of thanksgiving to which the people give their assent with Amen;

(c) communion is given and taken to 'those who are absent'.[21]
What is missing is the fraction which, however, must have taken place.
On the other hand we note that the celebrant is called 'president' and
that it is he who performs the eucharistic action.

In certain Reformed liturgies of the sixteenth century the fraction
was made at the words of institution and it may be asked why the early
church never adopted that position for it. The answer is, I think, to be
found in the fact that the church was precisely making the memorial of
the Last Supper and in the eucharistic prayer wished to dwell on the fact
and draw out its consequences. Now, after Calvary and the resurrection,
the eucharist was the 'memorial' (*anamnesis*) that made the power of
the whole redeeming work of Christ present to the community. Hence
the prolongation of the eucharistic prayer after the consecration, and we
may suppose that before the *epiclesis* of the Holy Spirit was introduced
(not generally until the fourth century), the fraction will have taken place
at that point.[22]

## *Holy communion*

This section of the Instruction does not in fact begin with one of its
more lengthy statements, but its doctrine can be gathered from its
interpretation of the rites that go to make up the communion act (GI 56,
b, c, i).

It is a curious fact of religious history that for centuries Christians have
not generally realized the full implications of the word 'communion'.
Yes, it means communion with the Lord, but this has been thought of
for the most part as a private conversation with him, often to the exclusion of other members of the Christian community. The Instruction is
concerned to bring back the fundamental and ancient connotation of the
word. It emphasizes that it means *koinonia* (inadequately translated
'fellowship'), which signifies communion with Christ *but also* with the
members of Christ, with the *community* that is assembled in church.

1. Thus, the sign of peace expresses the peace and unity of the
church, the mutual love that members of the church must have for one
another before receiving the one Bread, and it is also a prayer for the
peace and unity of the human family. The implications of this last
observation are far-reaching. It is meant to bring before the minds of
Christians, precisely at communion, that they are part of the human

family, that they have obligations to it and that at least they must pray for it. The Mass, in fact, is the vital centre of peace, love and unity in the world. The love that Christ had for mankind on the cross is mediated through the Mass to the world, even if it is not the only way it is so mediated.

2. The next statement deepens the notion of unity-in-fellowship: the fraction is not just a practical action to break the bread so that it may be distributed; it is the sign that we, though many in number, are by the one Bread, which is Christ, made one body, and the text refers to 1 Corinthians 10:7. This is one reason why the Order requires that the bread, or at least some of it, should be sufficiently large to be broken and that it should be broken before the eyes of the people, and so that some at least may receive communion from it. Here is one of the many instances in the reformed liturgy where we find a real revalidation of symbols. The practical will say, 'It does not matter whether the bread is broken or whether you can see it broken. You receive Christ all the same.' But they (and we) need to reflect that Christ himself thought this action to be of immense significance[23] and the early church saw it was so. The earliest name for the eucharist is 'the breaking of bread'.[24] Critics of the new liturgy often say that there has been a reduction of symbolism, that all is dull and pedestrian, but it would seem that their notions of symbolism are those of the allegorists of the ninth and subsequent centuries who overlaid the Mass with all sorts of arbitrary meanings. The symbolism of the Mass as Christ instituted it is what is all-important.

3. All this is spelt out in the communion act. The Instruction assumes that there is going to be a procession and it sees this and the chants that accompany it as means of promoting the 'spiritual union of the communicants' and of the brotherly love that exists (should exist) between them. As, then, the Christian people move towards the altar, singing chants taken either from holy scripture or from other sources, they are expressing in action the meaning of the whole rite: though many, they are being made one through the one Bread that is Christ.

Thus is brought back into currency by an official document of the church the most ancient and profoundest teaching on the meaning of holy communion. It will no doubt take time before this becomes the normal thinking of most Catholics and there will be (is) resistance to a change in one of the most intimate of people's devotional habits, but one can but feel that the change is long overdue. The practice of holy communion has too often been divorced from Christian living and the teaching given by the Instruction provides at least a point of entry into a fuller and richer use of holy communion.

Another aspect of communion is also high-lighted by the Instruction (GI 56, h). The people are to be communicated from the hosts consecrated at Mass 'to make it clearer that they are participating in the sacrifice that is actually being celebrated'. The Mass is a unity and communion is an integral part of it, and yet for many centuries there have been factors making for a separation of the sacrifice from communion. The fear of profanation in pre- and post-Carolingian times and the complications of the penitential system led to infrequent communion. All through the Middle Ages people did not receive it very often. One result was that the holy eucharist was divided into three things: Mass, communion and the adoration of the host (at the elevation, and towards the end of the Middle Ages, outside the Mass altogether). The strong recommendation of the Council of Trent to frequent communion did little to correct the situation and the custom of receiving it apart from the Mass grew. One of the greatest difficulties the early promoters of the Liturgical Movement had to overcome was to persuade both clergy and laity that communion is part of the Mass and normally should be received during it. Then, with the growing frequency of communion in this century, it was thought that there should always be a considerable reserve of hosts in the tabernacle and people even at Mass were communicated from that reserve. For a very long time now, from the time of Benedict XIV in the middle of the eighteenth century, recommendations have been made that the people should be communicated from hosts consecrated at the Mass. This recommendation has been renewed several times in recent years, by Pius XII in 1947 (*Mediator Dei* 128), by the Second Vatican Council (CL 55) and by the Instruction on the Eucharistic Mystery of 1967. The first battle has been won: people normally receive communion at Mass and in great numbers. Communicating attendance has largely replaced non-communicating attendance that was such a strange feature of Catholic life years ago. The second battle has still to be won, although the practice of communicating the people from hosts consecrated at the Mass is now very widespread. It is another case of fundamental symbolism that comes from the Last Supper itself. Jesus said 'Take and eat, take and drink' and what is needed is that the people should to be able to see the Mass-liturgy as a coherent whole coming from what Christ said and did at the Last Supper. Any practices that obscure the basic lines of the eucharist must be condemned by this principle.[25]

One of the more remarkable features of modern liturgical reform is that it has restored to the liturgy (not merely to the eucharist) the eschatological dimension. As the General Instruction says (240) communion from the cup expresses more clearly 'the relation of the eucharistic banquet to the heavenly banquet' and it refers to the Instruction on the Eucharistic Mystery of 1967 where we find a reference to Matthew 26:27–29, 'From now on, I tell you, I shall not drink wine until the day I drink new wine with you in the kingdom of my Father'. No doubt the first reference is to the eschatological banquet that is so frequent a figure for the consummation of God's work at the end (cf. Matthew 22:1 ff. etc.) and it is to this that three out of the four acclamations after the consecration and the phrase immediately before communion refer. But the church also comes into the perspective. The 'kingdom' begins to come into existence after the resurrection when we find Jesus present among his followers (Luke 24:13–35 and cf. Acts 1:4 and 10:41) with whom he had eaten and drunk. And we know that in the earliest days of the church there was a vivid sense of Christ as present among the gathered community. These words, then, refer to the church as the beginning of the kingdom, for it is through the celebration of the eucharist in the community of Christ that we shall come to celebrate the eternal banquet in heaven. A modern writer combines both perspectives very skilfully:

This eschatological perspective is an integral part of the eucharist. At the eucharist Christ appoints a kingdom unto the Church, which participates in it in advance, and in that communion with God which it involves; *the Church already sits at table with Christ to eat and drink with him* and enter into communion with him as in the Kingdom. As through the eucharist they participate in this communion of the Kingdom and are admitted to the table of Christ, *the faithful are assured of their entrance into the Kingdom of God at the Last Day* that they may enjoy eternal communion with the Lord. They receive the sign of their belonging to the coming Kingdom at the eucharist; they are given the pledge that they will be able to enter in and have the right to sit at Christ's table 'to eat and drink' with him in eternity.[26]

Expectation of the Last Day and the Triumph of Christ is the fruit of Christian hope and while we are used to saying that the eucharist is supremely the sacrament of love, both God's towards us and ours towards him and our neighbour, we can see now that it is also the sacrament of hope. This means not simply that we long for the consummation (and how many of us do!) but that through our celebration of the eucharist and our communion in the Lord we are working towards his final victory. The power of Christ's final victory is already, through the eucharist, exercising a sort of 'pull' so that we and the whole church are able to have a part in the working out in time and for the world of the divine plan of total salvation.

# *Notes*
~

[1] The elevation and the communion.
[2] **Synaxis** and **congregatio** are synonyms.
[3] Since there are witch-hunters about, perhaps I had better give the Latin for the last phrase: **substantialiter et continenter sub speciebus eucharisticis**, which literally is '**under** the eucharistic species'. For want of this proviso, I may be accused of holding the Lutheran theory of impanation! The phrases in italics represent the additions of 1970.
[4] G. Pasqualetti and S. Bianchi in **Notitiae**, 54 (May 1970), p. 177: **Nihil autem ex novo confectum est**.
[5] E.g. The 'Memorial of the Lord' says the same as 'eucharistic sacrifice', indicating perhaps that it is all a matter of semantics, though they go on to say that this phrase eliminates any notion that the Mass is merely a symbolic representation. It may indeed be wondered why the Constitution on the Liturgy avoided the word 'represented' which is found in the **Capitulum** on the Mass of the Council of Trent (Sess. XXII. Denz. 938, ed. 17a) which on the other hand did not use **perpetuaret** of Vatican II. As I remarked in **The Church's Worship**((London,1964), p. 133, n. 2) it seems to be a neutral word, deliberately chosen, perhaps to avoid words like **renovare**, which is to be found in the Proemium. 'Represented' is perfectly respectable. It was thought sufficient by the Council of Trent, it was used by St Thomas (ST III, 83, 1) and by at least one of his Jesuit commentators, Vasquez, in the sixteenth century.
[6] Dom Henry Ashworth in **Notitiae**, 53 (April 1970) points out that this description (to use a neutral term) of the Mass simply reflects 1 Corinthians 11:20-26: St Paul indicates that the eucharist was the **Cena Dominica** (GI 7), the people were gathered together (GI 7, the **synaxis** or **congregatio**) 'to make the memorial of the Lord' (Do this in memory of me) (GI: **memoriale Domini celebrare**). The

term 'The Supper of the Lord' (**Cena Domini**) was, of course, long current (cf. the **Missale Romanum**, Maundy Thursday) but Father Ashworth notes a peculiarly pregnant expression in the Leonine Sacramentary, which is older than the Gregorian: **ut et in caenae mysticae sacrosancto convivio**: 'in the holy meal of the mystical supper'.

7 Cf. CL 2.

8 See **ibid**. 14, 26–31, 34, 41, 42, 48, 50, etc.

9 The terms of the brief of Alexander VII condemning Voisin's translation of the missal are very severe: the people might not apparently know the sacred words of the Canon, even in translation. It is no comfort to learn that the document was canonically 'surreptitious', i.e. obtained on the false charge that the translator intended to say Mass in French! The condemnation exerted a baleful influence until it was withdrawn by Leo XIII at the end of the nineteenth century. (See L. Bouyer, **Liturgical Piety** (University of Notre Dame, USA, 1955), p. 51.)

10 There has been much writing about this in recent years. Apart from the Council documents and those of the popes insisting on the importance of the subsidiary function, there is, for example, the essay of Karl Rahner, 'Theology of the Parish' in **The Parish** (Eng. trans., Maryland, USA, 1958).

11 Luke 22:19. As against those who for long have held that the shorter reading, omitting these words, is the better one, I find the case put up for the longer reading by Jeremias (**The Eucharistic Words of Jesus**, p. 138) and Benoît (**Exégèse et Théologie** I, p. 163) completely convincing.

12 See, for example, Max Thurian, **The Eucharistic Memorial**, Part I: **The Old Testament** (London, 1960). After a close analysis of the OT material the author states that 'memorial' means recalling before God a past event of his saving mercy and through this 'memorial' making it present here and now. In Part II of the same work he applies this to the eucharist: 'The eucharistic memorial is a recalling of the Son to us, a recalling by us to the Father and a recalling to the Father for us'. We may add that because we are making the memorial according to the command of Christ, he makes himself present because like his Father in the Old Testament he is **faithful** to his covenant, to the new covenant of which the eucharist is the memorial. Thurian puts it this way: 'This memorial is not a simple subjective act of recollection, it is a liturgical **action**. But it is not just a liturgical action that makes the Lord present, it is a liturgical action that recalls as a memorial before the Father the unique sacrifice of the Son, and this makes Him present in His memorial, in the presentation of His sacrifice before the Father and in His intercession as heavenly High Priest' (pp. 35–6).

13 See Louis Ligier, 'From the Last Supper to the Eucharist' in **The New Liturgy**, ed. Lancelot Sheppard (London, 1970), pp. 136–40. In a brief phrase he sums up the meaning of **memoria-anamnesis**: 'It is the whole narrative-anamnesis which constitutes both celebration and action'.

14 See Letter to the Hebrews 10:7: 'I come to do your will'.

15 See Chapter 3.

16 **4 Sent**. 12: **Hostia illa perpetua est**.

17 Cf. CL 41, Decree on Priests 5, GI 7.

18 See the Instruction of 1970 where the point is re-emphasized.

19 We have used the ICEL translation here, which gives the version of the **Ordo Missae** of 1969, without, then, the revision. But on reflection I have felt that the revision neither adds nor subtracts anything from this perspicuous text and that

therefore it was best left in its simplicity. (Translation copyright © 1969, International Commission on English in the Liturgy, Inc. All rights reserved.)

[20] *The Shape of the Liturgy* (London, 1945), p. 48: 'Not all four actions are of equal importance: e.g. the placing of the bread and wine on the altar is very different from the later "offertory" '.

[21] Justin, *Apology* I, 65 and 67. The words of institution are suggested in 66 where he gives an account of Christian belief in the eucharist. He also mentions that a collection was taken at the end of the service—so collections are not a modern invention either!

[22] There is a fraction in the *Ap. Trad.* (xxiii) of Hippolytus but the bishop broke the bread immediately before giving communion. But this was an exceptional service: it was the first Mass of those who had been baptized and after the eucharistic prayer there was a series of blessings. In the place where he gives a specimen eucharistic prayer, there is an *epiclesis* of the Holy Spirit, the doxology and at this point the text comes to an end (iv). (Ed. G. J. Cuming, *Hippolytus, A Text for Students* (Grove Books, Nottingham, 1976), no. 4, pp. 10–11 and no. 23, p. 21.)

[23] See e.g. Luke 24:30–31: 'They knew him in the breaking of bread'.

[24] Cf. Acts 2:42 and many other places.

[25] For communion in both kinds for the laity, see below, Chapter 6.

[26] Max Thurian, *The Eucharistic Memorial*, Part II (London, 1961), pp. 66–7 (italics added). Theories on eschatology differ a good deal among the scripture experts and the note in Jerusalem Bible (*in loc.*) simply refers our Lord's statement to the end of all things. Thurian's view, which I have held for a long time, seems to be perfectly tenable and is, I think, the true meaning of this and similar statements in the gospel.

# The Structure of the Mass¹

~~~~~~

THE STRUCTURE OF the Mass as given in the *Ordo Missae* is the liturgical expression of the doctrine that is to be found in the General Instruction and this we have briefly considered. However, it is necessary from time to time to turn to the Instruction to discern the mind of the revisers, and this we shall do in what follows.²

The Mass, said the Constitution (CL 56), is made up of two parts: the ministry of the word and the ministry of the eucharist.³ Each of these parts is broken down into its constituent elements: the first consists of the three readings, the responsorial psalm, the Alleluia (or acclamation), the homily, the creed and the General Intercessions (GI 33). It is preceded by an entrance rite. The second consists of everything that runs from the presentation of the gifts to the completion of the communion rite, though the Order gives due prominence to its main elements: the eucharistic prayer and the rite of communion. It and the whole Mass is concluded with a brief rite of dismissal.

From this summary description the main lines of the Mass stand out clearly: fundamentally it consists of the proclamation of the word and 'the thanksgiving' with its necessary completion in holy communion. Nothing could be simpler, nothing nearer to the eucharist of the primitive church, and in the discussion about liturgical reform which some say must come from further experiment it is to be hoped that it will be realized that these are all indispensable elements and that the very order in which they occur is something that cannot be changed.⁴ Other elements, entrance rites and rites of dismissal, are variable and could be changed without any essential damage to the structure of the Mass. But, if we see things this way, it does mean that the revisers have been faithful to their brief which was given to them in the Constitution on the Liturgy (50): 'The rite of the Mass is to be revised in such a way that the intrinsic nature and purpose of its several parts, as also the connection between them, may be more clearly manifested, and that the devout and active participation by the people may be more easily achieved'. Keeping, then, the main structure of the Mass in mind, we can go on to consider its various parts.

## *The entrance rite*

Of the various elements that go to make up the entrance rite some are old and some are new, the oldest being the entrance chant and the collect.[5] The new elements, the greeting and the brief address, unfold the meaning and the purpose of the oldest elements. It is a traditional Christian belief that when the people come together for worship they are called by God—they are *ecclesia*, the assembly of God, the people of God, and his word is first heard in the entrance chant, especially when it is taken from holy scripture. The collect is the first prayer said by the president when they are assembled so that they may respond to God's call. But in the course of centuries not only have these truths been obscured by a faulty liturgical rite, but it has been felt that they were not sufficiently explicit. At the psychological level, too, there is a case for saying that if a crowd of people are to become a community they need to be made aware of their relationship to each other, they have to move from being a crowd to being a community. It is the first function of the president to help them to do this. Moreover, if worship is a Christian action (divine worship, as it used to be called) it has first to be a human action, and it is the most human thing in the world that celebrant and people should feel that they are related to one another. A first contact at this point, then, is of considerable importance.

By our standards now, the old Mass began almost brutally. The Mass began from cold. The priest appeared (sometimes out of a side-door on the sanctuary) with server or servers, went to the altar, turned his back on the people and then began the prayers. Sometimes the people could hear what these were and sometimes they could not. A few moments later he turned to them briefly to address a more or less hurried *Dominus vobiscum* and they did not see his face again until, on Sundays, he turned round to read the epistle and gospel in English and to preach to them. It was assumed that the people did not need any preparation for Mass, that they were fully aware of what the feast or Sunday was, of what texts would be read and so on. It was assumed that they were an instructed and devout congregation that was ready in all respects to celebrate the greatest act of worship that there is. Possibly this was true in some places and at certain times. It is no longer generally true and, in any case, we have discovered new needs in worship, and one of them is that there should be a relationship between celebrant and people.

If community then means a relationship between a group of people and a relationship between them and their leader, the Order has been faithful to its teaching as given in the Instruction. Here, right at the beginning, the Order of the Mass endeavours to create community, a community in which Christ is present and is going to renew his presence in a variety of ways. The Instruction sums up the whole matter very briefly: the entrance rites have the qualities of preparation and introduction, but, more purposefully and more concretely, they enable the people to realize they are a community and to prepare to receive the word of God and to celebrate the eucharist itself (GI 25). The purpose of the entrance chant in particular is to 'foster the sense of union of the gathered people' (GI 26). It helps to do this because, among other things, it introduces the whole community to the liturgy of the day and provides the accompaniment of the celebrant's procession to the altar (*ibid.*). It does indeed 'open their minds' and where minds are meeting in the same thoughts, expressed in song, there community is beginning to be formed.

The truth that the assembly is gathered by the word of God is made explicit in the greeting. This is especially clear in the first and longest: 'The grace of our Lord Jesus Christ and the love of God and the fellowship of the Holy Spirit be with you all', but it is also clear in the shortest and best known: 'The Lord be with you . . .' as the modern interpretation of this obscure phrase shows: 'He (the celebrant) expresses the wish that the Lord, or peace, or grace, should be with them (the people) in their worship, and they return his greeting specifying that the Lord (peace or grace) may be with him in the exercise of his ministry – should be with the special charism he has received so that he may worthily perform his duty'.[6] These phrases are precious reminders that the liturgical community is not just any kind of assembly and that the dialogue that takes place within it during celebration is a dialogue with God through the presence of his Spirit.

The General Instruction has no doubt about the nature of the worshipping community and sees in this first greeting a sign of God's presence with his people, who through it become a sign, a 'sacrament' of the mystery of the church. It thus echoes the Constitution's teaching that the celebration of the eucharist 'is the outstanding means whereby the faithful may . . . manifest to others the mystery of Christ and the real nature of the true Church' (CL 2 and cf. CL 41, 42).

The brief address that follows, apart from its psychological appropriateness, can also be seen as a communication of the Spirit to the community. The celebrant will select a phrase from the liturgy of the day to concentrate people's thoughts and to help them to realize that the Spirit is present with them. He may and should announce as briefly as possible the liturgical theme of the day or feast and will give such information as may be necessary about the penitential act and the eucharistic prayer that are to be used. It is regrettable that some celebrants are neglecting this opportunity to make contact with the people and some never seem to have used it at all. No doubt it is equally regrettable to overlay the liturgical action with floods of verbosity. Preparation of the texts and an effort towards economy of words will prevent that unhappy situation.

For centuries the Roman Mass had no penitential formula at all and then when it first acquired one (the *Agnus Dei* introduced by Pope Sergius I c. 700) it was rather the accompaniment to an action, the breaking of the bread, which in the papal rite was a prolonged affair. It was even later that a penitential act was introduced into the Mass (Psalm 42 with the *Confiteor*—missal of 1570), and even this was overlaid at High Mass by the singing of the introit. So far as the people were concerned there was no penitential act on such occasions.[7] It is not surprising, then, that in the discussions of liturgical experts that went on for nearly twenty years before the Council[8] various solutions were debated. It was agreed that the existing rite was unsatisfactory: the psalm made it more like a duplicated entrance rite and the length and doubling of the *Confiteor* made it unduly cumbersome. Its position in the rite, especially at High Mass, was also agreed to be unsatisfactory. But it was not so easy to see what should be done. One suggestion was that it should be put later in the Mass, either before the offertory, where in liturgies other than the Roman the kiss of peace takes place, or before the communion. Another, which has won the day, is that its form should be simplified and that it should be made part of the entrance rite of the Mass. It is a comprehensible solution: we need to be open to God both to hear his word and to receive his body and blood in holy communion. We have offended God in many ways and as we approach him once more we ask his forgiveness.

The relationship is primarily between God and the community. If we interpret the sign of peace now made before communion in the light of Matthew 5:23, 24, here reconciliation between the members of the community is the lesson that is given.

It does mean, however, that the entrance rite is somewhat over-loaded, and the whole situation is complicated by the retention of the *Kyries* in this place. This does ensure that the musical settings current for many centuries can still be sung where choirs are capable of doing so and on fitting occasions, though it does prolong the entrance rite unduly. It is indeed difficult to justify the presence of the *Kyries* in this place when they are taken as a separate piece. They are, of course, the remains of a whole litany which, as is well known, was shortened by Gregory the Great, at least for some occasions. However, they have been integrated into the third penitential act and have thus become part of a litany of repentance. This new arrangement offers interesting possibilities of musical development and pulls together this part of the Mass. The General Instruction indeed envisages a further development here and speaks of 'tropes' being inserted between the *Kyries* (GI 30), but it is a procedure which will have to be used with great discretion.

There is little need to say anything about the *Gloria in excelsis* here. It is not primitive to the Mass, it is true, but it is the means by which on great feast days the community, now 'gathered by the Holy Spirit', can express its joy, praise and adoration 'to God the Father and to the Lamb' as well as making supplication to him, as indeed the General Instruction says (GI 31). But it is perhaps appointed for use too often. Greater feasts, yes; every Sunday of the year, no.

The final element of the entrance rite and one that brings it to a climax is the collect, which is pre-eminently the prayer of the gathered community now 'aware that it stands in the presence of God' (GI 32). It is the prayer of the community but led by its president, who summons them to 'rehearse silently' their petitions which are then summed up by the president in the prayer that gathers or 'collects' the desires, aspirations and needs of the community and presents them to the Father through the Son in the Holy Spirit. The silence between 'Let us pray' and the collect itself is thus given its meaning and in practice it is important to give the people time to ponder on their petitions.

Through all the various and sometimes apparently disparate elements of the entrance rite, its purpose is clear. The people come and then by

~

God's word they are gathered into a community in which the Holy Spirit is present. This is the truth about the Christian assembly and the various texts are there to enable its members to realize that they are in fact gathered by the Holy Spirit and made one.

## *The ministry of the word*

The restoration of an adequate ministry of the word to the Mass-liturgy is one of the most satisfactory parts of the liturgical reform. Apart from a few of the older and greater feasts and seasons, the lectionary of the old missal was so jejune that it is a wonder that we were able to put up with it for so long. What is more, the way the Mass had come to be celebrated over the centuries and the use of the Latin, which ever-decreasing numbers of people understood, resulted in a devaluation of the importance of the word in the eucharist that led to a considerable distortion of the whole rite. From the beginning the eucharist has been celebrated in the context of the proclamation of the word and was always in antiquity regarded as an integral part of it.[9]

We shall see why this was so, but immediately it can be said that because it was neglected, the people came to think of the Mass as a holy action which they watched, as an object of adoration and as a means for 'getting' holy communion. Their piety did something to substitute for the approach that it is necessary to make when we worship God, but apart from that, the word, unintelligible and often inaudible, failed to touch their hearts. This is one of the reasons why the present pattern of the ministry of the word gives some people a good deal of trouble, and it may be admitted that the church has restored it just at a time when people are apparently becoming less capable of listening than at any time in the history of mankind. If defence of the new ministry of the word is necessary, it can be said that even the old Mass, when turned into the vernacular, provided a fair slice of reading material: epistle, gradual (sequence – and that interminable one on Corpus Christi), Alleluia, verse and gospel. What is more, these texts were often enough not related to each other in any coherent pattern. If imbalance between word and eucharist is the charge, the old Latin High Mass was a bad offender when it was sung *in full* – and how rare that was! A gradual and Alleluia with verse could take seven minutes, *Glorias* and creeds fifteen or more minutes when sung to elaborate settings. But, it is suggested, no one complained.[10]

The root of the objection to the new ministry of the word is to be found in the prevalent practice of people before the liturgical reform. Ordinarily they went to a low Mass, the murmuring of the Latin at the altar did not disturb them and they 'got on' with their own prayers or, as often as not, they just gazed around. Now that they are required to listen, they feel disconcerted.[11] In fact, there has been no change in the balance of the Mass. Simply, the ministry of the word has been made more coherent and more intelligible.

The first thing to be said about the new ministry of the word is that it provides a pattern for the absorption of God's word so that its message can become part of ourselves. The reading is proclaimed, facing the people, and they are enabled to respond to it by a psalm that continues the theme of the reading, turning it into prayer. A second reading, often giving moral instruction relevant to the Christian life, follows, and then comes the climax in the salutation to the coming of Christ in the word of the gospel, and the proclamation of the gospel. The purpose of the homily that follows is to expound the meaning of the texts and relate them to the life-situation of the gathered community. To the whole of the ministry of the word they make their assent of faith in the creed, and in the General Intercessions turn their reflections on the word into prayer for the church and the world. Reading, psalm, acclamation and response are the oldest elements of Christian (and, indeed, pre-Christian) prayer. If to these is added, as the Lectionary (no. 28) suggests, silent meditation after the readings or one or two of them, you have the combination of public and private prayer and the charge that the new Mass is a stream of verbiage is removed.

What then is the deeper purpose of the ministry of the word?[12] A full discussion would take us very far and it will be best to give the answer in the terms of the Constitution (CL 7, 33) and of the General Instruction (GI 33): 'in the liturgy God speaks to his people' and 'when the holy scriptures are read in church' Christ 'is present in his word'. First, then, through the readings (and, indeed, the other texts of the liturgy but preeminently in the scripture readings), God speaks to the assembled people. He is conveying his word just as really and, if we are willing to have it so, just as effectively as he did when he spoke through the prophets or when his own Son spoke to men. The words are the means, the envelope, the sign-sacrament of the saving truth that is to be found in God's word in itself. It comes in many forms, narratives, poetry, prophecy and the aphorisms of wisdom literature, and these different forms need to be understood if the essential meaning is to be discerned, for it is this that is of final importance.

The reading of the scriptures, then, at Mass is not just a form of giving information *about* God and his dealings with man, nor is it a kind of classroom instruction about 'the truths of faith' – for that purpose it would be supremely inefficient. What we need to realize before all else is that the reading of the scriptures in the Mass is an *event*, it is a happening, it is the intervention of God in the here and now, in the affairs and minds of this gathered community. In Hebrew *dabar* means *both* word and event and it is sometimes a little difficult to know which is meant. The Bible is a record of *both* events and words, words that were indeed indispensable to the interpretation of the events, but all told it was the events that mattered. For salvation history as a whole is action, the breaking through of God into this worldly order so that he can redeem it. But salvation history continues. It is not finished and will not be finished until the end of time. We are living in the last age, over which Christ is Lord and in which the Holy Spirit is present. God still intervenes in the world, the history of salvation is continued in the church and by the church and it is primarily in the liturgy, and nowhere more effectively than in the Mass, that it is continued.

The matter can be put in what perhaps are more conventional terms. Through the readings and other texts (especially the responsorial psalm) God communicates his grace. He offers himself to us once again. By the readings and the homily the people's minds are opened so that they may accept the word in faith. Through the whole ministry of the word their hearts should be stirred by love and it is perhaps the function of the homily principally to do this and, further, to draw people on to commitment. Within the context of the Mass this is made in the creed in which the people renew their faith in God, Father, Son and Holy Spirit. The event, the 'happening' then can be seen as the communication of grace which enlivens the faith and love of the hearers and stimulates them to action.

This is not a theology invented to fit the liturgy. It has always been presupposed, as we can see from the ceremonial that has surrounded the proclamation of the word in all liturgies. The Book of the Word has been (and is) carried in procession, surrounded by lights, saluted by incensations, reverenced in various fashions and all this would be sheer idolatry if it were not to be understood as a complexus of signs by which the Christian community bear witness to their belief in the presence of God in his word. For their part, the people hail Christ present in the gospel by Alleluia and acclamation, by the response they make as its title is proclaimed: 'Glory to you, Lord', and as it comes to its conclusion: 'Praise to you, Lord Jesus Christ'.

But as well as making God present to the people, the proclamation of the scriptures also unfolds to them 'the mystery of redemption and salvation' (GI 33). God has redeemed us through Christ, foreshadowing that redemption throughout the Old Testament and, as we can see now, bringing it ever nearer until it was finally achieved in Jesus Christ. The long and tortuous history of Israel is a record of the many ways in which God approached his people with love, offering them salvation. That history, however brutal and sordid at times, is also a gradual unfolding of God's nature, a *revelation* of what he was like, and if that revelation was always partial, it was in Jesus Christ that its meaning was made clear. It is in the light of Christ's revelation in the New Testament that we are able to understand the Old. The two march together and this is the fundamental reason why an Old Testament reading has been restored to the liturgy of the Mass.[13] It is through this use of the Old Testament, in conjunction with the gospel reading (and the two are usually related in the Lectionary), that the mystery of salvation will be unfolded to the people.

A third purpose given by the General Instruction (33) for the ministry of the word is the 'spiritual instruction' of the people. The Apostolic Constitution at the beginning of *Missale Romanum* refers to this (see p. 57 above) and we may ask how it will do it. The pope speaks of a better knowledge of holy scripture as a means of deepening the spiritual life, and if people are aware that in the scriptures they are in contact with God's word, that it is still communicating to them his grace and love, it will surely stimulate them to spiritual effort. The spiritual life is not *just* meditation; at its deepest it is action, the action of God in the depths of our being and a response to him from those same depths. It is on this that all else is built. God's word is then the *essential* nourishment; the early church lived by it, and as the years go by, and as people become ever more familiar with the scriptures, they will come to an ever deeper understanding of God and his saving actions and gradually enter into a closer union with him.[14]

## The homily

For a very long time the homily was regarded as an intruder in the Mass. Priests used to remove the maniple before preaching and some even the chasuble as if to say 'This has got nothing to do with what has gone before or is coming afterwards'. Nor, for the most part, had it. It was customary to preach at the High Mass on Sundays but low Masses were celebrated without a sermon, and the odd thing was that there were those who thought that the 'Solemn High Mass' (as some called it) with deacon and subdeacon positively excluded it. Nor was the discourse necessarily related to the texts of the day. It was an oratorical exercise that happened to take place during the Mass. Even when it was agreed that the sermon should at least be concerned with the Mass of the day, there was a curious notion that the Council of Trent had said that only the gospel was to be expounded. Hence the tired homilies that were so often repeated year after year. In fact, the Council of Trent said that all the texts of the Mass (meaning principally the 'Proper') were to be the subject of the homily.

The Second Vatican Council put an end to this unhappy state of affairs and the Constitution on the Liturgy has firmly integrated the homily into the liturgical action and insisted on its necessity (CL 35 (2) and CL 52). At the same time it has indicated in a general way its nature and function.

(a) It is part of the liturgical service, that is, in itself it is a liturgical action. Normally the Mass is incomplete without it.

(b) Its content should be drawn mainly from scriptural and liturgical sources. It is not a literary essay about Christian doctrine or morals, nor is it a discourse about general questions of the day.

(c) Its literary form is that of a *proclamation* of the deeds of God recorded in the history of salvation or of the mystery of Christ made present and active within the Christian, especially in the celebration of the liturgy.

Two things principally go to make up the liturgical homily:[15] its content and its form, namely proclamation.

1. The Constitution, not to mention other documents, leaves us in

no doubt about the *content* of the homily: it is primarily the scripture readings of the day, though seen in the context of the whole history of salvation. It is here that we learn of God's saving deeds and it is this that is 'actualized' in liturgical celebration: 'The liturgy is in fact nothing other than a way by which Christ, in the intermediate time that runs from Pentecost to the parousia, that is, in this eschatological time already in act, communicates the fullness of his divine life to individuals, reproduces his mystery in them and draws them into it'.[16]

This implies that the history of salvation is understood – it is the record of God's saving acts in Christ that are continued in the church – and that the scripture readings for the day are studied in this context.[17] The readings, again, are part of a liturgical context, feast, season or special occasion, and have a particular reference to it. These two factors, then, the history of salvation and the liturgical context condition the nature of the liturgical homily and so the use the preacher must make of the texts. A scripture expert's exegesis of them, apart from being unduly lengthy, is inappropriate, for it will almost certainly ignore the liturgical context. There must be a real penetration of the reasons why these particular readings are set for this day or occasion and the clue to this can be found through an attentive reading of the Bible and, where Old Testament passages are concerned, some understanding of scriptural typology.[18] A further clue will be found in an examination of the non-scriptural texts of the liturgy, of which the readings form a part, even if the most important part. It goes without saying that mere moralizings occasioned by the readings are totally inadequate to the situation.[19]

2. It is, however, *proclamation* that is decisive of the literary form of the homily, and the Constitution, as we have seen, says quite firmly that it is such. What, then, is it?[20]

The homily is proclamation first because it continues the proclamation of the scripture readings which themselves continue the *kerygma* of the New Testament. The gospels were *kerygma* or proclamation before they were written books, and it is widely agreed by theologians of the Catholic and Reformed traditions that it is in proclamation that the scriptures become the living word of God.[21] The models of *kerygma* are, as is well known, to be found in the New Testament, especially in Acts. Thus, in the first Christian sermon, Peter proclaims Christ, announces who he was, what he did and what he meant. He links this proclamation with the event that has just happened, and with a skilful use of the Old Testament[22] seeks to interpret the whole complexus of events in terms that his audience could be expected to understand. In a word, he proclaims the mystery of Christ who was sent by God and lived, died and rose again so that the sons of Israel might receive the Spirit whom Peter and his companions had already received. There was, too, the result: repentance, baptism and the coming of the Spirit (Acts 2:22–41).

The Constitution comes very close to this in its statement that the homily is 'the proclamation of God's wonderful works in the history of salvation, that is, the mystery of Christ' (CL 35 (2)).[23] The primary function, then, of the homily is to isolate the core of the Christian mystery set forth in the readings and clearly and succinctly to announce it to the people. But this will usually require elucidation and so we get exposition, what is called in the New Testament *catechesis* or *didache*. This will take as its point of departure the scriptural readings and its style will be conditioned by the language of the Bible rather than that of theological manuals. But both the proclamation and the exposition will have as their aim the deepening of the Christian life of the people and will thus have a practical issue. In the first instance, it will seek to lead them into the celebration of the eucharist – and this is called by the rather formidable word 'mystagogy', an initiation into the mystery – and beyond the liturgical celebration into the living of the Christian life in the world.

These four elements, it is agreed, go to make up the liturgical homily,[24] though it by no means follows that they must follow one after another in the order suggested above. It may indeed be that in a given homily one or two of these elements will play a much smaller part than others. Often on the greater feasts any extended exposition is unnecessary. It may be that any explicit leading of the people into the eucharistic celebration is unnecessary. Proclamation can often be combined with exposition and to the hearers these will be indistinguishable from each other. These are all matters of literary ability and pastoral sense that the preacher has to learn, not least from contact with people and knowing how their minds work. But this is what the church means by the liturgical homily and it is this style of preaching and this alone that is in tune with liturgical celebration.[25]

*The creed and the General Intercessions*

The creed, as we have said, is the principal assent of the people to the word of God proclaimed in the scriptures and in the homily. It brings to an end a process that has gone on since the beginning of the ministry of the word: God has been speaking, the people have been responding in various ways and now they sum up their response by a commitment of faith to God, Father, Son and Holy Spirit. As faith is more than an assent to a number of doctrines, so the creed is more than an audible recitation of those things that a Christian must believe. The General Instruction rightly calls it 'the profession of faith' (GI 43) and a profession of faith is an adherence to Christ as a living person as well as to all he taught and requires of us. Understandably, the Instruction insists that normally (*de more*) it is to be recited by all, either together or responsorially. Musical settings that take it away from the people are not suitable to its purpose and, anyway, are far too long for the likes of people nowadays.

Of the General Intercessions[26] three things are to be said:

1. It is part of the ministry of the word (GI 33). The people, opened up to the word of God and nourished by it, are now in a position to think of the needs of the church and the world and to pray for them. It is an interesting point of view, valid for prayer at any time. We do not rush into the presence of God to demand this and that. We listen to his word and try to discern his will. Then, humbly, we may address him. Practically, the Instruction thus indicates that the theme of the readings and the homily should be reflected in the intercessions. This, too, is a fundamental pattern of Christian prayer. We speak and we turn our speaking into prayer. The reflection of the word of the day in the prayer of the day is the condition of these intercessions remaining fresh, unstereotyped and in touch with the life of the people.

2. In these prayers the people exercise 'their priestly function' by praying for all mankind (GI 45). We are reminded of 1 Timothy 2:1, 2, 8, where the writer says that prayers, petitions, intercessions and thanksgiving should be offered for everyone and especially for kings, and others in authority, and of his conclusion 'I want all men to lift up their hands [the ancient gesture of supplication] reverently in prayer . . .'. These are the prayers *of the people*, under the presidency of the priest who introduces and concludes them, providing, incidentally, a classical

pattern of liturgical celebration. But since they are the prayers of the people they should have some part in them.[27] This may be done in various ways, but the people should at least be encouraged to send in their petitions. Normally, too, they will be announced by a lay-person with, of course, the people responding. This is a second condition of these intercessions remaining alive.

3. The form. A broad pattern of subjects is laid down (GI 45): prayers are to be made for the church, for earthly rulers, for those in any kind of need and for the local community. Normally the petitions will reflect these intentions but there is no need to be over-rigid about them. Circumstances alter cases and the emphasis can be now here and now there. What the church requires is that the intercessions should be concerned with the wider community and not concentrated on the particular concerns of the local community. These, too, play their part, and in practice the intelligent discernment of such local needs again ensures that the prayer is going to be alive. By experience one finds that the people are more alive to current needs, whether of the world or of the local community, than the clergy, and this is another reason why they should have a notable part in the intercessions. In detail, the prayer is made up of four parts, an introduction and a conclusion (both by the celebrant), the *invitation* to prayer (by a lay-person) and the response of the people. Of these a word needs to be said about the third.

In the booklet issued by the then *Consilium*[28] for guidance on these intercessions, the basic forms of these invitations to prayer are laid down and these make it very clear that they are invitations and not prayers. If they are prayers the lay-person is in fact usurping the function of the celebrant whose business it is to pray in the name of the community. The *Consilium* was in no doubt about this matter. What we have called 'invitations' are called in the booklet *propositiones intentionum*: intentions to be prayed for are proposed by the reader. They are not prayers themselves. The booklet lays down three possible forms: (Let us pray) *for* such and such *that* . . .; or simply (Let us pray) *that* such and such a favour may be granted; more simply still (Let us pray) *for* so and so. Different kinds of petition suggest the different uses of one of these three forms. They offer no difficulty and are beyond question the right ones to use. Fortunately a considerable degree of liberty is left open to the local clergy who within the limits laid down by the *Consilium* may compose their own prayers.[29]

~

It should be noted, too, that while the responses of the people on any given occasion should be the same (naturally to avoid confusion), they may be varied from one service to another and there is much to be said for doing so. The repetition of even short prayers, such as these, without variation soon becomes boring.

## The liturgy of the eucharist

The eucharistic liturgy should not be regarded as in some way cut off from the ministry of the word. As we have seen, word and eucharist have gone together since the beginning and one of the purposes of the proclamation of the word is to lead people into the fitting celebration of the eucharist. Even the General Intercessions may legitimately be regarded as an anticipation of, and, indeed, a sharing in, the Great Intercession that from one point of view the Mass is.[30]

Yet, of course, the eucharistic liturgy has an identity all its own and the General Instruction (48) lays out its principal phases: the preparation of the gifts, the eucharistic prayer and the fraction and communion.

### The preparation of the gifts

As is well known, the offertory rite of the Roman Mass of the 1570 missal was elaborate and yet at the same time inadequate for its purpose. Fundamentally, it was a *priestly* rite. The celebrant said and did almost everything and the prayers he was required to say, if adverted to by the people, were somewhat misleading. They spoke of the bread and wine as a 'sacrifice' which was 'offered', giving the impression that there was an offering here somehow independent of the act of offering that occurs in the eucharistic prayer. In many places the offertory was known as the 'Little Canon'. In the new rite the emphasis is wholly different.

First, the rite has been renamed. It is a presentation and a preparation. The offerings (bread, wine, money and possibly other things) are merely brought to the altar (*afferuntur*) and the Order recommends that this should be done by the people. It goes on to say that although the link between the bread and wine presented by the people in former times and the elements that are now placed on the altar has been broken, the gesture none the less retains a spiritual significance (GI 49). So the emphasis is on preparation rather than on offering. The gifts are considered to be set apart so that they may be used in the *eucharistic* offering. They have no intrinsic value and only acquire value when they become part of the eucharistic offering. They are signs of the people's desire to give themselves in eucharistic worship, and since self and life and work are really one, they are signs, too, of the surrendering to God of what man has. This is the sense of the prayers of offering now said over the bread and wine. These prayers, which are modelled on Jewish forms of blessing prayers, state the all-important truth that all we have comes from God's bounty. Of ourselves we have nothing. Yet the desire of self-giving is so strong and psychologically so necessary to us that we feel we must make the gesture. Bread and wine are offered in view of the eucharist ('that it may become the bread of life . . .') so that the offering is at once a plea for the coming of Christ to the community in the eucharistic action and a thanksgiving for all that we have and are, but a thanksgiving that will only acquire any value when it is enfolded in the self-offering of Christ.[31]

If the rite is called 'the preparation of the gifts', its description might be extended, 'that are brought to the altar by the people', for though the Order makes no obligation of it, it urges that they should be brought to the altar by the people. How this is to be done and, in some churches, whether it can be done at all, are practical matters to be decided by the local clergy. The important thing is to see the rite as yet another sign of community. The action is to be a *procession* accompanied by a chant. It is here that the people, usually through a representative group, are able to express the gesture of offering we have spoken of and, as the Instruction observes, to unite with the bread and wine their money or even other gifts in kind that are to be given to those in need (GI 49). This is an important aspect of the whole Mass and of the presentation of the gifts in particular. The Christian community exists to worship God but also to serve the world, and a community that is shut in on itself is not making the sign of the church that the Constitution says it should. The whole validity of a money offertory at this point has been questioned,[32] but if at least part of the offerings, of whatever kind, are given away, the practice is not only fully justifiable but continues the practice of the church in its first days.

What in any case needs to be avoided is any suggestion that we have anything to give to God, and the consequence must be that the liturgical arrangement of the offertory must be sober and never allowed to get out of hand. In the recent past there has been a tendency to over-rate it, perhaps because the offering, the real offering, that takes place during the eucharistic prayer was obscured by a silent canon which left the people no room for expression.

## The eucharistic prayer

The most interesting point the Order makes about the eucharistic prayer is that 'it is the centre and climax of the whole celebration' (GI 54). It is to be noted that it does not say this of the consecration which, *theologically* speaking, may be regarded as the climax of the eucharist (though one has doubts: the theology of the eucharist that has been based on what can be called the 'consecration mentality' has been far from happy). In so doing the Order returns to the oldest tradition of eucharistic celebration. For centuries, roughly up to the eleventh, Christians were not concerned about 'the moment of consecration', and until the addition of the elevation of the host at the end of the twelfth century, they were largely unaware when it occurred. Until this time, then, the church thought of the whole eucharistic prayer as the *action* which was to achieve the purpose for which it was instituted. We are reminded of this by the phrase in the missal of certain insertions into the Roman Canon, *infra actionem*, which is found in the Gelasian Sacramentary, in all medieval missals, in that of 1570 and retained in the latest edition.[33] The whole eucharistic prayer was regarded as effecting the eucharist and this meant that the early church had a much wider and, as one may think, a deeper understanding of it. They saw the prayer not just as bringing about the presence of Christ but as making the great thanksgiving-memorial that made the great redeeming actions of Christ present and enabling the community to enter into them. They did not at all sharply distinguish 'real presence', 'sacrifice' and 'communion' (as was common in the later Middle Ages); they saw the eucharistic prayer as effecting the whole *opus redemptionis*.[34] The prayer, and the action, ran from thanksgiving through consecration to memorial, offering, intercession and communion. All this and much more is the content of the action that is set in motion by the eucharistic prayer.

We have, then, to do with action and the eucharistic prayer unfolds the various phases of that action which constitutes the essence of the eucharistic celebration. The Order (GI 55) gives a liturgical analysis of the eucharistic prayer which is really a description of the principal phases of the action. They are as follows: Thanksgiving, acclamation, *epiclesis* (or invocation), the words of institution, *anamnesis* (or memorial), offering, intercessions and doxology. To these could be added proclamation. Merely to list the various parts of the eucharistic prayer is to reveal how much richer it is than has been commonly supposed for many centuries.

*Proclamation*

The proclamation of God's word does not cease with the reading of the scriptures and the homily. The church has taken into herself God's message and now, almost exclusively in her own words, proclaims the meaning of the message. In the Roman tradition this is done in the first place by the 'preface' and the most plausible interpretation of that word (Lat. *prae-fatio*, a speaking out before God and his people) is that it means 'proclamation'.[35] In the Eastern tradition much of the first part of the anaphora is given over to a proclamation of the saving works of God, resuming the main phases of the history of salvation. This proclamation, with which is combined the invocation of the divine names, continues the action of the ministry of the word and shows that the eucharistic celebration itself is part of the history of salvation carrying it forward until the *parousia* which is announced in the acclamation after the consecration.

But it is also the proclamation of the church's *faith*.

> The eucharistic prayer is the principal proclamation made by the church of what the eucharist is. It has an absolutely crucial teaching function, for it is here in the first place that we must look for the faith of the Church in the eucharist. It is to this prayer we must go if we would know what the church wishes to affirm about the eucharist. . . . We discover too what the church is saying about herself, for as we know from the Constitution on the Liturgy, the eucharist is the principal expression of the church's life and activity and the manifestation of its true nature. The church is not primarily an institution or a society that has parallels with earthly societies. It is above all a communion, a *koinonia*, which is lifted up to God through the eucharist, the dynamic centre of the

church's unity, in praise and thanksgiving to the Father. It is in the eucharist that the community, the *Qehal Jahve*, is actualized and is able to lay hold of the saving work of Jesus Christ and so make itself, if only slowly and with pain, what he would have it be. The church, it has been said often enough, makes (celebrates) the eucharist; it is even truer that it is the eucharist that makes the church.[36]

All this and indeed much more the church is saying about the eucharist and herself, though not everything can be said in one eucharistic prayer. Hence the need for several.

*Thanksgiving*

Thanksgiving, eucharist, is the dominant note of the prayer and takes us right back to its institution when Christ brought the sacrament into being in the course of the 'thanksgiving' that he pronounced at the Last Supper: Mark 14:22, 23 (*eulogēsas* over the bread and *eucharistēsas* over the cup); Luke 22:19, 20 (*eucharistēsas* over the bread); Matthew 26:26, 27 (*eulogēsas* and *eucharistēsas* as in Mark).[37]

The origins of 'thanksgiving' are to be found in the prayers of blessing that Christ pronounced at the Last Supper. These were two: a very brief blessing of the bread at the beginning of the meal and the longer one for the blessing of the cup. Even before the end of New Testament times, it would seem, the former had been swallowed up by the latter and the consecration of both bread and wine took place during the one prayer called *eucharistia*. But the second table-blessing was no ordinary one. The Last Supper was a Passover celebration (whether exactly a Passover meal is another question) and the eucharistic prayer over the cup contained special elements appropriate to the occasion: God's passing-by, the *midrash*, that is the account of the Exodus given to the guests by the head of the family, the eschatological passage, the expectation of Elijah and the verses speaking of the pouring out of wrath over the nations who know not God.[38] If we take this view, says Ligier,

> it is easy to reach a conclusion by situating the principal stages of the Last Supper within the framework of the Passover meal or *seder*. The verses of Luke 22 (15–18), the words of the Master and the first cup corresponded to the 'blessing of redemption' which

was already followed by a cup. In accordance with the Passover tradition, in it Jesus expressed his joy in taking part in this Passover; but instead of then, according to custom, showing his desire to take part in the approaching festivities he stated that for him this was the last Passover before the coming of the Kingdom. Then came the rite of the bread, coinciding with the blessing of the unleavened bread,[39] since it occurs directly afterwards and marks the beginning of the festal meal. Lastly, the consecration of the chalice, postponed to the end of the meal according to the traditions of Paul and Luke, occurred at the time when the father of the family offered the long prayer of thanksgiving. It was only after saying it that Jesus offered the cup and said the sacramental words in the presence of his apostles, at the moment when they were getting ready to recall the verses of wrath. Christ the Redeemer had transformed the cup of wrath into the chalice of mercy for the multitude of nations.[40]

What emerges from all this is that the eucharistic prayer derives from the Jewish table-prayer of 'blessing', though all the elements of the latter are completely transformed. But it is this prayer that gives the Christian prayer its dominant character: it is a proclamation of thanksgiving (blessing) for the wonderful works of salvation that are recalled in greater or less detail in the course of it. In the Christian prayer the saving deeds of God wrought through Christ continue the recalling of the saving events of the Old Testament and lead naturally into the narrative of the institution. Even this, then, exists in the perspective of thanksgiving, as does the *anamnesis*, the making of the memorial with offering that follows the words of institution (see Eucharistic Prayers II and III). The prayer ends in *doxa*, giving glory to God through the Son in the Holy Spirit. *Doxa* is always associated with 'blessing', 'thanksgiving' and 'praise' which, with petition, are found in Jewish prayers of blessing (*berakoth*). They are also found in the Christian eucharistic prayers in different ways.

*Acclamation*

Although the eucharistic prayer is uniquely the prayer of the president of the community and although he, in the name of the people, voices the thanksgiving, there is also within it a certain dialogue. The greatness, the glory and the love of God are proclaimed in the first part of the prayer and the people make their response with the *Sanctus*, which is a hymning of that same glory and love. But the dialogue goes on at an even deeper level. The church recalls and makes present the saving deeds of God so that she may receive into herself the 'eucharist', the thanksgiving of Christ, her head. For it is only then that she can return, bearing her gift of thanksgiving, to the Father through the Son and in the Holy Spirit. This response is made in the acclamation after the consecration, in the doxology at the end of the prayer and finally in the communion.

## Epiclesis *or invocation of the Holy Spirit* I

The Jewish prayers contained supplication and the eucharistic prayer has one of a rather different kind. Since the fourth century the Roman Canon has had a prayer beseeching the Father to accept the offering of the community so that it may become the body and blood of Jesus Christ.[41] In the three new prayers there are invocations of the Holy Spirit asking that the people's offerings may become the body and blood of Christ.[42]

The importance of this supplication is that first it invokes the work of the Holy Spirit in the eucharistic action and secondly it integrates the 'offertory' into that same action. The gifts the people have presented as the sign of their self-giving are now to be integrated into the offering of Christ which the eucharistic action makes present. In the New Testament view (cf. Romans 12:1, 2, etc.), self-offering, the offering of one's whole life and activity, is always associated with sacrifice and here in the eucharist it receives expression.

## The institution narrative

The words of institution are the heart of every known eucharistic liturgy with the possible exception of the eccentric liturgy of Addai and Mari.[43] They constitute of course the real *anamnesis* of the Mass, for the church is here doing visibly what Christ commanded her to do at the Last Supper 'in memory of' him. This is the reason why they are effective. This has not always been understood by some of the critics of the new Order, and no doubt the passage (GI 55) has been 'edited' in the version of the

General Instruction to be found in the *Missale Romanum* (1970)[44] to satisfy these critics.

The Order of 1969 (GI 55) then says this:

(a) In the words (narrative) of institution the Last Supper is made present (*repraesentatur*) by the words and actions of Christ;

(b) in the Supper, Christ instituted the 'sacrament of his passion and resurrection';

(c) this he gave to his apostles, namely his body and blood under the appearances of bread and wine;

(d) at the same time he left to them the command to perpetuate the same mystery.

We note the identification between the 'narrative of institution' and 'the words and actions of Christ'. It is these that make present what Jesus did at the Last Supper. But what Jesus made present at the Last Supper was much more than bringing about a Real Presence under the appearances of bread and wine, more, in fact, than constructing a sign that was simply a memorial of his death. As the gospel narratives make clear, our Lord's mind was moving on towards the future, to the passion and the death, but also to the resurrection and the glorification. Indeed, he was looking on to the kingdom that would come into existence as a result of his death and resurrection, and all this was his redeeming work. When, then, he said 'Do this in memory of me' he was not restricting his vision to the passion and the death. The eucharist was to be in memory of *him* suffering and dead, yes, but also risen, ascended and glorified with his Father. The eucharist is the sign, the sacrament, the mystery of all this. St Paul, whose whole experience was of the risen, glorified Christ, had no doubt about it. For him the celebration of the eucharist was a proclamation of the redeeming death of Christ until he should come again. This, in fact, is what Jesus commanded his apostles to do so that the 'sacrament of his passion and resurrection' might be perpetuated in the church.

This, it seems to me, is a perfectly satisfactory way of speaking of the 'words of institution' or consecration, and I believe it to be thoroughly traditional. The church perpetuates the sacrament of the passion and resurrection precisely by saying and doing what Christ did at the Last Supper. She has nothing else to do. As Maurice de la Taille said a very long time ago, the 'newness' of the sacrifice of the Mass is totally on the part of the church: the power (of the Mass) is totally on the part of

Christist.[45] The church has nothing to handle but the *sacramentum*, but Christ committed himself to it—it is the sign of the covenant, the new covenant—he is faithful to his promises and when the church, in obedience to his command, constructs the sign, makes or celebrates the sacrament, then Christ with all his redeeming power is present to her.

What, however, has changed the perspective for Catholics of the Roman rite is the introduction of three new eucharistic prayers which may be used severally as alternatives to the Roman Canon. We shall consider each of them lower down. What needs to be said here is that though in the narrower sense the words of institution (what scholastic theologians have called the 'form') are the same in all four prayers, the narratives in which they are set are different in each case. That of the Roman Canon retains its elaborate description: Jesus took bread into his hands, he looked up to heaven (Matthew 14:19) and the Supper took place on the *day* before he suffered (a peculiarity of the Roman rite). The second takes from Hippolytus the phrase (that comes from John 10:18) saying that Jesus freely accepted his death, while the third adds no more than that it was on the *night* before he died that Jesus took the bread and cup. The fourth is markedly Johannine (John 13:1ff.): Jesus loved those who were his own and the eucharist is the proof of his love. To the words over the cup it adds 'filled with the fruit of the vine'. These variations will not only enrich people's notions of the eucharist but will be a constant reminder that the New Testament accounts themselves vary, each one throwing a different light on the mystery of eucharist.

As for the words of institution in the narrower sense, authority decided that they should be uniform in all four prayers. It was said that this was for pastoral reasons, presumably not to confuse the people. But the four longer narratives are already there to confuse them (if anyone is going to be confused) and one must suppose that all Catholics are aware that the New Testament accounts differ from one another. However that may be, two things have happened to this set of words: 'which will be given up for you' have been added to 'This is my body' and the famous (or notorious) 'Mystery of faith' has been removed from them in the Roman Canon and appears in the acclamation after the consecration. The first is borrowed from Luke 22:19 (and cf. 1 Corinthians 11:24, margin, *klōmenon* = 'broken') and underlines the sacrificial aspect of Jesus' action ('This is my body which is to be delivered over to suffering and death for you'). This must be said to be a distinct enrichment of the rite and from a literary viewpoint it provides a better balance with the words over the cup. The removal of the words *mysterium fidei* from the words over the cup occasioned, it will be remembered, a considerable outcry, though needlessly. It was certainly not a confession of faith in the Real Presence. If it had been, it ought to have appeared in the words over the bread too, and in any case it was not until the twelfth or thirteenth centuries that the word 'mystery' was used of the Real Presence. Before that it meant the whole mystery of salvation or of the eucharist. That the words are an interpolation is certain, they seem to have come in somewhere during the sixth century, though how they got there is a matter of scholarly speculation.[46] The insertion of these words into the acclamation is a very happy stroke and the responses of the people very evidently interpret their meaning: they acclaim the mystery of salvation, death, resurrection and second coming (the last in all but one).[47]

## *The* anamnesis *or memorial prayer*

The words of institution are the real *anamnesis* of the eucharist. By these words that come to us from Christ we at once recall and make present his redeeming action. But the church from the time of the earliest eucharistic prayer we possess (that of Hippolytus, c. 215)[48] has always and everywhere drawn out the implications of the *anamnesis* in a prayer that bears that name. Verbally it varies a good deal but the sense is always this: by making the memorial (*anamnesis*) the church is brought into the presence of the redeeming Christ who suffered, died, rose again, ascended to the glory of his Father whence he will come again at the end of time. The power of the redeeming events is available to the church, she is able to 'make his sacrifice her own' and he unites her self-offering to his own. So the church is able to say: 'We make this sacrifice in the memory of Christ, we recall his passion, death, resurrection and ascension'[49] and so we are able to offer 'from your own gifts to us'[50] the bread that is now the Bread of Life and the cup that is now the Cup of Salvation, namely the 'holy and perfect sacrifice',[51] Jesus Christ our Lord.

But the theme of thanksgiving is to be understood to be there, too, and this is often made explicit. This is very marked in the liturgy of St John Chrysostom. After the phrase 'we offer you your own of what is your own', the choir (or the people) cry out: 'We praise you, we bless you, *we give you thanks*, Lord . . . '. But it is also found in the third eucharistic prayer: 'we offer you in thanksgiving this holy and living sacrifice'.[52] Objectively, the sacrifice of Christ by which he took away the sin of the world is the cause of all Christian rejoicing and 'eucharist'; subjectively, here in the Mass he makes his self-offering available to the offerers and they, thus being united with him, give thanks for the 'work of redemption' that is taking place within them. *Anamnesis*, offering and thanksgiving all go together.

In the presence of Christ's offering, however, we have 'to learn to offer' ourselves so that through him our Mediator we may be drawn day by day into an ever more perfect union with God and with each other.'[53]

## Epiclesis *or invocation of the Holy Spirit* II

As far as we know, the Roman Canon has never had an invocation of the Holy Spirit. The third prayer (*Supplices*) after the consecration is certainly a prayer for the acceptance of the sacrifice and for the fruitful reception of holy communion on the part of the worshippers. But all efforts to show, by reconstruction, that it contained an invocation of the Holy Spirit have proved vain. Nor is it possible to show that the earliest eucharistic prayers had one. It is true that it is to be found in the present text(s) of the *Apostolic Tradition* of Hippolytus, though its authenticity has been contested.[54] The *epiclesis* of the Holy Spirit in this place is generally considered to have come into the prayer during the fourth century in the Syrian area.[55] In the light of all this it cannot be said, then, that an *epiclesis* of the Holy Spirit is a *necessary* element of the eucharistic prayer. But if we see the eucharist as the sacrament-sign of the church, there is a high appropriateness in having such an invocation. The church is the Spirit-filled body of Christ, in that body the Holy Spirit is regarded as the animating principle and it is to him that the fruitfulness of Christ's saving work in the hearts of Christians is attributed. Now that people can *hear* the invocation they become aware of the work of the Spirit in their midst and the eucharist becomes a more adequate sign of the church. From a practical point of view, the insertion of *epicleses* of the Holy Spirit into the Roman rite will do much to remind Western Catholics of the work and importance of the Holy Spirit in the church. To this extent it should have an ecumenical value, for the East has always had a stronger grasp of this truth than the West.

But what is the exact purpose of this *epiclesis*? There is no need here to go into the very vexed question of the consecrating power of the invocation of the Holy Spirit if only because the *epicleses* inserted into the last three eucharistic prayers for use in the Roman rite have carefully avoided all suggestion of consecration.[56] In the eucharistic prayers added to the Roman rite we find three elements: 1. the church asks that through the reception of holy communion 2. all may be filled with the Holy Spirit so that 3. all may be made one in Christ. The *epiclesis* of Eucharistic Prayer III sets this out most clearly: 'Grant that we, who are nourished by his body and blood, may be filled with the Holy Spirit, and become one body, one spirit in Christ' (cf. 1 Corinthians 12:12, 13). Eucharistic Prayer IV adds 'into the one body, *a living sacrifice of praise*', thus relating the offering of the people to the sacrifice of Christ. This seems to echo the General Instruction (55, f) which remarks that in the memorial the church offers the Victim to the Father in the Holy Spirit. So there is the upward and downward movement of the Holy Spirit, upward so that the very work of the church, the offering, is effected in the Holy Spirit and downward, for it is through his operation that the communion can become fruitful in the hearts of men.[57]

*The intercessions*

As we have seen, the Jewish form of blessing-prayer admitted supplication – it usually came towards the end of it – though it is impossible to say whether this influenced the insertion of intercessions into the Christian eucharistic prayers. They may not have been there from the beginning and the sample prayer given by Hippolytus does not contain them. On the other hand Justin[58] has them, though *before* the eucharistic prayer begins, and there are references to prayers for various categories of people in the works of Tertullian. But if they were not included from the beginning the church soon saw the appropriateness of interceding for the needs of mankind during the eucharistic prayer. Perhaps the best statement of the matter is to be found in the *Mystagogical Catecheses* of Cyril of Jerusalem.[59] This moment is most appropriate to make intercessions since the 'spiritual sacrifice' (*pneumatikēn thusian*) has just been accomplished and 'over the victim we call upon God and pray and offer it for all who are in need, for the peace of the church, for the well-being of the world, for rulers, for armies, for the sick and the afflicted'. 'While the holy and dread sacrifice[60] is present' those who are prayed for 'greatly profit' from its offering.

The General Instruction (55, 9) yields a similar though less impressive teaching: the church at this moment celebrates the eucharist in union with the whole church both earthly and heavenly (Cyril includes this, too) and makes the offering for all its members, both living and dead, who are called to share in the redemption and salvation of Christ acquired by his body and blood. Unlike Cyril it does not emphasize the presence of Christ's sacrifice, yet the sense that intercessions should be made within the eucharistic prayer is ancient in the Western church. It was the sense of Pope Innocent I's letter (415) to Decentius of Gubbio, and it is clear from the same letter that some time before Innocent (perhaps not very long before) the intercessions had been brought within the Roman Canon. There they still are, distributed before and after the consecration, though the *Memento* of the dead did not become a fixed element of the prayer until after the Carolingian adaptation of the ninth century. The Roman Canon thus made the point, at a very early date and in a manner wholly liturgical, that intercession during its course is of special efficacy.[61]

The compilers of the new eucharistic prayers have preferred to place the intercessions after the consecration, no doubt to make clear the fundamental character of such a prayer: it is a single prayer, made up of proclamation, thanksgiving and praise, taking up in its course the enactment of the 'thanksgiving' which is the memorial of the Lord's passion, death and resurrection. Intercession, however appropriate within the prayer, is a sort of consequence of the pleading of the Lord's sacrifice and is therefore better placed at the end.[62]

As for the content of these intercessions, the Roman Canon is notably rich. It has a strong sense of the communion of saints and its lists of saints are nicely graduated (thought by some to be the work of St Gregory the Great), though one could wish that they had not been so rigidly fixed. The ability to insert either the saint of the day or the saint of the place of celebration would help to make the prayer live for the time and the place. The emphasis, too, on the power of the intercession of the saints is more clearly marked in the Roman prayer than in the others ('May their merits and prayers gain us your constant help and protection'). That of EP II is briefer, less explicit, though in intention all-inclusive. It is difficult to understand why the laity were not included with the clergy, for the phrase 'have mercy on us all' is hardly sufficient. Mary and the saints are merely mentioned, though the earthly church is seen as joining with them in the praise of God. The intercessions of EP III have evidently been carefully thought out. They run out of the offering of sacrifice, they are explicitly inclusive of the universal church and of the local church gathered for worship and they end with an eschatological emphasis ('We hope to enjoy for ever the vision of your glory') that is so strongly marked in all the new liturgy. This part of the intercession is preceded by another in which the prayer of Mary, of the saints and of the saints of the place and the feast is sought. The commemoration of the dead is particularly rich and expresses a truly Christian theology of death. The intercessions of EP IV, if shorter than those of EP III, are none the less rich. Pope, bishop, clergy and laity are all prayed for explicitly and an ecumenical dimension is given with the prayer for 'all who seek you with a sincere heart'. The prayer for the dead is also generous in its scope: 'all the dead whose faith is known to you alone' – and how many there must be of that kind! The last petition is for the perfecting of the communion of saints when all, 'freed from the corruption of sin and death', will sing God's glory with every creature through Christ our Lord.

These intercessions must be said to be one of the most valuable additions to the liturgy of our day. It is one thing to be told from the theological manual or catechism that the Mass is a 'sacrifice of impetration' (language that tempts one to go heretical without further ado) and it is another to hear the eucharist being pleaded for the well-being of the whole church and the world.

## The doxology

The eucharistic prayer began with giving praise and thanksgiving to God through Jesus Christ. Now it ends with giving God the glory through the Son and in the Holy Spirit for the showing forth of his continuing love made present in the eucharist. The church has received Christ's 'thanksgiving' into herself with the co-operation of the Holy Spirit. The covenant has been renewed, the bridal relationship between Christ and his church has been strengthened and the Spirit, with a new infusion of life, has come to her again. So she can now through Christ her head and Bridegroom and in the Holy Spirit give all glory and honour to the

Father. This is made particularly clear in the doxology of the Roman Canon which seems to bear a family relationship to that of Hippolytus: 'Glory and honour to you (the Father) through him (Christ), with the Holy Spirit in the holy church, now and for ever'.[63] The fragmentary prayer of Der-Balyzeh combines the doxology with a prayer for communion and in language lies somewhere between that of Hippolytus and that of the Roman Canon: 'Give (thy servants) the power of the Holy Spirit, the confirmation and increase of faith, the hope of eternal life to come, through our Lord Jesus Christ. Through him, glory to thee, Father, with the Holy Spirit for ever.'[64] With this seems to be related the doxology in the Sacramentary of Sarapion: 'Through him (Christ), glory to thee and power, in the Holy Spirit, now and for ever and ever'.[65] There are others, and I have quoted one or two here to show that if the Roman doxology is good, it is not unique, and it is perhaps a pity that for pastoral reasons the Roman version is the only one used in all four eucharistic prayers. Variation, of course, offers musical difficulties and this is one of the texts the celebrant is urged to sing,[66] but the single text rather limits the possibilities of musical settings that at least *some* celebrants could sing and that could be of considerable interest.

From the time of Justin the Martyr the people's response 'Amen' has been given at this point and usually in a loud voice or in song. It is the affirmation of the people to what has been done in the eucharistic action; by this response they express their participation in the thanksgiving and in the offering of Christ. The revisers have set their face against repetitions in the liturgy, but perhaps there was a case here for at least a triple Amen, which musically can be very effective and is easier for the people to sing.[67]

## The communion rite
~

One of the undeniable advantages of the new Order is that it has made it perfectly possible to see, without explanation, what are the great structural lines of the Mass: the ministry of the word, the celebration of the eucharistic memorial and the communion. It has thus replaced the old 'three parts of the Mass': the Offertory (which you had to be present for to avoid mortal sin), the Consecration and the (Priest's – sic)

Communion. And even the liturgists' division of the Mass into the Mass of the Catechumens and the Mass of the Faithful is now shown to be inadequate. Revision of the communion rite was very necessary, for no part of the Mass was as confused as this. Missals continued the heading *Canon Missae* over the whole section giving the communion rite, the breaking of the bread that came during the embolism of the Lord's prayer, the elaborate signing of the chalice with a portion of the host, the *Agnus Dei* that had become completely divorced from its original purpose (an accompaniment to the breaking of the bread which in the papal rite was very elaborate – and lengthy) and the kiss of peace (restricted in fact to the clergy) embedded in the celebrant's private prayers before communion.

The new Order now makes it quite clear that the communion rite begins with the Lord's prayer, and even the printers have been instructed to put here the heading *Ritus Communionis*. All is now orientated towards the act of communion: the whole community prays the Lord's prayer, asking for the Bread of Life and that their sins may be forgiven so that, as the Instruction says, holy things may be given to those who are truly holy.[68] The embolism has with advantage been shortened and the action goes straight to the sign of peace which is prefaced by a prayer giving (part of) its meaning and the sign of peace is extended to the whole community. The bread is now broken during the *Agnus Dei*, as it was when Pope Sergius I introduced it into the Mass at this place and for this purpose *c.* 700. A single prayer of preparation follows and after the invitation the community move in procession to the altar for communion. It is a comprehensible pattern.

In the copious commentary provided by the Instruction (56, a–k) certain features stand out. The church is concerned to emphasize brotherly love, the spirit of reconciliation that goes with it and the unity of Christians who are made one by the one Bread that is the body of Christ.

In the Lord's prayer we ask for our daily bread which for Christians is principally the body of Christ. Perhaps Western Christians ought to ask also that through the generosity and ingenuity of modern man the people of the Third World should be fed. The reconciliation theme is not prominent in the commentary here, though it is implicit in all it has to say about the communion act itself. We should do well to recall that, as the Lord said, when we are bringing our gift to the altar and if we

~

*110*

remember that a brother has something against us, we should first be reconciled with him and only then may we offer our gift (Matthew 5:23–24).[69] If through the strength given us in holy communion we could go out and be reconcilers in the secular community we should be doing no more than is implied by the whole eucharistic action.

The sign of peace and the fraction are closely associated. The first is seen as a prayer for the peace and unity of the church and of the whole of mankind (here the reconciliation theme appears) and as an expression of mutual love among the worshippers before they receive the one Bread that makes them one body in Christ. At this point the Instruction quotes 1 Corinthians 10:17, and remarks that the fraction is not merely for practical purposes to divide the hosts for the communicants but that it has this significance: we, though many, by communion in the one Bread of Life are made the one body which is Christ.

This is very satisfactory teaching and coming in a document that is primarily practical is very gratifying. But practice still limps behind preaching. Until the bread that is used for the people is much more substantial and the portions larger it is difficult to make the rite of the fraction as significant as the church now says it should be. For concelebration larger altar-breads have become common (though their papery quality is not satisfactory) and we now need something of the kind for the communion of the people. Such bread could be broken and the breaking would be visible to the people. If the ceremony were somewhat prolonged, so much the better. For far too long the people's communion in the Roman tradition has been too clinical. Small white 'hosts' which bear little resemblance to bread are hastily inserted into the mouths of the communicants. The whole rite is done as quickly as possible. There are, no doubt, practical difficulties to be overcome – there always are – but, as the Instruction observes (56, h), there are certain things that are highly desirable in themselves and that even if difficult should be done. At least some of the bread the people receive should be broken from the large host or hosts. This is now required by the *Ordo Missae*. What is necessary is larger and more substantial altar-breads.

The mingling of the consecrated bread and wine, about which the Instruction is completely uninformative, has been retained, though its significance is not at all apparent. Its history is extremely complicated and cannot be gone into here.[70] The Order has retained the rite but has simplified the text, removing the awkward word *consecratio* (which probably witnessed to primitive notions of consecration by contact) and turning it into a prayer for the communicants.

In the new Order the administration of communion to the people is quite elaborate and the commentary in the Instruction rich in content. The communion act is a *procession*, one of the three of the Roman rite (entrance, 'offertory' and communion), it is accompanied by song and *together* these express the unity of the communicants, their spiritual joy and brotherly love. Holy communion is no longer, therefore, *at this point* an act of private devotion; it is the action of the community whose members are praying that they may be drawn into a closer unity with Christ and through him with their fellow-worshippers and with all their fellow Christians throughout the world. In recent centuries we have reflected too little on the meaning of the word '*com*-union' which expresses one of the deepest truths about the church, namely that it is *koinonia*, a sharing of the common life of the body of Christ, the church. The church is communion long before it is institution and at a much deeper level than can be created by juridical bonds. Of this *koinonia* holy communion is the most conspicuous and pregnant sign. It is at this moment that the church is made one and as St Thomas Aquinas said seven hundred years ago, the ultimate, the *real* effect of the eucharist is the unity of the mystical body.[71]

This teaching remains true *however* communion is administered, though it is an interesting reflection on the power of liturgical gestures that where the communion procession has been absent, the notion that holy communion is an act of private devotion has prevailed. The communion procession is then not merely a matter of good order in the assembly (though that has its importance), it is a symbolic gesture signifying that communion is the action of the community, that by it its members are drawn more closely to each other and in practice it should give them an awareness of their solidarity with those outside their community. The communion procession should therefore be regarded as a normal part of the Mass and not as a ceremonial extra.

The rite of administration of communion is rich in meaning: the celebrant shows the host to the people and *invites* them to receive communion: 'This is the Lamb of God . . .' (John 1:36) to which has been added, from Revelation 19:9, 'Happy are those who are called to the (wedding) supper of the Lamb' and the people respond with further words from the gospel: 'Lord, I am not worthy . . .' (Matthew 8:9). It is interesting to observe that the whole invitation and final preparation for communion are in the words of scripture. The formulas of administration ('The body of Christ . . . the blood of Christ') with their response 'Amen' are very ancient, being found already in the writings of St Cyril of Jerusalem in the East and of St Ambrose in the West.[72] The latter's comment is the best interpretation of the phrase: 'Not idly therefore do you say "Amen" for you are confessing that you receive the body of Christ. When, then, you present yourself, the priest says "The Body of Christ" and you answer "Amen", that is, it is true. *What you confess with your lips, keep in your heart.*'

As is well known the *manner* of receiving the eucharist has varied in the course of ages. The earliest records show that the people stood and received the bread in their hands and drank from the cup.[73] From the ninth century in the West, to avoid profanation and out of respect for the Sacrament, people were communicated directly into the mouth. Even later, from the thirteenth century onwards, the custom of kneeling for communion came in. Habits and ways of thinking are changing again and now there is a great desire among the laity to receive in their hands and standing. The latter has become very common and the bishops of a region may give permission for the former.[74] Standing may be regarded as no more than a convenience and the natural thing to do when people are walking in a procession and singing. Communion in the hand is also the more natural way to take food and is a gesture helping people to remember that the eucharist is a meal.

The desire for communion in both kinds is even greater and the documents on this matter since (and including) the Second Vatican Council are numerous.[75] In certain communities, mostly of religious, full use has been made of the permissions so far granted. Bishops have, however, been sending in repeatedly petitions that the facilities should be extended. This has now been made possible by the last Instruction (1970) issued by the Congregation for Worship. This gives permission to local conferences of bishops to determine, within the limits set out in the document, when communion in both kinds may be given. The tendency seems to be setting that communion in both kinds should be normal practice and communion in one kind abnormal, that is, practically impossible on account of the great number of communicants. We have not yet arrived at that situation and meanwhile it seems worth saying that in smaller parishes communion in both kinds should present no very great difficulty and certainly at week-day Masses, where the number of communicants is small, one would have thought that it ought to become normal practice. As people learn to appreciate the significance of the practice, it is likely to be extended. But the documents insist on instruction beforehand and certain lines of it are suggested in a semi-official commentary attached to the 1970 Instruction.

While this, as might be expected, draws attention to the traditional doctrine, summed up at the Council of Trent, that communion under either kind is sufficient and that the whole Christ is present under the appearances of either the bread or the wine, it is interesting to observe that instead of the metaphysico-theological principles that have been to the forefront for centuries to justify communion in one kind, it now appeals to *significance* and *symbolism*. Communion in both kinds expresses more fully what Christ did at the Last Supper when he said 'Take and eat' and 'Take and drink'. The communicants, that is, at least in principle, the whole community, are making a more *exact* memorial of what Christ did at the Last Supper. Likewise, the practice shows up more clearly that the eucharist is a *meal*—at a meal one both eats and drinks—and in this way, too, the memorial aspect of the eucharist is made clearer. There is an even deeper reason for it. In celebrating the eucharist the church gives thanks so that she may receive within herself the self-giving of Christ by which he not only redeemed mankind but gave praise and glory to his Father (John 17). The bread that was broken and 'given up' for us is certainly a sign of that self-offering, but it is more vividly expressed by the significance of the blood 'which is to be poured out for you and for all mankind for the taking away of their sins'. As the Old Testament had it, 'the life is in the blood' and Jesus was visibly indicating the pouring out of his life when he took the cup and said 'This is the cup of my blood of the new covenant which is to be poured out for you'. If this is our understanding of the sacrificial nature of the Last Supper and of the Mass, which is its memorial, then it follows that the communicants, by receiving the cup, will be associated all the more closely with Christ's sacrifice, with his self-giving, which enables the Christian to give himself and his life to the Father.[76]

In fact, communion in both kinds has, as far as one can tell, caused no difficulties among the people. They see the point of it very quickly and in a country such as ours, where communion in both kinds has been customary in other Christian churches since the Reformation, they are more familiar with it than Christians of some continental countries who have had no knowledge of it at all. At the same time, an extension of the practice would give much better opportunities for instruction and so would deepen the people's appreciation of the Mass.

Communion in the hand is now widespread in the church[77] but among traditionalist Catholics it seems to raise more objections than communion from the cup. No doubt it is a change from a practice that is some thousand years old and devotional habits, especially those connected with the reception of holy communion, change very slowly. This is very understandable but it is also clear from experience that there has been a faulty instruction about the manner of Christ's presence in the eucharist. Some people show themselves to be unable or unwilling to distinguish between an altar-bread and a 'host'. What lies at the bottom of this attitude is a failure to distinguish between the *sign* and the reality it signifies (the body of Christ). Sight, taste and touch are in the eucharist deceived, said the author of the *Adoro te*, it is *faith* that perceives the reality. On the other hand, bread and wine are there precisely to support the senses; they are *signs*, symbols, telling us that here is the Bread of Life and the Cup of Salvation. It is not necessary to go to the long and elaborate treatise of St Thomas on the eucharist to learn that when we touch the sign we do not touch the Body. The teaching is for all to read in the Corpus Christi hymn, generally attributed to St Thomas, the *Lauda Sion*: when you break the host you do not break the Reality; only the sign (the bread) is broken and such a fraction in no way affects him whom the bread signifies.[78]

However, as the document sent to bishops on the subject and made public in 1969 observes, what touches the people so closely must be dealt with very carefully.[79] In this Instruction we note that the bishops are given permission to allow communion in the hand with proper safeguards. All danger of irreverence is to be avoided and conditions for a proper respect for the Real Presence are laid down. Previous instruction is one of them and such instruction would, one thinks, enlighten those who do not wish to receive in their hands. As the Instruction makes clear, no one is to be pressed to do so. Still, there are considerable numbers of people who do wish to receive in their hands—it seems a more natural and adult way of taking food, even when it is the body of Christ—and it would seem that permissions should be granted more readily than they are at present. Anglicans receive in the hand and *their* reverence is very striking. It is difficult to suppose that ours would be less.

The rest of the communion rite nicely balances the needs of public worship and private devotion. During the procession there may be song and then, when it is over, there is silence. If there has been no singing during the procession, the silence may be concluded with a chant sung by all.[80] Two observations may be made here.

1. While it is highly desirable – and should be normal practice – that the people should take part in the communion chant, it is also perfectly proper that the choir should sing more elaborate chants that are calculated to assist the private prayer of the people. If the texts are familiar there is no reason why they should not be in Latin and this would ensure a place for Latin and certain kinds of music in our present liturgy. It goes without saying that the music should be of good quality and that the choir should be capable of singing it *well*. It is difficult to see the virtue of badly-sung music. Mass is not the time, nor is it the function of the choir, to mortify other people's flesh.

2. People probably need to be taught that *silence* as such is a good and prayerful thing and we all know that there is too little of it in the modern world. Sometimes they do not profit sufficiently from the silence after communion because they are saying words, even if only in their minds. Silence if willed leads to prayer, prayer that is quite wordless, a mere dwelling on the reality of God.

Anyway, this silence and other periods of silence that are permissible in the new rite, e.g. after the readings, should be treasured and if they do play the part in the celebration that they should, the complaint of some (quite unjustified) that the modern Mass is 'all talk' would fall to the ground.

### The dismissal

Since the Last Gospel and the Leonine Prayers were dropped, some have complained that the Mass comes to an end rather abruptly. There is some truth in this and no doubt they will not be consoled to be told that before 1570 it was even more abrupt. There were no Leonine Prayers, there was no Last Gospel and no blessing (both these being uttered by the priest, if at all, on his way back to the sacristy). The Roman Mass has always ended abruptly and the reason is that Rome (and the other great centres) saw the Mass as *the* eucharistia. The Mass is the 'thanksgiving' of the church which she is able to make to God through Christ and once she had asked in the prayer after communion for the effects of communion in the assembly she thought that the action was over: *Ite, missa est!*

But devotional habits change[81] and the church, in the new missal (pp. 495–506) has provided blessings *in addition* to the postcommunion prayer. These are combined with prayers (*orationes super populum*) which were a normal feature of the Mass in the Gelasian Sacramentary but which survived only for Lent in the Gregorian Sacramentary. Those in the new missal are of good quality and a translation of one or two of them may be of interest to the reader.

1. (For Paschaltide): The celebrant addresses the people: 'Bow your heads for the blessing.' He continues (and the prayer is addressed *to the people*):

> By the resurrection of his only Son, God has graciously redeemed you, making you his adopted children;
> may you always rejoice in his blessing.
> By Christ's redeeming work you have received the gift of perpetual freedom.
> By his grace may you be co-heirs with him in eternal life.
> By faith and baptism you have been raised to a new life;
> may you, by your good life here below, be united with him in the heavenly city.
> And may the blessing of almighty God, Father, Son and Holy Spirit. . . . [82]

2. (For any Sunday in the year):

> May the God of all consolation guide you through life so that you may enjoy his peace and blessing.
> May your hearts be untroubled, established in his love.
> Rich in faith, hope and love, may you pass through this present life, doing good and rejoice at the end in the happiness of eternal life.
> And may the blessing. . . .

For ordinary use also there is the Aaronic blessing (Numbers 6:24–26) and the passage from Philippians 4:7: 'May the peace of God which surpasses all understanding keep your minds and hearts in the knowledge and love of God and of his Son, our Lord Jesus Christ'.

One feels that a judicious use of these blessings will do much to take away the reproach that the Roman Mass ends too abruptly.

# Critical observations on the new Order of the Mass

It will, I trust, be clear that I have given a positive evaluation of the new Order of the Mass. But liturgy-making is a human activity and consequently fraught with imperfection. No liturgy that ever was is perfect, if only because it can never adequately express the mystery of the eucharist and of the church of which it is the sign. In the last chapter of this book I have considered liturgy in the context of the modern world and I have suggested certain requirements of a liturgy that will, I believe, be suitable to that world. There is a number of smaller matters that deserve comment and that is done here.

## The introductory rites

The main criticism of the Order here must be that it is unduly cumbersome. Normally, it is made up of eight different elements, some of which seem to duplicate each other: the sign of the cross, the greeting, the brief address, the confession with absolution, the *Kyries*, the *Gloria* and the collect. The sign of the cross and the greeting *could* have been alternatives and, as I have suggested above, the confession (combined with the *Kyries*) could have been placed at the end of the General Intercessions.

## The preparation of the gifts

The insertion of 'offertory' prayers, as of obligation, has unduly complicated what is, according to the General Instruction and the Roman tradition, an essentially simple rite. Apart from the prayers over the bread and the cup, the rest are for the private devotion of the celebrant. Perhaps they could have been prescribed for celebration when there is no procession, on weekdays, for instance, but as it is, it is difficult to combine them with the procession.

*The eucharistic prayers*

The chief criticism that is to be made of these is that they do not reflect the daily concerns and life of people today who in various documents are exhorted to offer themselves and their work through Christ to God. There are one or two references to the created universe, but they are insufficient and make little impression. Nor, as we shall see, is the balance corrected by the new prefaces.

*The rite of communion*

This is much improved but there is one feature, whose significance is heavily underlined by the General Instruction (GI 56), that still appears as a secondary rite. The bread is broken so that all, receiving from the one loaf, may become one body in Christ. The original place of the fraction was immediately at the end of the eucharistic prayer, a place it retains in one Western rite, the Ambrosian. Its place in the Roman rite is due to the exigencies of papal ritual. After the doxology the Pope left the altar, went to the throne and there sang the Lord's prayer. Gregory the Great wished to sing it over the consecrated elements and moved the fraction to where it is now. It is to be supposed that such a return to tradition was too much for the responsible authorities who felt that, apart from a certain straightening out of the rite, it had better be left alone.

The significance of the mingling with its accompanying (though revised) text remains obscure. It is a rite that could have been omitted without any impoverishment of the communion act.

# Notes
~

1 GI 7-57.
2 It is likely that the Order was worked out first and that the Instruction was then written as a liturgical commentary on what had been done.
3 I use the word 'ministry' instead of 'liturgy' as the former has a long tradition in the English language. For me it has no theological overtones at all.
4 See J. D. Crichton, 'Liturgical Forms', *The Way*, special number (Autumn 1970).
5 If we take the old (pre-1955) Good Friday liturgy as being the liturgy of the church of Rome in the fourth century, we see that it began without either. The entrance chant and the collect would both seem to have been added to the Mass in the fifth

century. (See J. A. Jungmann, **Missarum Sollemnia**, French trans., vol. II, pp. 72ff.)

[6] Paulinus Milner, OP, '*Et cum spiritu tuo*' in **Studies in Pastoral Liturgy**, ed. Placid Murray, OSB (Dublin, 1967), pp. 202–10.

[7] In practice, of course, they read the **Confiteor** out of their books and those who were 'liturgical' tried to lend an ear to the text of the introit. Psalm 42 with a confession was used in the later Middle Ages but the former was usually said either in the sacristy or on the way to the altar.

[8] E.g. at Lugano (1953), Assisi (1956).

[9] See Oscar Cullmann, **Early Christian Worship** (London, 1953), pp. 26–31. The view, still widely held, that the ministry of the word was added to the eucharist in some dark period between, say, AD 80 and AD 150 (Justin's **Apology**) seems to rest on a confusion between a word-service, probably very free and informal, and the synagogue service, something analogous, that may well have influenced the Christian service of the word as we see it when it emerges into history. After all, Christ instituted the eucharist in a context of dialogue and conversation, the 'prayer of blessing or thanksgiving' was almost certainly long and was a proclamation of the saving deeds of God, and if even only some of the discourses of St John (13–17) were uttered at the Last Supper, as is generally supposed, this would indicate that the eucharist was celebrated in a context of the word. In any case, there is Acts 20:7–12 recording that St Paul did celebrate it in the context of a service of the word.

[10] In fact, ordinary people just contracted out and in certain continental places where you could witness these performances, the local people just drifted in for twenty minutes or so and then drifted out.

[11] There is another objection that goes deeper. The modern Mass strongly suggests that the congregation should be involved, they are constantly being invited to commitment and those who have regarded the Mass as the ritual of a private club are naturally very upset.

[12] Cf. Hubert J. Richards, 'God's Word in the Liturgy' in **The Mass and the People of God**, ed. J. D. Crichton (London, 1966); Paulinus Milner, OP, 'The Purpose and Structure of the Liturgy of the Word' in **The Ministry of the Word**, ed. P. Milner (London, 1967).

[13] The only exception is the Easter season, for then the church is celebrating its birth from the crucified and risen Christ. Hence the readings are from Acts and Revelation (Apocalypse), which have been used at this time since the fourth century (cf. certain sermons of St Augustine).

[14] It cannot be said with absolute certainty that the nourishment of the spiritual life is the purpose of the **second** reading, usually from St Paul, but more often than not it serves this purpose. For the purpose of preaching it often has to be neglected, but no doubt as years go by and as the main themes of salvation-history become more familiar we shall be able to pay greater attention to it.

[15] The word 'homily' apparently means 'familiar discourse' and is suggestive of a certain approach to preaching at the liturgy, but it does not seem to offer grounds for a distinction between 'sermon' and 'homily'. St Leo's discourses on the feasts of the year are called **sermones**, at least in the printed editions, and it is difficult to distinguish in St Augustine between **sermones** and **homiliae**.

[16] See C. Vagaggini, **Il Senso Theologico della Liturgia** (Rome, 1958), pp. 27, 33, 85–6, 369, etc.

[17] For the history of salvation see CL 5, 6, 7, 8 and a commentary in J. D. Crichton, **The Church's Worship** (London, 1964), pp. 27–41.

[18] See, for instance, J. Daniélou, **The Bible and the Liturgy** (London, 1956) and modern introductions to the Bible.

[19] At least one book of commentaries on the readings has appeared that falls into this category. On the other hand, the **Commentary on the Sunday Lectionary** (3 vols, Liturgical Press, 1986) by Peter Coughlan and Peter Purdue, one a liturgical expert and the other a scripture expert, has entirely the right approach and, though short, provides the right orientation for the preacher. The combination of the **two** expertises should be noted.

[20] See J. D. Crichton, 'The Nature of the Liturgical Homily' in **The Ministry of the Word**, ed. P. Milner (London, 1967), pp. 27–44; the same: 'The Function of the Homily at Mass', **Liturgy** (April 1967), pp. 25–33.

[21] Oscar Cullmann, 'Scripture and Tradition' in **Divided Christianity** (London, 1961), pp. 7–33.

[22] At least six quotations–which, of course, may have been the work of St Luke.

[23] 'History of salvation' and 'mystery of Christ' are separated by **seu** in the Latin, the weakest of distinguishing words, and best translated 'that is'.

[24] See J. Gelineau, 'L'homélie, forme plénière de la prédication', **La Maison-Dieu**, 82 (1965).

[25] The above is not to be regarded as a recipe for constructing homilies. The four elements should normally condition their shaping but, of course, the preacher is left complete liberty to shape his discourse as he thinks best for the circumstances in which he is working. It should not be thought that the liturgical homily is a piece of disincarnated biblico-liturgical theology without connection with the life-situation of the people. It must speak to them as they are and where they are.

[26] This is the translation ICEL have opted for and it is a good one. A possible alternative is 'Prayer for the whole world' (**oratio universalis**) which may be thought to be a little cumbersome. In England the title is 'Bidding Prayers', which seems to be deliberately archaic.

[27] The revised Holy Week Order in the **Missale Romanum**, 1970, uses these words of the newly baptized who, it is envisaged, are taking full part in the eucharist for the first time.

[28] **De Oratione Communi seu Fidelium** (Vatican, 1965).

[29] The **Missale Romanum** (1970), pp. 893, provides some specimens of these general intercessions and has naturally used the forms given above though it has opted for the use of the second and third forms rather than for the first. Since the **Missale Romanum** is an official book, the obligation to follow it seems clear.

[30] This would seem to be the sense of the somewhat tortuous statement that Pope Innocent I (died 417) made in his famous letter to the Bishop of Gubbio which is so difficult to interpret. He wanted the intercessions to take place in **ipsis mysteriis**, during the eucharistic prayer, and said this was the Roman (indeed apostolic) custom. On the other hand, the question whether the General Intercessions belong to the ministry of the word or to the ministry of the eucharist is a little difficult to determine historically. In the fourth century (**Apostolic Constitutions**, viii, 8), there were prayers (and a blessing) for the catechumens who were then dismissed. The rest were apparently regarded as the 'prayers of the faithful', as they are still so called in modern Roman documents.

[31] J. C. Buckley puts this point very well: 'All is gift, free and unmerited, on the part

of God. All we can do is to thank him and our offering can only be thanksgiving.' See 'Money and the Offertory' in **The Mass and the People of God**, ed. J. D. Crichton (London, 1966), p. 97. This thanksgiving element is clearly expressed in the people's response, 'Blessed be God for ever', for understood, and in Jewish blessings expressed, is the phrase 'for all his wonderful works'.

[32] See J. Duncan Cloud, 'The Theology of the Offertory Collection' in **op. cit.**, ed. J. D. Crichton, pp. 108-21.

[33] For the Gelasian Sacramentary see **Liber Sacramentorum Romanae Aeclesiae Ordinis Anni Circuli**, ed. L. Mohlberg (Rome, 1960).

[34] Prayer over the Offerings for Maundy Thursday, Evening Mass, and formerly 9th Sunday after Pentecost. It is found in the Gelasian Sacramentary (nos. 170, 1196) belonging to the seventh century and therefore expressing the ancient theology of Rome. The Constitution on the Liturgy (2) thought good to use it as a summary definition of the liturgy and in particular of the eucharist.

[35] Cf. J. A. Jungmann, **Missarum Sollemnia** (French trans., Paris, 1954), vol. III, p. 12.

[36] See J. D. Crichton, 'The New Eucharistic Prayers', **Liturgy** (October 1968), p. 90.

[37] There seems to be little difference in meaning between the two words. **Eulogein** is closer to 'blessing' (Lat. **benedicere**), the 'saying of good things' about God which was very much the Jewish way of 'giving thanks'. However, the use of the two words in Matthew and Mark would seem to indicate the existence of the separate and differing 'blessing' prayers said over the bread and the cup at the Last Supper. Luke, and more particularly Paul (1 Corinthians 11:24), have put both under the one term 'thanksgiving' (so L. Ligier, 'From the Last Supper to the Eucharist' in **The New Liturgy**, ed. L. Sheppard (London, 1970), p. 118).

[38] Ligier, **op. cit.**, p. 123.

[39] With the formula 'Blessed be you, Lord, our God, king of the world, you have made us holy by your commandments and have commanded us to eat unleavened bread'. As Ligier points out (**op. cit.**, p. 125, n. 46), this formula opened the way for Christ to insert 'a new commemoration' into it (Do this in memory of me), a point which Paul and Luke emphasized in their accounts of the institution.

[40] **Ibid.**, pp. 124-5. Ligier goes on to show that supplication (intercessions) and **epiclesis** are both suggested by the Jewish texts. It is not our purpose, however, to give a complete literary analysis of the eucharistic prayer but merely to indicate its nature.

[41] St Ambrose, **De Sacramentis**, IV.

[42] This invocation before the consecration seems to be an Alexandrian or Egyptian peculiarity. See **Prayers of the Eucharist, Early and Reformed**, ed. R. C. D. Jasper and G. J. Cuming (OUP, New York, 1985), 'Sarapion, The Euchologion', p. 34, and 'Liturgy of St Mark', p. 43.

[43] At least in the state in which it survives at present. For text, in translation, see Lucien Deiss, **Early Sources of the Liturgy** (London, 1967). It may be of the third century (Botte) or of the fifth century (Raes). Dom Botte thinks it once had the words of the institution.

[44] The revised version runs: 'The narrative of the institution and **the consecration**. The sacrifice is effected by the words and actions of Christ. This sacrifice he instituted at the Last Supper when he offered his body and blood under the appearances of bread and wine and gave them to his apostles to eat and drink and left to them his command to perpetuate the same mystery.' The translation given in

the ICEL (1969) text runs as follows: '*The narrative of the institution*: the Last Supper is made present in the words and actions of Christ when he instituted the sacrament of his passion and resurrection, when under the appearances of bread and wine he gave his Apostles his body to eat and his blood to drink and commanded them to carry on this mystery' (translation copyright © 1969 International Commission on English in the Liturgy, Inc. All rights reserved).

The differences between the two are obvious. In the revised text 'consecration' and 'sacrifice' are inserted—corresponding with the obsession some have that if these words are not included every time the eucharist is spoken of, the statement will not be orthodox—the 'sacrament of his passion and resurrection' is removed, thus weakening the theology of the passage and it is at least suggested that the **narrative** of the institution does not effect the eucharist, as the Order of 1969 (Latin) says. In this thinking a narrative cannot be the 'form' of a sacrament. On the other hand, the ICEL translation hardly does justice to the Latin. Since the version of 1969 is thoroughly traditional in the best sense, we propose to follow it here.

[45] **Mysterium Fidei**, Elucid. XXIII (Paris, 1921 ed.), p. 296. And again: **Novitas sacrificii Missae respectu crucis desumenda est tantum ex parte Ecclesiae**: the newness of the Mass-sacrifice is to be found only on the part of the church. Further on he says that 'the church makes her own' the sacrifice of Christ (p. 299).

[46] B. Capelle, **Travaux Liturgiques**, II (Louvain, 1962), pp. 283–4.

[47] ICEL's translation of the first is very successful. It has turned a mere statement into an enthusiastic acclamation. ICEL has often been the target of bitter criticism. It is right to give credit where it is due. On the other hand it is odd that in English we have **four** acclamations and that there are only three in the **Missale**.

[48] And perhaps St Paul's 'announcing the death of the Lord' indicates a primitive **anamnesis**.

[49] In most prayers the second coming is mentioned.

[50] Roman Canon **de tuis donis ac datis**, which echoes the **ta sa ek tōn sōn**, lit. 'your own from your own', of the liturgy of St John Chrysostom, a phrase used also in Alexandria, it would seem, and that expresses the truth that the church has nothing of her own to offer.

[51] Roman Canon.

[52] In EP II it is less emphasized: 'We thank you for counting us worthy to stand in your presence and serve you'.

[53] CL 48; GI 55, f, and see above, Chapter 3.

[54] Botte (ed. Münster, 1963) strenuously maintains its authenticity and Dix (**Shape**, p. 158, and his ed. of **Ap. Trad.** (1937), pp. 75 ff.) is strongly inclined to reject it. If one is allowed a view in so learned a controversy, I would say that the passage is authentic. In any case, Dix's willingness to cut about liturgical texts to suit his own notions does not seem to be a very happy method of dealing with them, even if his analyses are sometimes illuminating.

[55] See the Mystagogical Discourses of St Cyril of Jerusalem, **Catéchèses Mystagogiques**, ed. A. Piédagnel (Paris, 1966), III, 3, 5. Does the existence of an **epiclesis** of the **Logos** (the Word) in the Sacramentary of Sarapion (**c.** 350) witness to an uncertainty about the whole business?

[56] The solution of the problem whether the **epiclesis** is consecratory probably depends on an assessment of what the Easterns held in the fourth century and later about the 'moment of consecration'. It is generally held that in the fourth century

and until a good deal later the 'moment of consecration' was not isolated. The whole prayer, enshrining an action, the action of the church, was regarded as consecratory. This was certainly so in the West, as the reference in the Roman Canon to the elements as **sacrificia** before the consecration suggests. Indeed, the whole notion was extrapolated into the 'offertory' as the ancient prayers over the offerings also suggested.

[57] This is suggested by GI 55, c, where it says that the **epiclesis** is an invocation that the Victim may become the source of salvation to those who receive holy communion.

[58] **Apol.** I, 65, and cf. 1 Timothy 2:1, 2.

[59] V, 8, 1–8; 9, 6–7; 10, 10–12. I assume, with the latest editor, Piédagnel, the high probability that these catecheses were Cyril's, though possibly worked over by his successor, John.

[60] 'Dread' = 'hair-raising', literally, a word much used in liturgies coming from the Syrian region and found also in St John Chrysostom.

[61] If one may refer to the 'moment of consecration' business again, it seems clear that for Pope Innocent the main point was that the intercessions should be within the prayer, though it did not matter to him whether they were before or after the consecration. This fits in with the whole tenor of the Roman Canon.

[62] The Roman position, intercessions **before** the consecration, is not unique. They are found in the same position in an ancient Alexandrian prayer—one more instance of the strange similarities between Rome and Alexandria which liturgical scholars have noticed for years. (For a discussion of the Alexandrian prayer, see L. Bouyer, **Eucharistie, Théologie et Spiritualité de la Prière Eucharistique** (Tournai, 1966), pp. 191–6.)

[63] Trans. Brian Newns in **Liturgy** (January 1968), p. 14.

[64] Lucien Deiss, **Early Sources of the Liturgy** (Eng. trans., London, 1967), pp. 193–4. It is described as a 'communion prayer' in this edition, with what justification I do not know.

[65] **Early Sources of the Liturgy**, p. 129.

[66] Instruction on Sacred Music (1967), nos. 7, 16; and cf. GI 19.

[67] If, of course, the celebrant says the doxology perfunctorily or drops his voice, there will hardly be any reply at all. The commentary of GI 55, h, seems hardly adequate. The people confirm and conclude the giving of glory to God. Rather, they give their assent to the whole eucharistic prayer and action.

[68] This phrase comes from the liturgy of St John Chrysostom where it is said immediately before communion. It is one of the oldest expressions used in connection with the reception of the eucharist, and one could wish that it had been introduced into the revised liturgy, either as an alternative to or in conjunction with the **Ecce, Agnus Dei**.

[69] In Orthodox practice it is the custom to do this before confession. See J. D. Crichton in **Penance: Virtue and Sacrament**, ed. J. Fitzsimons (London, 1969), pp. 28–9.

[70] It derives from **two** minglings in the papal rite of the **Ordines** (I and II), the earliest of which represents the mingling of the **Sancta** consecrated at a previous Mass (to signify the continuity of the sacrifice). The formula accompanying the mingling in the 1570 missal seems to have been inserted by a Syrian pope (unknown) and the mingling of the consecrated bread and wine was seen as the re-uniting of the body and blood of Christ, as it were a 'resurrection' taking place on the altar (the Syrians were much given to an exaggerated realism). But, more

satisfactorily, it remains as a prayer for communion in the whole Christ. (See **The Church at Prayer**, ed. A. G. Martimort (Eng. trans., new ed.), II: R. Cabié, **The Eucharist** (Liturgical Press/Geoffrey Chapman, 1986), pp. 111–13.)

[71] The expression occurs throughout his treatise on the eucharist: ST III, qq. 73–83.

[72] **Catech. Myst.** V, 21, 5; **De Sacramentis**, IV, iii, 25. In a note to his edition of **De Sacr.** (**Des Sacrements, des Mystères**, Paris, 1961), Dom B. Botte notes that it occurs in the third century, in a letter (3) of Pope Cornelius (died 252). Cf. Eusebius, **Hist. eccles.** 6, 43.

[73] It would seem that at Alexandria in the time of Clement (**c.** 200) some walked up to the altar and communicated **themselves** there. But this may have been an abuse as Clement mentions the custom only to disapprove of it. See R. Berger, **Kleines Liturgisches Wörterbuch** (1969), s.v. 'Kommunion', p. 225.

[74] See p. 115 for the Instruction.

[75] CL 55, **Ritus Communionis** . . . (1965) **Eucharisticum Mysterium** (Eng. trans., **Instruction on the Eucharistic Mystery** (CTS, 1967)), repeated in **Ordo Missae** and **Missale Romanum** (1970). The latest document is of 1970 from the Congregation for Worship: **Instructio de Ampliore Facultate s. Communionis sub utraque specie administrandae.**

[76] See **Notitiae**, 57 (September–October 1970), pp. 326–8. The last consideration is my own. The commentary goes on to say that part of the catechesis should show that the practice of not communicating people from the cup is to be explained on historical and practical lines. Dogmatic considerations did not come into play—at least not until the fourteenth century. In a note at the end it remarks that if communion by intinction is chosen as the **safer** way of communion, this is not to be regarded as the **better** way.

[77] For **some** permissions, see **Notitiae**, 6 (June 1970).

[78] It is almost impossible to emulate in English the succinctness of the hymn's statement: 'Nulla **rei** fit **scissura**; **signi** tantum fit fractura; qua nec status nec statura **Signati** minuitur.' It has been to me a perpetual surprise that the teaching of Aquinas on the Presence of Christ in the eucharist has not, apparently, entered ordinary Catholic consciousness. And whenever modern theologians or priests (some of them) are accused of irreverence or diminishing the doctrine of the Real Presence, one suspects that the objectors have not absorbed Aquinas's doctrine.

[79] **Notitiae**, 5 (1969): **Instructio de Modo Communionem Administrandi,** pp. 347–351. It was based on a questionnaire sent to all the bishops of the world, and in **Notitiae** is followed by a letter in the vernacular from the then President of the Congregation for Worship, Cardinal Gut.

[80] Other combinations are permissible according to GI 56, i.

[81] Not, however, as much as some people think—and say. I can remember the clergy more than sixty years ago deploring the neglect of the people who did not stay to 'make their thanksgiving' after Mass—and this is just the time when some would have us think that people were so very devout and did. I suspect it was those who had servants to get their breakfast who stayed!

[82] One notes with gratification that this longer form has been chosen. It is so much easier to translate into acceptable English.

~

# The Eucharistic Prayers

~~~~~~~

ITHOUT DOUBT THE biggest change brought about in the Roman rite of the Mass is the addition of five eucharistic prayers, or eight if we count the three for Masses with Children. Since the late fourth century, when the Roman rite becomes visible, there was only one eucharistic prayer, known as the *Canon Missae*, the Canon of the Mass, so called because it was the 'rule', fixed and unchanging. As the revision of the liturgy went on in Rome and as ideas were developing it was felt that other eucharistic prayers were necessary, first the better to express the extent and depth of the mystery of the eucharist and secondly to increase devotion, for the continual repetition of the same text does not conduce to it. There was much discussion about the Roman Canon itself, whether it was to be revised, or even entirely re-written. After prolonged consideration it was decided that since the Roman Canon hangs together and if you move one part the rest falls to pieces, it must remain as it is, a venerable witness to our forefathers of the fourth and fifth centuries who compiled it. It was also agreed that other traditions should be drawn on for the composition of new eucharistic prayers. An Eastern tradition is represented in Eucharistic Prayer IV, which conforms very nearly to the tradition of Antioch (compare the eucharistic prayer that bears the name of St John Chrysostom) though it is older and of rather different provenance.

A more ancient tradition, this time Roman, provided another model. This was the prayer that is found in the *Apostolic Tradition* of Hippolytus, who was a Roman priest living in the early third century. His prayer is the oldest extant and long before Vatican II it had been the subject of much scholarly investigation, and its simplicity attracted the attention of many pastoral liturgists also. The scene was thus set for the compilation of new eucharistic prayers.

~

# *The Roman Canon or Eucharistic Prayer I*

As said above, this has been retained though one or two slight changes
have been made. In the institution narrative to the words over the bread
the phrase from Luke 22:19 has been added: '(this is my body) *which will
be given up for you*' (also found in the Hippolytus prayer). The puzzling
phrase *mysterium fidei* which occurred in the words over the cup has
been removed and incorporated into the invitation to 'proclaim the
mystery of faith'. This is followed by *three* acclamations[1] of the people,
to be used at choice. They underline that the assembly is celebrating
the whole mystery of redemption, passion, death and resurrection.

New insertions (embolisms) have been provided for special occasions
such as marriage and ordination, though this is really a return to a pre-
Gregory practice.

The needs of translation have revealed some difficulties that were
in fact long known to scholars. After the *Sanctus* the Roman Canon
continues *Te igitur* ('Thee therefore . . .') and it is very difficult to know
what this section refers back to. The translators have tried to get over
the difficulty with a sentence that cannot be said to be very happy: 'We
come to you, Father, with praise and thanksgiving through Jesus Christ
your Son'. It is not clear whether we *come* to the Father through Jesus
Christ or whether we are offering praise and thanksgiving through Jesus
Christ. However, as the Roman Missal in English is undergoing revision
we can hope that this sentence will be re-written.

At the end of the same section we find the words 'offer . . . for all
who hold and teach the catholic faith . . .'. In the Latin this undoubtedly
refers to bishops, who are responsible for holding the true faith that
with love is the bond of unity of the church. As such, the phrase does
not include the laity or even priests. Whether it *ought* to is altogether
another matter.

In the list of saints St Joseph was inserted at the request of Pope John
XXIII while the Council was sitting.

For a very difficult text beginning *Quam oblationem* which contains
words like *adscriptam* and *ratam* the translators opted for a paraphrase
and have produced an excellent and evocative text (cf. John 4:24): 'Bless
and approve our offering; make it acceptable to you, an offering *in
spirit and in truth*'.

We might note the translation of the section immediately after the words of institution: 'Father, we celebrate the memory of Christ, your Son. We, your people and your ministers, recall his passion. . . .' This is a laudable effort to convey the meaning of *anamnesis*, the name this part of the eucharistic prayer bears. The church, led by its priest, is *recalling before God* the saving work of his Son, Jesus Christ, and so making it present to those 'who offer to you, God of glory and majesty, this holy and perfect sacrifice, the bread of life and the cup of eternal salvation'.

I hear it said and I read from time to time that 'no one' now uses the Roman Canon. I wonder how people know. It is certainly a difficult text, and perhaps its main weakness is that after the 'Preface' it nowhere refers to thanksgiving. There are obscurities here and there though the English translation has ironed out some of them. On the great feasts of the year when there are special insertions that 'actualize' it, it seems appropriate. One could wish however that the little section *Per quem haec omnia* before the doxology had been removed. In spite of scholarly opinion to the contrary it is almost certain that once it or a similar passage was *outside* the eucharistic prayer and was a blessing e.g. of oil for the anointing of the sick.[2] The ending of the prayer would then run much more smoothly.

## Eucharistic Prayer II
~

This is based on the prayer of Hippolytus (see above) but there have been several changes. The Hippolytan prayer runs from the opening dialogue to the doxology without interruption of any kind. There is no *Sanctus*, there was of course no elevation of the bread and the cup, there was no invocation (*epiclesis*) of the Holy Spirit before the words of institution and those words and the doxology have been brought in line with those of the Roman Canon and the other eucharistic prayers. There are other changes too. Some phrases in the original like 'fix the term' are incomprehensible and the *epiclesis* of the Holy Spirit after the *anamnesis* is very obscure in its wording though not in meaning. The revisers then either omitted certain phrases or re-worded others to make the prayer understandable to modern Christians.

As we examine the prayer we note that the term 'Preface' is a misnomer. Prefaces are a feature of the Roman rite of a later time and

~

Hippolytus's prayer is all of a piece. There are no 'joins' in it. Taking up the response of the people 'Let us give thanks to the Lord' it begins 'We render thanks . . .'. It then goes on to mention the 'beloved Son, Jesus Christ' (cf. Colossians 1:19) through whom we give thanks. His saving work is briefly recalled, his birth from the Virgin Mary, his death and resurrection. The next passage is an addition by the revisers 'And so we join . . . Holy, holy, holy Lord . . .' to accommodate the *Sanctus* which of course is absent from the Hippolytan prayer. This is followed by a post-*Sanctus*, 'Lord, you are holy indeed', which leads to a first *epiclesis* of the Holy Spirit, also absent in this place from the original text. Hippolytus is again taken up with a phrase that introduces the institution narrative. After that comes the *anamnesis*, which is close to the original, the words 'life-giving' and 'saving' being added to the words 'bread' and 'cup' respectively. This is to underline the essential sacramentality of the eucharistic offering. The thanksgiving here is very brief: 'We thank you for counting us worthy *to stand in your presence and serve you*'. In the original these words seem to refer to the newly ordained bishop (for whom the prayer was written), to the ordaining bishops and to the presbyters standing around. Some scholars hold that that is so. Others contend that the 'we' who offer and give thanks are the same as those 'who stand before you' and pray for the coming of the Holy Spirit. In the circumstances in which we now use the prayer the second view is the more comprehensible. The second *epiclesis* follows immediately and is a prayer for the unity of the communicants.

The intercessions are also an addition though in what is perhaps the earliest eucharistic text, the *Didache*, there is a prayer for the unity of the church. Whether there were intercessions in the liturgy of Hippolytus it is difficult to say. They are to be found in the earliest description of the eucharist, that of Justin the Martyr c. 150, though they come before the eucharistic prayer and are quite separate from it. They were in fact the 'Prayer of the Faithful', which seems to be referred to in 1 Timothy 2:1, 2: 'I urge that supplications, prayers, intercessions and thanksgivings be made . . .'.

Reviewing this text one accepts that it was necessary to include the *Sanctus* for pastoral reasons: people would have been much disturbed to find a eucharistic prayer without the *Sanctus*. But since it is essentially a sung text, permission might have been given to omit it when the assembly was too small to sing it.

~

It is more difficult to accept the insertion of a pre-consecration *epiclesis* of the Holy Spirit. It has no part in the thinking of the prayer of Hippolytus in this place. It seems to have been inserted for theological/apologetic reasons, as we shall see when considering the next two eucharistic prayers. For Hippolytus the *epiclesis* was a prayer for the communicants that they might be made one through the Holy Spirit.

The simplicity and clear pattern of this prayer have made it a great favourite, perhaps because it has been found to suit a wide variety of congregations, even children. It is generally thought to be suitable for weekday celebrations but there is no reason why it should not be used on Sundays.

## Eucharistic Prayer III

This is a new composition and its genesis was painful and long-drawn out in the discussions that went on for months in the committee of the *Consilium* appointed to deal with eucharistic prayer. The protagonist was Dom Cipriano Vagaggini, theologian and scholar, who presented elements of it in his book *The Canon of the Mass and Liturgical Reform* (Eng. trans., 1967). As it appears in our missal now and even if it can be shown to have touches from the Mozarabic (Old Spanish) liturgy, it is well within the Roman tradition. It requires Prefaces and like the Roman Canon emphasizes the sacrificial element of the eucharist. Yet at the same time it shows the influence of new thinking about the shape of the eucharistic prayer: its second section forms a firm link with the Preface (as the Roman Canon does not), it has an *epiclesis* of the Holy Spirit after the institution narrative and it groups all the intercessions at the end.

The first section after the Preface embraces the whole of creation, sees the Holy Spirit at work in everything, and reminds the congregation that it is God who has gathered them together so that they can make a perfect offering to his name. This phrase thus brings back into one of our eucharistic prayers the phrase from Malachi (1:11) that is found in the earliest Christian references to the eucharist.

In the next section the gifts of the people are incorporated to be sanctified by the Holy Spirit so 'that they may become the body and blood' of Jesus Christ. This leads immediately to the words of institution and from there on to the *anamnesis*, the 'memorial' of the death, resurrection and ascension of Christ, with which is combined a prayer for his second coming, so strongly marked in our post-Vatican II liturgy. With the theme of memorial are combined those of 'offering' and 'thanksgiving'.[3]

The second *epiclesis* unites the theme of acceptance by God of the 'Church's offering', which, it is emphasized, is identical with the sacrifice of the cross, and prays that the whole assembly, and indeed the whole church, may be filled with the Holy Spirit 'and become one body, one spirit in Christ' (Ephesians 4:4).

The eucharistic prayer is now joined to the intercessions by what Louis Bouyer has called (a phrase from) 'one of the finest prayers over the offerings of the Roman Missal (*Ille nos tibi perficiet munus perfectum*)': 'May he make us an everlasting gift to you'. Through the gift of the Lord to us we can become a perfect gift offered to him. This is perhaps an echo of Romans 12:1 where St Paul urges us to offer our very bodies as a living sacrifice, i.e. our whole selves, body, mind and spirit, to God, for such will be holy and acceptable worship.

The intercessions are somewhat elaborate but are inclusive. The church in worship prays for the pope, for the local bishop, for all bishops and priests '*with*' the entire people God has made his own. The people gathered in church are prayed for as are 'all God's children' throughout the world. We pray for 'departed brothers and sisters', a petition that is extended in Masses for the dead in a text that is uplifting and moving.

As one reads the Latin original or a literal translation one comes to the conclusion that the ICEL translators have done a very good job. In the second section they very correctly translate 'we bring you these gifts', they are brought (the verb is *deferre*, not *offerre*) to be made holy and then transformed into the body and blood of Jesus Christ; that is, the elements the people have brought and that have been placed on the altar are now to be *offered* through being united with the self-offering of the people who through the grace of God are able to join themselves with the once-for-all offering of Christ.

The translators have however not translated *sacranda* (gifts) 'to be consecrated' or at any rate have seen that notion covered by 'make them holy'. It remains however that this text is a 'consecration *epiclesis*' or perhaps better, a prayer that the gifts will be consecrated. It is a

~

pity however that the translators were unable to do in English what Vagaggini did in Latin to avoid the word 'Victim', a word that has been so generalized as to lose its liturgical character: 'Recognize *him* who in your mercy, reconciled us to you'. 'See him' seems unduly curt and spoils the rhythm of the English phrase: 'See the Victim whose death has reconciled us to you'. However, perhaps the ICEL people will be able to do something about it.

This eucharistic prayer seems to have won a wide acceptance but it is a pity that it now seems to be used every Sunday or almost every Sunday. It is gradually ceasing to make the impact it should, which is an indication that we badly need more eucharistic prayers, especially for the long series of Sundays of the Year.

## *Eucharistic Prayer IV*

In many ways this is the most interesting of the additional eucharistic prayers, if only because its content is so rich. It is profoundly biblical and it takes a good deal of time to trace all the scriptural references so many of which are implicit. Here if anywhere we are aware that we are 'praying out of the Bible'. Another feature is that it is firmly in the tradition of the Eastern churches, in fact, of those prayers that derive from Antioch like those named after John Chrysostom and Basil. It is agreed by scholars that this prayer was drawn up by the great St Basil of Cappadocia and that it was used in Egypt before being expanded into the anaphora of St Basil still in use of course in churches of the Byzantine rite. Ecumenically it shows that the Western church can pray at the centre of its liturgy in the accents of the Eastern churches.

According to scholars this prayer was brought to Egypt about the middle of the fourth century. Long known, at least to scholars, it was, as it were, re-discovered and published in a good text just before the Second Vatican Council. It was thus an early candidate for consideration when it was decided that further eucharistic prayers should be added to the missal. It is known as 'The Alexandrian Anaphora of St Basil' or sometimes (and for short, as here) as Proto-Basil. It exists in Greek and partly in Coptic and a full translation will be found in *Prayers of the Eucharist* (ed. R. C. D. Jasper and G. J. Cuming, London, 1975; 2nd ed., New York, 1985). It should be noted however that this ancient prayer was used as a *model* for EP IV. It is not a translation or a reconstruction of it.

As we consider it – and use it – we find that it has an internal logic, a certain inevitability of pattern that is devotionally satisfying. After an ascription of praise and thanksgiving, in which all created beings and things are included, the prayer moves to the heavenly liturgy with which the church on earth joins in singing 'Holy, holy, holy Lord . . .'. After a link passage the text then resumes in its own way the history of salvation from the creation of human beings, through the Fall, the giving of the Covenant, to the coming of the Son of God in the fullness of time born of the Virgin Mary through the intervention of the Holy Spirit. There follows a brief recalling of the ministry of Christ, his passion, death and resurrection and the sending of the Holy Spirit 'to complete his work on earth'. This leads to the first *epiclesis* of the Holy Spirit, who is asked to sanctify the offerings lying on the altar so that they may become the body and blood of Jesus Christ 'as we celebrate the great mystery which he left us as an everlasting covenant'. This is obviously a reference back to the Last Supper (cf. Mark 14:24 and par.) and through it to the old covenant mentioned earlier in the prayer. With three very condensed references to John 3:16, 17:1 and 13:1 the prayer leads in the institution narrative, which is a little different from the other prayers. The *anamnesis* has no special features but the prayer for acceptance has: 'We offer you *his body and blood*, the acceptable sacrifice which brings salvation to the whole world'. This has been much remarked upon by both Catholic and Anglican scholars. If we compare the phrase with, for example, the Roman Canon we see that there it is very clear that 'the body and blood' is the *sacramental* body and blood, for all the church has is the sacramental sacrifice to offer: 'We offer to you, God of glory and majesty, this holy and perfect sacrifice; the *bread of life* and the *cup of eternal salvation*'. This is regrettably not clear in EP IV. It is however a little mitigated by the introduction to the intercessions: 'Lord, look upon this sacrifice which you have given to your Church; and by your Holy Spirit gather all who share this one bread and one cup into the one body of Christ, a living sacrifice of praise' (again a reference to Romans 12:1). Here we have to do with the sacramental bread and the sacramental wine whereby alone we are able to enter into the once-for-all sacrifice of Christ.

The intercessions are very comprehensive: we remember before God not only all who are in church but also 'all who seek you with a sincere heart', namely the living, and among the dead, 'all whose faith is known to you alone'. The prayer ends with a strong eschatological emphasis: we ask that we may enter into our inheritance with Mary the Mother of God, with the apostles and saints, and we look forward to the kingdom that has no end when, freed from the corruption of sin and death, we may sing the glory of God with every creature through Christ our Lord. This leads to the doxology.

This is a fine prayer, in many ways the best we have got, but it is a pity that its use is restricted by rubric. With its fixed 'preface' it may not be used on any day, season or feast with their own prefaces. Apart from that it could be used very appropriately in the Easter season.

The pattern of Proto-Basil, even if not complete, is clear: it runs from the proclamation of praise and thanksgiving for the creation through the recalling of the history of salvation to the institution narrative, the *anamnesis* and the *epiclesis* of the Holy Spirit. In the Antiochene tradition, still in use of course, this is always the place of the *epiclesis* and it is the only *epiclesis*. In the version we have, an *epiclesis* of the Holy Spirit has been inserted *before* the institution narrative. Why this was done it is difficult to say. It is said that it was done 'for theological and pastoral reasons and represents a return, justifiable or not, to the Alexandrian anaphoral structure'.[4] The thinking seems to have been like this. The Roman Canon is notoriously without an *epiclesis* of the Holy Spirit. The Eastern traditions, Syro-Antiochene and others, always have an *epiclesis* of the Holy Spirit but *after* the institution narrative where it is a petition for the change of the bread and wine into the body and blood of Christ and for a fruitful communion. It is highly desirable that there should be an invocation of the Holy Spirit (or rather an invocation to the Father that he should send him) but the Eastern *epiclesis* asking for consecration after the institution narrative would confuse and disturb people. The decision therefore was made to insert an *epiclesis* before the institution narrative that would be a prayer for the sending of the Spirit so that the bread and wine may become the body and blood of Christ. The second *epiclesis* is a prayer for the communicants that they may make a fruitful communion.

There is of course something to be said for the 'pastoral' viewpoint but I suspect that a little more thought could have produced a more acceptable solution, at least for this eucharistic prayer. A differently worded second *epiclesis* might well have got over the difficulty.

It must be said however that the insertion has been made very elegantly. The section about God's saving works 'through Jesus Christ' is brought to an end with a mention of the completion of the work of redemption by the sending of the Holy Spirit and there follows immediately the petition, 'Father, may this Holy Spirit sanctify these offerings. Let them become the body and blood of Jesus Christ our Lord.'

As for the ICEL translation it must be said to be generally good. The first part, the praise and thanksgiving for creation, is unduly staccato; in two lines there is a colon, a comma and a full stop. By contrast the Latin runs smoothly. In the second part, the recalling of the history of salvation, we have the word 'man' over and over again, standing for *homo* which means a human being. It must be said that the very exclusive language here makes it difficult to use the prayer for fear of offending those (and there are many) who are sensitive about exclusive language. I understand that an emended translation was sent to Rome but was rejected. Lastly, there is the intrusive 'through whom you give us everything that is good' which ultimately derives from the Roman Canon (*Per quem haec omnia . . .* ) and is found in EP III and here where it has no place at all. If it were removed the last words of the last paragraph of EP IV would be 'through Christ our Lord' upon which the doxology would follow immediately.

## The Eucharistic Prayers for Reconciliation, I and II
~

These prayers were drawn up for use in the Holy Year of 1975 which had for its theme Reconciliation and was thus linked to the new Rite of Penance (December 1973). Their use was extended to other occasions, e.g. Lent, by Pope John Paul in January 1983. Commentary on them could be very extensive but all that can be given here are some general remarks.

Generally speaking, the first prayer is concerned mostly with the inner peace of the church and the reconciliation of sinners with the church: 'Father, look with love on those called to share in the one sacrifice of Christ. By the power of the Holy Spirit make them one body,

~

healed of division.'[5] In the Holy Year, the Jubilee Year of Redemption (1983) and in Lent, this was and is appropriate and understandable. This is in fact worked out in the course of the prayer of which the dominant note could be said to be unity; thus in the preface: ' . . . through your Son, Jesus our Lord, you bound yourself even more closely to the human family by a bond that can never be broken'.

As for the 'shape' of the prayer it can be said to represent the new form of the Roman rite: preface (in this case proper to each prayer), *Sanctus*, first *epiclesis*, institution narrative, *anamnesis* and second *epiclesis*, and the intercessions. If that is so it provides a sufficiently flexible form for the redaction of further eucharistic prayers.

In detail we note that the first section after the *Sanctus* takes up the word 'holy', first used of God and secondly of ourselves: God made it possible for us to be holy as he is holy. The prayer asks for the sending of the Holy Spirit so that the gifts 'may become for us the body and blood of your beloved Son, Jesus Christ, in whom we have become your sons and daughters'. There is then a link passage which echoes John 3:16 (as in EP IV) and recalls the 'indestructible covenant' of the cross of which the eucharist is the sacrament-sign. The section ends with a reference to the Passover (Luke 22:15) and so leads into the institution narrative. This differs a little from the narrative in the other eucharistic prayers, stressing the 'after supper' of St Paul, and the words over the cup show the unity between the reconciliation wrought by the cross and its sacramental celebration in the eucharist: 'At the end of the meal, knowing that he was to reconcile all things to himself by the blood of his cross, he took the cup, filled with wine . . . '.[6]

In the *anamnesis* we first remember 'Jesus Christ our Passover (who is) our lasting peace'. This I think is the only time this title is used in a eucharistic prayer, the only time when the church remembers Jesus in person. The prayer continues as the memorial of the death, resurrection and second coming of the Lord and speaks of offering the sacrifice 'which restores man to your friendship', which may be another reference to the rite of penance which speaks of sin as the loss of friendship with God. There follows the second *epiclesis* (see above) and then the intercessions which most appropriately emphasize unity in the terms of 'communion in mind and heart' with the pope and the (local) bishop, the laity being included in the 'us' and the 'we' who are all praying together, awaiting final freedom from death and the new creation when the whole redeemed community will give thanks 'with Christ our Lord'.

The second prayer is more direct in style, less wordy, and likely to make a deeper impression on the assembly. Its vision is also wider: it is a prayer for the ending of strife and division in the world. So it is that in the first part we thank God who gives his Spirit to change hearts, to bring enemies together, to put an end to strife and bring forgiveness. In the passage after the *Sanctus* there is a recalling of the saving work of Jesus, the Son of the Father; he is a hand stretched out to sinners, the way that leads to peace with God: 'God our Father, we had wandered far from you, but through your Son you have brought us back . . . therefore we celebrate the reconciliation Christ has gained for us'. The prayer then moves to the first *epiclesis* and the institution narrative.

The *anamnesis* begins with a phrase that seems to be unique in eucharistic prayers: 'Lord our God, your Son has entrusted to us this pledge of his love'. This of course refers to the giving of the eucharist at the Last Supper with which the Mass is identical and so we are able to celebrate the memory of Christ's death and resurrection and offer to the Father 'the gift you have given us, the sacrifice of reconciliation'. The second *epiclesis*, which follows immediately, is brief and seems to be a little negative: 'May he (the Holy Spirit) take away all that divides us'; but union and communion are strongly emphasized in the classical intercessions that follow: 'May the Holy Spirit keep us always in *communion* . . .' with the pope, the local bishop, all the bishops and all the people, so that the church may be a sign of unity and an instrument of God's peace throughout the world. The intercessions finally look on to the 'new heavens and the new earth' (cf. 2 Peter 3:13) when all of every race, language and way of life may share in the one eternal banquet with Jesus Christ the Lord (cf. Revelation 4:9 and Matthew 22:10 and par.).

This second prayer, it seems, might be used much more often than it is. We live in very troublous times when there is much strife and bitterness and as dreadful events unfold week by week a prayer for reconciliation would meet the needs of the people.

## Eucharistic Prayer for Masses with Children

As for baptism with its Order for the Baptism of Infants, so for the eucharist we now have eucharistic prayers, three, specially devised and written for children when with adults (in greater or lesser numbers) they celebrate the Mass. It has been described as a 'historically significant change'[7] and so it is. At last children are no longer thought of as 'little adults' but as persons with their own needs, their own way of going to God and their way of worshipping him. A eucharistic liturgy in the hands of sympathetic and informed people can make the Mass a devotional act of worship for children. In this connection it is useful to recall that if the priest-celebrant is not capable of talking suitably to children (and not all have the gift) a trained adult (a teacher) may deliver the homily.

In these eucharistic prayers there are several features that are unusual. Only some of them will be noted here.

These prayers were not written in Latin but in modern languages (French and German) and were offered as models with considerable scope for adaptation. The Directory for Masses with Children (1973) asked that the many and various language groups should seek the abilities and gifts of catechists, teachers and others skilled in speaking to and working with children. How far they have been successful must remain a matter for discussion.

There are other features of the prayers that prompt the thought that they might be harbingers of the future. In prayers I and II the *Sanctus* is divided by a text from the 'Blessed is he . . .'. In I the acclamation is delayed until after the *anamnesis* section (which could easily be done in EP III and IV of the missal). In the model there is no first *epiclesis*, though there is in the ICEL version. The second prayer has a longish 'preface' in which love is emphasized calling for a repeated response 'Glory to God in the highest' or something similar. When sung these responses can be very effective. Likewise in the *anamnesis* and what follows various responses are suggested. If the purpose is practical, to hold the children's attention, it also leads to devotion.

In the third prayer we note a likeness to the Roman Canon: instead of an invocation of the Holy Spirit before the institution narrative there is a prayer that the Father may bless the gifts of bread and wine and make them holy (there is of course an *epiclesis* of the Holy Spirit after the narrative). There are three acclamations in the sections after the *anamnesis* such as 'Glory to God in the highest' or something similar. It is noteworthy that in the intercessions there is no commemoration of the dead. Finally, there are special insertions for use in the Easter season.

The effectiveness of these prayers will greatly depend on their handling. The many suggested responses need to be sung, introduced by the celebrant with the cue (sung) where it is provided. The prayers need to be carefully enunciated if the children are to take in their content or at least the main parts. And this raises a pedagogical question. For whom exactly were these prayers drawn up? There is a considerable difference between an eight-year-old and a twelve-year-old. For the former these prayers seem to be too long, too wordy, though it would seem that the latter can profit from these prayers very well. Prayer I for instance has a long opening section thanking God for creation, recalling the saving work of Jesus Christ and ending with intercessions for the pope, the bishop and a mention of saints and angels (somewhat reminiscent of the Roman Canon). All this is rather a lot for young children even if interrupted by a divided *Sanctus*. Nor do children seem impressed by the many adjectives inserted into the English texts: 'wonderful', beautiful', 'kind' etc. Some at least could be eliminated without detriment to the prayers. Indeed I think all these prayers could be shortened to their advantage and the benefit of the children. Their attention-time is short![8]

To the eucharistic prayers studied above may now be added another. As long ago as 1973/74 the church in Switzerland received permission to use a prayer drawn up in French, German and Italian on the occasion of a synod. Subsequently its use was permitted in no less than twenty-seven countries though for some strange reason not in English-speaking countries. Since various translations have been made in the course of time into modern languages, with inevitable differences of meaning, the Congregation for Worship and the Sacraments thought it necessary to revise the prayer (slightly) and to issue an official edition in Latin.[9]

First, the Congregation lays down rules for use. This prayer may be used with the formularies of the Masses (and prayers) for Various Occasions (as in the English Missal, pp. 788–852). Among the occasions are Masses for the pope, for the bishop, for a General Council, for a synod 'and for a spiritual or pastoral gathering'. This last could cover a very large number of celebrations!

Indicative of the occasions when the prayer may be used are four special Prefaces (e.g. evangelization, a national celebration) which are to be used appropriately. With them is a series of intercessions to be used in conjunction with the Prefaces severally. Thus the Preface for the

Unity of the Church carries with it the intercession for the same purpose.

The pattern of the prayer conforms to what now seems to be that of the reformed Roman rite: Dialogue, Preface, *Sanctus*, link passage *Vere Sanctus, epiclesis* of the Holy Spirit I, the institution narrative, the *anamnesis* with offering, *epiclesis* II and intercessions.

One or two points of interest deserve mention. After the *Sanctus* there are *two* petitions: the Spanish *Vere Sanctus* and a new one referring to the Benedictus, *Vere benedictus*: 'Blessed indeed is your Son who is in our midst and gathers us together by his love'. The last phrase echoes the *Ubi caritas* of Maundy Thursday. The revisers have retained the *Qui pridie* of the Roman Canon but have combined it with a phrase from the *Pange lingua* hymn: *Qui pridie quam pateretur, in supremae nocte Cenae . . .'.* (Literally 'the *day* before he suffered, on the night of the Last Supper'; the French had 'Vigil', as had the Italian, the German omitted it! In English 'eve' might do.)

The *anamnesis* is slightly Romanized, at least in the Latin, *Unde et nos. . . .* But what follows is somewhat similar to a phrase in the first Eucharistic Prayer for Reconciliation: 'Therefore, Holy Father, *we remember Christ your Son and our Saviour*', a direct recalling of Christ, who, as the prayer goes on, was led by the Father through the passion, death and resurrection to his exaltation at his right hand. While thus praying, the assembly offers to the Father 'the bread of life and the cup of blessing' (cf. 1 Corinthians 10:16). It is the *sacramental* bread and wine that is in question, as in the Roman Canon.

Again reminding one of the Canon, the second *epiclesis* refers to the 'oblation' the church is making in which 'we show forth the paschal sacrifice of Christ . . .'. There follows the petition that the 'Spirit of love' will come upon the members of Christ whose body and blood they are going to receive. Then come the intercessions mentioned above and the doxology. One rejoices to note that the phrase from the Roman Canon 'Through whom you give us everything that is good' has been omitted.

This is a prayer of good quality and in the Latin it is both concise and full of meaning. If its use seems restricted it is a welcome addition to the corpus of eucharistic prayers. Moreover, if we look at the Roman Missal in the section of Masses for Various Needs we find that those 'Needs' are no fewer than forty-six. This means that during the course of the year there will be many occasions when it can be used, even during the week, though there must be an assembly of the people. But while grateful for the generalized permission to use this prayer one cannot but regret that, special occasions apart, it will not be possible to use it during the very long series of Sundays of the Year. The officials of the Congregation understandably seem anxious that the existing four eucharistic prayers should be used regularly and they speak of more and better catechesis of the people (what about the clergy?) so that they shall understand the prayers better. Maybe so, but it is not just a question of understanding. It is a question of boredom, for both priest and people. In effect, EP III and II are most often used on Sundays, the rubrics (which need changing) rule out EP IV, and the Roman Canon, if appropriate on certain great feasts and seasons, is not much liked for regular use. Nor is it as easy to understand as the officials seem to think. By comparison with the other eucharistic prayers, it seems to many, if not most, unduly complicated and lacking in certain respects. For instance, after the Preface the Roman Canon nowhere mentions thanksgiving. The pattern is very different from that with which the people are familiar; it is all broken up into little bits and they are now used to something that flows and is clear in pattern, something with that 'noble simplicity' of which the Constitution on the Liturgy (34) speaks. This new prayer, which is not to be grouped with the 'Four', could very well be used on Sundays if shorn of its special Prefaces and intercessions. It is however against the law to do so; only special circumstances justify its use.

## Notes

[1] Four in English.

[2] See the Prayer of Hippolytus (ed. G. J. Cuming, **Hippolytus, A Text for Students** (Grove Books, Nottingham, 1976), no. 5, p. 11).

[3] The comment of H. Wegman is appropriate at this point: 'We do not ask God to take cognizance of our memorial, but to recognize in our offering the memorial of his Son's death. We pray to him to assure us that our celebration is truly a commemoration of Jesus. The death and the resurrection are thus at the heart of the eucharist' (see E. Mazza, **The Eucharistic Prayers of the Roman Rite** (Eng. trans., Pueblo Publishing Co., New York, 1986), p. 140).

[4] See Mazza, **op. cit.**, p. 171. See also his long note 120, on the Alexandrian tradition. Of eight texts examined only one has two **epicleses**, one consecratory and the other sanctificatory.

[5] A curious turn of phrase: literally it is 'freed from all division'.

[6] **Aliter**, 'filled with the fruit of the vine'.

[7] Mazza, *op. cit.*, p. 238.

[8] To Mazza's book (much the most important) referred to above add **The New Liturgy**, ed. Lancelot Sheppard (London, 1970), essays by experts on the four eucharistic prayers of the Missal of 1970. For the question of the insertion of the **Sanctus** into the eucharistic prayer see Bryan D. Spinks, **The Sanctus in the Eucharistic Prayer** (CUP, 1991). See also Edward Matthews, **Celebrating Mass with Children** (London, 1975),

[9] See **Notitiae**, 301 (August 1991), 8, pp. 388–478.

EIGHT

~

# The Calendar

~~~~~~

I T WAS EVIDENT once the liturgical reform, initiated by the Second
Vatican Council, got under way that sooner or later a new missal
would be needed. What has perhaps been forgotten is that the
radical revision of the calendar promulgated by Pope John XXIII in 1960
rendered a good deal of the existing Roman Missal obsolete so that even
without a council a good deal of revision would have had to be made.
A calendar is an integral part of liturgical celebration. It largely dictates
how and when a liturgical book is to be used and hence the new Roman
Missal has its calendar (pp. 100–12).

By nature a calendar is a dull enough document, nothing more than
a long list of feasts to be observed at certain times and, what is even more
boring, a body of usually complicated rules dictating the precedence or
otherwise of certain festivals. The *Calendarium Romanum* issued by the
Congregation for Worship in 1969, and now attached to the *Missale
Romanum*, is a document of a very different kind. If you looked at (and
still more, used) the calendar of about eighty years ago, you would have
got the impression that the church was mainly concerned to celebrate
the feasts of saints.[1] An ordinary saint's feast (a double, in technical
language) could obliterate the celebration of Sunday and usually did.
There were a considerable number of votive Masses that could be
celebrated on Sunday and the ferial days of Lent were usually overlaid
with votive Masses of the 'Holy Winding Sheet' and such like. It was
Pius X who restored the celebration of Sunday, and during the next fifty
years there was gradual pressure to ensure a better observance of Lent.
By the *Simplification of the Rubrics* (1955) it became possible to choose
the daily Lenten Mass in preference to a saint's feast[2] and the *Corpus
Rubricarum* of 1960, by upgrading the Lenten ferias, made it possible
to celebrate the Mass of the day almost throughout Lent.[3]

The old, unhappy order of things was decisively abolished by the
Constitution on the Liturgy (102–108) and by the Calendar of 1969
which has faithfully interpreted the injunctions of the Council.[4] The

~

143

former (CL 108) said that 'the minds of the faithful must be directed primarily towards the feasts of the Lord whereby the mysteries of salvation are celebrated in the course of the year. Therefore *the proper of time must be given the preference which is its due* over the feasts of the saints, so that the entire cycle of the mysteries of salvation may be suitably recalled.' This the Calendar has carried out. A simple inspection of it is sufficient to show that now the celebration of the mysteries of salvation dominates the whole year. A few figures will indicate the change of emphasis. Up to 1960 there were over three hundred saints' feasts in the calendar, not counting those of the Lord, Our Lady, the apostles and certain New Testament saints. In the new Calendar there are only sixty-three obligatory celebrations of saints and ninety-five *ad libitum*.[5] What is even more significant is that Sundays have now an almost unique position in the Calendar. They may only be superseded by 'solemnities' and feasts of the Lord, and in Advent, Lent and Paschaltide they have absolute priority. With the celebration of the Lord's paschal mystery on Sunday is closely linked that of the liturgy of Holy Week, and it is to this that we now turn.

In the Introduction to the Calendar we find exactly the same emphasis as is to be found in the Constitution on the Liturgy.[6] Like all the other new liturgical documents it sets what formerly would have been a piece of dry legislation in a liturgico-theological context. During the year the church celebrates the 'saving work' of Christ on certain days and of these celebrations that of Holy Week/Easter is the most important, though it is this same paschal mystery that is celebrated every Sunday of the year. At these times the church 'makes the memorial' (*agit memoriam*) of the passion and death of Christ for, as the Constitution said (CL 102), by so doing, the mysteries of redemption are in a certain way made present to the people who are thus enabled to lay hold of them.

There was some debate years ago about when the Liturgical Year began, whether on the First Sunday of Advent or some other time. The Calendar does not even glance at this debate. The paschal celebration of the Lord's passion and resurrection (at Eastertime) is the culminating point (*culmen*) of the whole Liturgical Year, it has absolute precedence over all other feasts or celebrations, it is put first in the list of precedence (59 (1)) and, to re-establish that it is a unitary celebration of the one Passover, it has been renamed. It is not merely the *Sacrum Triduum* (lit.

'sacred three days') but the *Paschal Triduum* and 'begins with the Evening Mass of the Lord's Supper (on Maundy Thursday), is centred upon the Paschal Vigil and ends with vespers on Easter Day' (18). Thus is restored to us in its full significance the most ancient celebration of the Christian church.[7] The impression has been finally removed that we were merely celebrating three holy days that 'commemorated' the last events of Christ's life. The three days form a whole in which the church celebrates the whole paschal mystery which is reflected (and participated in) in different ways throughout the period.

Next in order of importance comes the celebration of the Christian Sunday (4). This is the first and original (*primordialis*) feast of the church, celebrated by the apostles, and from which even the annual paschal celebration derives.[8] It is a festal day and should be kept as such. Because it is the weekly celebration of the paschal and saving mystery it has precedence over all feasts of saints (except a very few of the highest rank) and in Advent, Lent and Paschaltide it has absolute precedence over every kind of feast however great.[9] There are a few apparent exceptions during the year (Holy Family, Baptism of the Lord, Holy Trinity and Christ the King), but these are all 'feasts of the Lord', at least in the broad sense, and for the most part fit in well with the Sunday celebration of the paschal mystery. Other exceptions found in some countries, Epiphany, the Ascension and Corpus Christi, which are celebrated on the Sundays following the feast, are due to the exigencies of local situations: these feasts cannot be kept as real holidays, so the bishops of those countries have transferred these feasts to the following Sunday. There is much to be said for this policy.

Second only in importance to the annual and weekly celebration of the paschal mystery is the time after Easter (22–26). This is the oldest known season of the church's year. It is the sacred Fifty Days, already in existence in the second century, long before anything like Lent had evolved. It was regarded as a continual celebration of the paschal mystery and as St Athanasius called it 'The Great Sunday'.[10] Its observance, too, is kept intact by the rules of the Calendar and, as will be seen in a later chapter, the revisers have gone to great lengths to enrich this season of the year with new texts, for both the Sundays and the days of the week.

The season consists of seven Sundays that are evidently to be counted as 'Sundays of Eastertide'. 'Low Sunday' (as it has been called for long in the English tradition) is Easter II, since the Easter Octave ends with the

Saturday. The following Sundays are numbered III, IV, V, VI, VII and Whitsunday is the last day of the *Pentecostē* or Fifty Days. Its octave, ancient as it was, is suppressed[11] and there can henceforth be no doubt that Pentecost, the Easter season, ends with Whitsunday.

Lent, as we have observed, had already been restored to its original observance – at least as far as the calendar is concerned – but the teaching of the Introduction unfolds its meaning: it is a preparation for the celebration of the paschal mystery. The main features of this preparation are the (organized) catechumenate and works of penitence. In addition, its limits are sharply defined: it runs from Ash Wednesday to the evening Mass of Maundy Thursday exclusively. The sense of such a limitation is that on Thursday evening the church begins the celebration of the paschal mystery. Passion Sunday has been abolished[12] and the Sundays re-numbered accordingly from I to V, the sixth being what has been called for centuries Palm Sunday. This day is the prelude to Holy Week and the last act of Lent is the consecration of the Holy Oils at the morning Mass of Maundy Thursday (27–31).

It is necessary perhaps to say that the catechumenate element of Lent is not just an archaeological revival. In several countries now the catechumenate has been restored to meet a new pastoral need, and the *Order* (or *Rite*) *of Christian Initiation of Adults* appeared in 1972 (ICEL translation, 1985). Nor is what the Introduction calls 'the keeping of the memorial of baptism' an archaeological attitude. As we have learnt in more recent years, baptism is a beginning and not an end and we have to live out its implications throughout our lives.

Lent, too, is a privileged time and its observance is now virtually uninterrupted.

Thus are established the main lines of the church's year, and it is plain for all to see that it is essentially a celebration of the redeeming work of Christ.

'The church recalls the whole mystery of Christ throughout the year' (17), but the one mystery is broken down into its various aspects. Of these the most important is Christmas, which runs from the celebration of the Lord's birth beginning on the eve of 24 December to the Sunday after Epiphany or after 6 January if the latter feast is kept on a Sunday (32–38). Christmas retains its octave (apart from Easter, the only one in the year). The 'mysteries' of the infancy are kept (Sunday after Christmas is the feast of the Holy Family and the scripture readings of the season concentrate on what might be called the pre-history of Jesus) and it comes to an end with the beginnings of the public ministry at the Baptism of the Lord. The season is marked (1 January) by the celebration of the oldest feast of Mary as the Mother of God.

Advent (39–42) has until now been somewhat ambiguous in significance, no doubt thanks to the very various sources from which it was derived.[13] The new Calendar dispels the ambiguity and states firmly that Advent is made up of two elements: a preparation for the first coming of Christ, celebrated at Christmas, and secondly the season when *by means of that event* we are led to look for his second coming at the end of time. The season is to be kept in a spirit of devotion and joyful expectancy. The penitential element is thus suppressed.

The season has two clearly defined parts, the first running from its beginning to 17 December and the second from that date until 24 December. This second part is totally taken up with the preparation of the coming of Christ in his nativity, and Mary, Joseph and John the Baptist have a prominent place in it.

To all this there remains only to be added the time of the Sundays of the Year which, says the Introduction (43–44), are celebrations of the 'mystery of Christ in its fulness'. There are thirty-four such Sundays, the exact number in any year being dictated by the date of the First Sunday in Advent. Some may regret the disappearance of their ancient titles 'Sundays after Epiphany' and 'Sundays after Pentecost'. The new system is, however, simpler and may be easier to fit into a liturgical year for which there will one day be a fixed Easter.

The new arrangement for Rogation and Ember Days (45–47) reveals that the church now realizes that a liturgy based on a Mediterranean culture is not adapted to a church that is universal, many parts of which have a quite different cycle of natural life. The Introduction also realizes, but perhaps not sufficiently, that vast areas of the world are no longer agricultural. These occasions are described as times when the church prays for harvests, the work of man's hands and for the different needs of mankind. They are also times of thanksgiving (45). Now they are to be adapted to the different conditions of time and space and local conferences of bishops are to determine them and to work out forms of service. Mass-formulas are provided for these occasions in the new missal (Masses and Prayers for Various Occasions, III: 25–31).

This change, which was adumbrated in the *Corpus Rubricarum* of

1960 (346–7), presents an opportunity to work out suitable services for these occasions. A Bible Service is the obvious solution, but now that we have a form of Divine Office much more suitable for use by the people, it would be very appropriate to compose intercessions to be used in conjunction with the morning and evening offices of the new breviary. This should be perfectly feasible as the new breviary makes it possible to combine an office with the Mass. Praise, intercession and eucharist combined into one service would be a most suitable liturgical expression of these occasions and should ensure that a sufficient number of people attends them.

There remains the question of the *Sanctorale*, the calendar of saints, an infinitely contentious subject. A writer in *La Maison-Dieu* (no. 100, December 1969) gives a useful hint to help keep a sense of proportion: he says that it is naïve to suppose all the saints of paradise are or ever were in the calendar, that no human action is entirely free from arbitrariness and choices are always disputable.[14] Within the limits the revisers set themselves, one notices a genuine effort to make the calendar universal, both geographically and chronologically. Geographically, all five continents are now represented if, in the nature of the case, somewhat thinly: Japan, North America, Oceania and Africa (Uganda) all being represented by martyrs and South America by St Martin Porres ('very popular with Negroes and coloured people' says the commentary, p. 75), St Turibius, Archbishop of Lima, as well as St Rose of the same place. England in particular appears with the feast of St John Fisher and St Thomas More, which may be celebrated everywhere in the church on 22 June. The commentary on them suggests that their example of fidelity should be offered to Christians of our time. St Bede, however, has been reduced to only a permitted celebration, though St Boniface of Devon retains his status, no doubt on account of his importance as the apostle of the Germanies.

Chronologically, the selection of commemorations covers the whole period of the church's history from the beginning until recent times. There is noticeable a certain emphasis on the early martyrs whose acts are authentic and those with dubious legends for the most part disappear. St Cecily, 'on account of her popularity', is a notable survivor, even though her legend is one of the most questionable. The Fathers of the Church are well represented and so are the 'Doctors'. Among the chief casualties are a number of early popes who appeared in former calendars as martyrs and who are now known not to have been so. Perhaps the chief weakness is the representative value of the more modern saints, or rather, the failure of the church to produce really great characters in the last hundred years or so. No bishop later than St Charles Borromeo (sixteenth century) seems to rate an obligatory celebration, and although he was a great man in his time, he was very much of his time.

The total picture is a little odd and one is led to ask whether the canonization processes are all that they should be. Great numbers of holy foundresses have been canonized (or beatified) in the last one hundred and fifty years and only two bishops.[15] St John Vianney stands out in solitary glory as the one parish priest, and there are no modern married women. What is supremely anomalous is that Cardinal Newman, a man who has had more influence in and outside the church for a hundred years, should be kept, apparently interminably, waiting in the wings.

However, the austerity of the saints' calendar is mitigated by the suggestion that here, too, diversity in unity is part of the vision of the church, and it rests with regions, dioceses, and religious families to construct their own local calendars. This has always been so, but this document gives the matter a notable impetus. Here in England, where we have an exceptionally rich hagiography (thanks to men like St Bede), where we have a roll of saintly men and women reaching from the earliest centuries until the seventeenth, it would seem to be our bounden duty to construct a calendar that will reflect the long tradition of English (and British) sanctity. If such a calendar were carefully constructed, I believe that the sixteenth-century martyrs could be incorporated without offence to anyone. Perhaps, too, some way could be found of honouring men of traditions other than our own: for example, Keble for the Church of England and Wesley for the Methodists.

To conclude, the new Calendar is broadly satisfactory, its teaching is important and of considerable pastoral value, and the balance held between the celebration of the Year of the Lord and that of saints is about right. What the future will hold is anyone's guess and no doubt attempts will be made once more to infiltrate saints' feasts into the Proper of Time. It is to be hoped that they will be resisted.

Much of the Introduction is naturally taken up with technical matters (e.g. 8–16, 49–55 (local calendars), table of precedence, 59), which are hardly of general interest. It is well enough known by now that the highly complicated system of the former calendars has been very much modified since 1955. Clashes of feasts and interweaving octaves are now a thing of the past. The new Calendar has sought to exclude such confusion in the future by working out a quite simple system of precedence. There are three classes, described as 'solemnities', feasts and 'commemorations',[16] these last being either obligatory or *ad libitum*. Particular (i.e. local or 'religious') calendars have, broadly, to harmonize with the general calendar (49–55). The rules seem to be sufficient to prevent any undue invasion of the Proper of Time while at the same time making provision for local celebrations. One of the features is that locality, as in so many other documents, is firmly written into the system. For example, the general rule is that only saints with a genuine local attachment are to be celebrated in any diocese or region.

However, the whole matter of keeping saints' feasts of minor grades (obligatory commemorations and the permitted ones) needs re-examining. The rules (referred to in Chapter 11) do preserve one principle that is very important: normally the daily course of scripture can be read on such days. But in effect the observance of these minor days does mean that it is only priests and religious who keep them. Even with the now-established custom of evening Masses the people are for the most part not able to do so. On the other hand the calendar would certainly be bleak without saints' feasts. I do not see any solution to the problem unless it be that local saints are celebrated locally, whether in the parish or the diocese (on the assumption that we have smaller dioceses) and that these celebrations are truly festivals, marked by some 'secular' rejoicing. This would indeed keep before people that 'feasts' are festivals, and we can be well content that most of the saints in the general calendar are 'commemorations'.

# Notes
~

[1] When in the nineteenth century some bold spirit suggested that saints' feasts should be reduced in number, he brought down on his head the fulminations of Abbot Guéranger who said the holy Catholic faith was being attacked.
[2] See J. B. O'Connell, *Simplifying the Rubrics*, a commentary on the Decree *Cum Nostra* (London, 1955).
[3] The exceptions were great feasts like that of St Joseph, the Annunciation and a few others.

~

[4] All sorts of wicked things have been said of the **Consilium** and of the Congregation for Worship that has superseded it. A prolonged examination of the work and documents of both convinces me of their astonishing fidelity in interpreting the decrees of the Council. If charges are to be brought against them, they must be fairly laid at the doors of the bishops who by an almost unanimous vote brought the Constitution into being.

[5] For these statistics see *La Maison-Dieu*, 100 (1969) and J. D. Crichton, 'The New Calendar', *The Tablet* (10 January 1970), pp. 46–7.

[6] **Calendarium Romanum: Normae Universales de Anno Liturgico et de Calendario**, numbered in articles from 1 to 61 (Vatican Press, 1969), pp. 11–22.

[7] For an account of how the paschal liturgy was broken down into **two** 'three days' (Thursday, Friday and Saturday/Sunday, Monday and Tuesday, the old 'Days of Devotion'), see Balthasar Fischer in **Paschatis Sollemnia** (Freiburg im Breisgau, 1959), pp. 146–56; for a more summary account see J. D. Crichton in **A Catholic Dictionary of Theology** (London, 1967), s.v. 'Easter, the Feast of', pp. 202–4.

[8] CL 108. For some commentary on the Christian Sunday, see J. D. Crichton, **The Church's Worship** (London, 1964), pp. 203–5.

[9] These are to be celebrated on the previous Saturday (5).

[10] Quoted *in loc.*, *Epist. fest.* 1 (PG 26, 1366).

[11] It was in fact a pseudo-octave and the week was originally concerned with fasting, prayer and the offering of the first-fruits of the harvest (cf. P. Jounel in **The Church at Prayer**, ed. A. G. Martimort (Eng. trans., new ed.), IV: **The Liturgy and Time** (Liturgical Press/Geoffrey Chapman, 1986), p. 61).

[12] The title is combined with that of Palm Sunday.

[13] The penitential element seems to have come from Spain and the famous **Rotulus** of Ravenna seems to indicate a season of expectation of the first coming of Christ. Rome was late in adopting the season. See P. Suitbert Benz, **Der Rotulus von Ravenna** (LQF, 45; Münster, 1967). For the provision of prayers for seventh-century Rome in the Gregorian Sacramentary, **Das Sacramentarium Gregorianum**, ed. D. Hans Lietzmann (LQF, 3; Münster, reprint of 1967), nos. 185–193.

[14] This and the following paragraphs on the saints first appeared in **The Tablet** (10 January 1970) and are reproduced with permission.

[15] Add St John of Avila.

[16] The Latin is **memoriae** and presents difficulties of translation though it is a term long used in the monastic calendar. 'Commemoration' as above gives to older people the sense of a second feast, kept on the same day, and commemorated in the Mass and the office. Since this practice is virtually obsolete, 'commemoration' can do service and since the term is applied only to saints' feasts, whose **historical** entry into heaven is being 'commemorated', it is not inappropriate.

# NINE

# The Roman Missal of 1970: A Description of Its Contents

~~~~~~

CLERICS HAVE probably forgotten that there was once a time in their lives when the old missal appeared to be a very complicated book and that when as laymen they were 'following the Mass with a missal' they had considerable difficulty in finding their way about it. Even after they were ordained many, regrettably, never explored its content sufficiently and neglected large parts of it. However, they got used to it and on coming to a new missal will no doubt renew some of their youthful dismay. For though the new missal does in some ways follow the pattern of the Roman missal that was based on the *missalia plenaria*[1] of the eleventh century, its arrangement is somewhat different from that of the 1570 missal. Further there are certain *new* features that make some description, however summary, a necessity.[2]

Physically the *Missale Romanum*[3] is a very beautiful and noble book. The paper is of excellent quality, the typeface agreeable and easy to read, the rubrics are in a true terra-cotta red and what is more important than all, the lay-out of the pages is generous – plenty of space around the individual items. Normally, the texts of a Mass lie before one: no turning over is necessary. The binding is solid and opens very well in almost all parts. With the various documents, already mentioned, that come at the beginning, the whole book makes a volume of 966 pages.[4]

The first feature that will strike the reader is that it is fundamentally a sacramentary in the tradition of the Gelasian and Gregorian. It is without lectionary and contains the prayers to be used at the eucharist. It differs only in pattern from the sacramentaries in that it has included the entrance and communion texts.[5] Its spine is, of course, the Liturgical Year (as set out in the Calendar)[6] and the 'Proper of Time' is organized around the great feasts and seasons of Advent, Christmas, Lent and Paschaltide, ending with Whitsunday.

~

## The Proper of Time

*Advent.* As before, there are four Sundays which retain their old introits and communion texts but are endowed with four new collects. For weekdays there are six new Mass-formulas for the days from the beginning until 16 December with collects (and other prayers) for every day in the week. From 17 to 23 December there is a Mass-formula for each day.

*Christmas* begins with 24 December, Christmas Eve (the Mass intended only for use in the evening). Christmas Day has the midnight, dawn and day Masses as usual (alternative introit for the midnight Mass). The rest of the period is provided with the formulas for the feast of the Holy Family, the solemnity of Mary the Mother of God, and three ferial Masses for 29, 30 and 31 December. (The feasts for 26, 27, 28, for England 29, and the *memoria* of 31 December are to be found in the 'Proper of Saints'.)

There is a Mass-formula for II Sunday after Christmas, which is followed by those for Epiphany and the Baptism of the Lord. Six ferial Masses with alternative collects to be used before and after Epiphany are provided for the days from 2 January to the Saturday before the Baptism of the Lord.

*Lent* follows with a Mass-formula for every day as before, but there is a proper preface for each Sunday of Lent, included in the Sunday texts.

*Holy Week.* The liturgy of Holy Week from Palm Sunday to Easter follows.

*Eastertide.* Mass-formulas are provided for the ferias in Easter week and for the seven Sundays of the season. The Ascension appears after VI Sunday and Pentecost (with a Saturday evening Mass and the Mass of the day) concludes the Easter season and the Proper of Time. The formulas for ferias during the weeks of Easter time appear after the feast of Pentecost.

*The Sundays of the Year.* Thirty-four Mass-formulas for these Sundays are placed next. It is to be noted that alternatives are given for the communion verse, the second for the most part being taken from the gospels and to be used when the gospel text appears in the Mass for the day.

*The Solemnities of the Lord* (occurring during the year). These consist of the feasts of the Holy Trinity, of the Body and Blood of

~

Christ (formerly Corpus Christi), the Sacred Heart and the Kingship of Christ.

*The Order of the Mass.* This appears at this point, rather less than halfway through the book. It consists of the Order of the Mass with the people and that when there are no people present. It includes 51 of the prefaces out of the 84 all told, the rest appearing in their proper places in the course of the missal. The four eucharistic prayers appear after the prefaces and before the Rite of Communion. An appendix follows, giving the alternative greetings of the Mass, the alternative acts of penitence, alternative beginnings and conclusions of prefaces that may be used in the making of vernacular versions, the alternative acclamations after the consecration, the Solemn Blessings (to which we have referred) and Prayers over the People which may be said before the blessing at any Mass during the year.

*The Proper of Saints.* This runs from 1 January to 31 December (not from November–December as in the old missal). Each solemnity and feast has a proper Mass-formula and almost every *memoria* has at least a proper collect.

*The 'Commons'.* This has been completely reorganized. It is made up as follows: Dedication of a Church (regarded as a feast of the Lord), the Blessed Virgin Mary, Martyrs, Pastors, Doctors, Virgins, men and women saints (six formulas), religious (two formulas), those conspicuous for works of mercy, educators or simply holy women. If it be thought that these last groups are superfluous, the intention is that they should be used as models for the construction of Mass-formulas for local calendars (cf. Instruction *De Calendariis*, 1970).

*Ritual Masses.* This is a new title and to all intents and purposes a new section. All the sacraments and some other ecclesial acts may now be celebrated within the Mass and this section provides for this new situation. It has Mass-formulas for the various stages of Christian initiation, the catechumenate, baptism, and confirmation. There are others for ordination, for the administration of Viaticum, for weddings (three formulas), wedding anniversaries (also three), for the consecration of virgins and for the renewal of religious vows.

*Masses and Prayers for Various Occasions.* Although the old missal had a section something like this, this is really new both in its texts and in the variety of occasions it provides for. The Pope in his Constitution refers to it specially as showing the concern of the church for all the needs of modern man. There are three sections that cover what are substantially public needs and may be used in public Masses. A fourth section gives formulas for more private needs (e.g. for a family) and may not normally be used in public Masses. There are 46 titles in all and many of them show the influence of the Second Vatican Council, some of their texts apparently being taken from council documents.

*Votive Masses.* These, says the General Instruction (329), are to serve the devotion of the people (and so not primarily the devotion of the priest). The texts given are for Holy Trinity, the Eucharist, the Name of Jesus, the Precious Blood, the Sacred Heart, Our Lady (a reference is given to the Common), Angels, St Joseph, Apostles, Sts Peter and Paul, one Apostle and All Saints. It will be seen that this section is much reduced and the slightly bizarre Masses for things like the Holy Winding Sheet or the Holy Lance and Nails have gone.

*Masses for the Dead.* This has been not only completely revised but completely re-thought. It is now an immensely rich anthology of scripture texts and prayers about Christian death, clearly reflecting its paschal character in accordance with the Constitution on the Liturgy (81). Not only this, but every possible category of person has been thought of. There are Masses for popes, bishops, priests (and deacons), of course, but also for a young person ('May he enjoy perpetual youth in heaven'), for one who has been suddenly taken away, for one, on the other hand, who has died after a long illness and, not to mention others, for a child and for parents who have lost an unbaptized child, and for a still-born child.[7]

*Appendix.* The appendix gives the formulas for blessing water (it may be done in place of the penitential act in the Mass on Sundays), specimens for the General Intercessions (for every season of the year and for funerals), the preparation before Mass and thanksgiving after it (the prayers are the traditional ones, so traditional that the one beginning *Ad mensam* still bears the title *Oratio Sancti Ambrosii!*, only the list is a little shorter), the plainsong for various texts of the liturgy, and finally three indexes: one, alphabetical, of all the 'celebrations' (i.e. solemnities, feasts, etc.), two, of the prefaces (necessary because some of them may be used on a variety of occasions) and three, a general index of the whole book. (The ICEL edition has a slightly different order.)

It will be seen that the job has been done competently and efficiently and represents a quite herculean labour.

## Collects

A missal, however, which is the euchology or prayer-book of the church is going to stand or fall by the quality of the prayer-texts that are to be found within it. The revisers were fully aware of this and in the General Instruction is indicated their sense of its importance:

> Among the prayers that belong to the priest the eucharistic prayer has first place because it is the climax of the whole celebration. After that come the prayers, that is the collect, the prayer over the offerings and that after communion. These prayers, said by the priest who presides over the people, acting in the person of Christ and in their name and in that of the whole people, are directed to God. They are therefore rightly called presidential prayers (GI 10).

We must then give these prayers some consideration, though it is manifestly impossible to consider them all, especially when we remember that there are 187 collects from the beginning of Advent to the last Sunday of the year, not counting Holy Week.[8] There are of course, in addition, prayers over the offerings and those after communion. We shall confine ourselves to some remarks on the collects and one or two brief comments on the prayers over the offerings.

An examination of the Proper of Time reveals that from Advent to Pentecost all the Sunday collects are 'new' (even those from the Gregorian Sacramentary for Advent have been replaced) and one is immediately prompted to ask: where do they come from? A brief investigation showed that some have come from the Gelasian Sacramentary, though it is very difficult to discover how many since the lists of *incipits*, now regularly printed in modern editions of sacramentaries, do not always or often give the clue. Mgr Jounel, who was on the sub-commission for the redaction of the new missal, tells us that they made a complete investigation of all the sources of the Latin liturgy, the Gregorian, the Gelasian (in both its editions), the Verona (or Leonine) as well as the Ambrosian books and those that are compendiously called

'Gallican'.[9] Wherever they found prayers of good quality they laid them under contribution for the formation of the new euchology.

This does not mean, however, that they have merely 'lifted' prayers from the ancient sources. Anyone who has browsed in, say, the Gelasian or the Leonine Sacramentaries, knows that the texts are often visibly corrupt, that the 'authors' were often content with an approximation to what they wanted to say and, indeed, were sometimes the victims of the *cursus* which dictated what they in fact said. The revisers, then, have corrected them in the light of all that is known of this kind of prayer and especially by comparing the versions as they appear in different sources. But they have also done something bolder. Discreetly but quite firmly they have adapted the prayers wherever they judged that they could enrich their content and improve their message. If the purist is inclined to shudder, let it be said that an examination of the revisers' work fully justifies their procedures.

Thirdly, the revisers have used the sources as a quarry from which to build new prayers. They soaked themselves in the prayer-language of the sacramentaries so that they were able to recall almost at will phrases that have been incorporated into new prayers which, in fact, are entirely in the best Roman tradition.[10]

A good example of the first kind of correction and adaptation is to be seen in the collect for Easter Day, long known to have been 'edited', perhaps by St Gregory. The only way to show the methods of the revisers is to set out in Latin the three variations of the prayer.

| Missal of Pius V (and Greg) | Missale Gallicanum Vetus (and Gel) | Missal of Paul VI |
|---|---|---|
| Deus, qui hodierna die, per Unigenitum tuum, aeternitatis nobis aditum devicta morte reserasti, | | |
| vota nostra quae praeveniendo aspiras, etiam adiuvando prosequere. | da nobis, quaesumus, ut qui resurrectionis dominicae sollemnia colimus, per innovationem Spiritus *a mortis animae* resurgamus. | da nobis............. ........................ ........................ ........................ *in lumine vitae* resurgamus. |

For some reason, unknown to us, the last part of the prayer was diverted from asking for a paschal grace into something that looks like an anti-Pelagian prayer. The phrase 'that we who celebrate the mysteries of the Lord's resurrection' is obviously more appropriate to the day and the petition that follows from it is the right sort of thing to ask for at this time: 'By the renewal of the Spirit may we rise . . .'. But the revisers were rightly not very happy with *a mortis animae*, from the death of the soul. This is too restricting and not quite in harmony with Pauline teaching. So the revisers adapted the prayer very slightly, putting in *in lumine vitae*. This is a slightly ambiguous phrase, but it does suggest baptism (and St Paul, Romans 6) and the consummation of the Christian life, resurrection to the light of glory.[11]

A few further examples of collects will give a notion of what I believe to be distinct improvements. It has been observed for instance[12] that the old Sunday collects of Lent never mentioned Christ. This has been rectified and each Sunday of Lent is provided with a new collect that reflects the gospel readings of Year I. Thus for the Second Sunday of Lent we have this:

O God, you commanded us to listen to your beloved Son.
May our hearts (*interius*) be fed with your word
so that our minds may be purified
and we may rejoice at the sight of your glory.

A prayer that perfectly reflects the message of the gospel of the day. For the Fifth Sunday of Lent the message is turned in the direction of the paschal mystery soon to be celebrated in Holy Week:

Lord our God, out of love for all mankind
your Son gave himself up to death;
by his grace, may we remain in that love, readily following his
example.

The Second Sunday of the Easter season (formerly 'Low Sunday') is provided with a rich and rather long prayer. It is from a Gallican source, *Missale Gothicum* (no. 305).[13] It will be best to give it in the Latin:

Deus misericordiae sempiternae
qui in ipso paschalis festi recursu
fidem sacratae tibi plebis accendis,
auge gratiam quam dedisti,
ut digna omnes intellegentia comprehendant,

quo lavacro abluti, quo spiritu regenerati,
quo sangine sunt redempti.

If the last three phrases can be translated as they demand, they will bring
a note of splendid (but still prayerful) rhetoric into our liturgy.

God of unfailing love,
by their celebration of the annual feast of Easter,
you kindle the faith of the people that is dedicated to you;
increase in them the grace you have given
that they may grasp with their minds and hearts
the richness of the baptism wherewith they have been washed,
the depth of their inward renewal
and the price by which they have been redeemed, the blood of
  your Son,
Jesus Christ our Lord. . . .

Another prayer, for the Ascension, breathes yet an earlier world:

Fac nos, omnipotens Deus, *sanctis exsultare gaudiis,*
et pia *gratiarum actione laetari,*
quia Christi Filii tui *ascensio est nostra provectio,*
*et quo processit gloria capitis,*
*eo spes vocatur et corporis.*

The phrases underlined are from a sermon of St Leo, *De Ascens.* I (PL
54, 396) and in effect a passage from that sermon has been shaped into
a prayer giving the essential meaning of the feast. Here is a rough
translation:

Almighty God, through your goodness
we rejoice with great joy
and give thanks in gladness of heart:
the ascension of Christ your Son spells our exaltation,
for the Body in hope aspires to the glory
which the Head now enjoys.

Of the two masses provided for Pentecost, the first, for the Vigil (to
be said in the evening), stresses that the celebration of the paschal
mystery is 'contained within the fifty days', thus clearly indicating that
Paschaltide ends with Pentecost; and the second, for the day, emphasizes

the *missionary* task of the church. The collect asks that the gifts of the Spirit may be diffused throughout the world and that what was achieved through the divine mercy by the preaching of the gospel in the beginning may now be achieved by the work of believers. For the Vigil Mass there is an alternative collect which asks that the light of God's splendour may come upon us and that 'the light in which we see your light' (*lux tuae lucis*—cf. Psalm 35:10) may be strengthened by a new illumination of the Holy Spirit. The postcommunion prayer of the former missal which was so difficult to translate has gone and is replaced by a much better one, directly related to holy communion.

The main corpus of collects of the old missal are distributed throughout the Sundays of the Year. The best have been kept and those no longer used in Paschaltide are put into commission here. But even here we see the hand of the revisers, to the benefit of the prayers. The collect for XIV Sunday, the fine *Deus, qui in Filii tui humilitate iacentem mundum erexisti*, has been edited to its advantage. In the former version we prayed to be delivered from the falls that bring eternal death (*perpetuae mortis casibus*). The revisers turn it into a more Christian prayer: may we be delivered from the slavery of sin (*a servitute peccati*). It is a small touch but well worth making. On the other hand, the collects for this time are a little colourless, and some very brief, which makes their use in the liturgical assembly somewhat questionable. They are over so quickly that the people cannot grasp them. It was a pleasure, then, to come across a collect that has taken the twofold commandment of the New Testament and turned it into a prayer: 'O God, you set the fulfilment of the law in the love of you and our neighbour; grant that we may keep your commandments and so come to eternal life.' Although very slight, the last touch suggests Mark 10:17–22 (the rich young man: 'what must I do to inherit eternal life'). This again is a prayer that has been adapted, much to its advantage, from the Verona or 'Leonine' Sacramentary where it is confused and obscure. The revisers have made it more direct and more Christian.[14]

Another collect that is improved is that for the feast of the Holy Trinity. In the old version (generally attributed to Alcuin) the confessing of the trinity and the adoration of the unity in majesty was gloriously unclear, whether in Latin or English, as the celebrant rolled it out. The new version has added the 'processions' of the Word and the Spirit, but we are still asked to confess the true faith by acknowledging the trinity (of persons) and by adoring the unity (of nature) 'in the power of majesty'. The fact that I have had to add 'persons' and 'nature' shows how obscure the text is, and I just do not know *precisely* what is meant by *in potentia majestatis*, which must apply to all three persons and not to 'nature'. The whole prayer, I suggest, could have been dropped and something quite new excogitated. There is a strong case for dropping the whole feast.

The whole Mass for Corpus Christi (as no doubt we shall go on calling it) remains the same. Evidently no one was disposed to change it and that is a witness to the excellence of the work of St Thomas Aquinas. However, the collect is the only one I have noted in the whole missal that is addressed to the second person of the Trinity and then under the appellation *Deus*.[15] On the other hand, both the feast of the Sacred Heart and that of Christ the King retain their address to the first person of the Trinity.

~

The collects for the Proper of Saints are extremely interesting and for the most part entirely new. In the old missal they were among the poorest texts in the missal. Either they repeated phrases again and again, and often from the Common, or they wandered on more like a baroque sermon than a collect. What is striking about the new collection is that in almost every case the prayer is closely related to the life of the saint and singles out, usually with great perception, the distinguishing mark of his life and work. Here are two examples, interesting because, in the old missal, they were both long, weary prayers, and the first retailed the legend of St Raymund flying about on his cloak (a legend attached to a number of other saints, too): the prayer says that St Raymund was conspicuous for his compassion for sinners and for the (Christian) captives who were enslaved by the Saracens; the petition, very neatly, is that we may be released from the slavery of sin and do what is pleasing to God.

The second is for the feast of St Francis of Sales: by God's grace Francis could be all things to all men for the salvation of souls (both phrases were in the old prayer but embedded in a mass of verbiage), and we pray that we may imitate the charity of God (a reference to his great book *L'Amour de Dieu*) by always serving our brethren.

Even the collect for St Thomas Aquinas has been shortened, re-written and, I think, improved: he was notable for his zeal for holiness and his ardent study of doctrine; may we understand what

~

he taught and imitate him in what he did.

Sometimes the prayers are very concrete and in translating them you have to be careful. This is illustrated by the collect for St Paul Miki and Companions, martyrs (6 February). The Latin says: '*per crucem ad vitam vocare dignatus es*' which might seem no more than a cliché drawn from stock. Then you remember they were the Martyrs of Nagasaki and that they *were* crucified, so you must translate literally: 'you called Paul and his companions to undergo crucifixion and so enter life'.

Another prayer is an example of what can be done when the long and rich tradition of the Catholic liturgy is remembered and drawn on. It is again for modern martyrs, those of Uganda, Saint Charles Lwanga and Companions:

> The blood of martyrs is the seed of Christians.
> Lord God, we ask that the blood of your martyrs, Charles and
>     companions,
> which they poured out on the field that is your church, may con-
>     tinually
> produce an abundant harvest to the glory of your name.

This, we are told, is based on a prayer from the neo-Gallican missal of the eighteenth century,[16] but we also notice the phrase that is owed to Tertullian (an African!) *c.* 200: 'the blood of martyrs is the seed of Christians'. So this prayer reaches from the end of the second century right up to present times and this is surely what is meant by *tradition*. The revisers have drawn on the *whole* Christian tradition of prayer and by so doing have immeasurably enriched our euchology. We can indeed drive the origins of the prayer back even further, for the simile of the church as a field is related to the parable of Matthew 13:24–30.

In some cases the prayers seem to be entirely new. Thus the collect for Sts Perpetua and Felicity, which briefly and tellingly recalls their (authentic) *acta*: they overcame the torture of (their) death, despising the persecutor; the petition is that we always grow in the love of God. This again is another touch one notices in the collects of martyrs: they are conspicuous examples of *love*; it is love and not the tortures that made them saints. In all this one marks a return to the ancient theology of martyrdom which saw them as the supreme examples of holiness because of their *imitatio Christi*: like him they suffered death out of love of God and their fellow men.

~
162

Poor St George, who the world has convinced itself has been virtually kicked out of heaven, has been given a new and very splendid prayer that is from an ancient source:[17]

> Magnificantes, Domine, potentiam tuam, supplices exoramus,
> ut sicut sanctus Georgius dominicae fuit passionis imitator,
> ita sit fragilitatis nostrae promptus adiutor.

> We glorify you, Lord, in your power and we humbly ask
> that as saint George imitated Christ in his passion,
> so he may always be a ready helper in our weakness.

Here, quite clearly, is the *imitatio Christi* theology of martyrdom and this, the prayer suggests, is the essential thing about St George. All legends are left behind, but on the other hand the prayer is a great deal 'warmer' than the one in the old missal.

The collect for St Benedict (now 11 July) is very skilfully constructed and manages to get in three key phrases from his Rule:

> Deus, qui beatum Benedictum abbatem
> *in schola divini servitii* praeclarum constituisti magistrum,
> tribue quaesumus,
> ut, *amori tuo nihil praeponentes,*
> *viam mandatorum tuorum dilatato corde curramus.*

Benedict is a Master in the school of divine service – the service of God. Then a bold adaptation: for the *nihil operi Dei praeponatur* of the Rule the revisers have substituted *nihil amori praeponatur*, 'that we may put *God's love* before everything else' and so run in the way of the commandments with generous hearts.

What others will think of such a procedure I do not know. I find it completely acceptable that it should be possible to turn into prayer parts of the Rule of one of the greatest spiritual guides of the Western church. Among other things the revisers have made of it a prayer that all Christians can pray, and that surely is required in a liturgy that is intended for all.[18]

One or two small observations must conclude our treatment of the Proper of Saints. It will be remembered that St Vincent of Paul had a rather long and cliché-ridden prayer. Now it says exactly the same only in about half the number of words: he was notable for his concern for the poor and for the clergy: may we love what he loved and do what he taught!

Finally, the prayer for St Thérèse of Lisieux has been re-written while retaining all its substance. God opens his kingdom to the humble and to little children (a clear reference to the gospel) and we pray that trustfully (like St Thérèse) we may follow the way she went and so, by her intercession, come to the revelation of God's glory (as she did). Moreover, the prayer is now addressed to God the Father, which makes it not only a better prayer but much more appropriate to the saint whose message was so very much the fatherly love of God for mankind.

~

One turns to the section providing texts for various occasions and needs with some interest. It is said to be the newest part of the missal and in the sense that a great many more occasions are provided for than in the old missal this is true. It is also clear that Vatican II has influenced the composition of a number of the prayers, especially those on the church, but the general picture given is still that of a largely agricultural society. Earthly rulers are provided for and even the United Nations, but there is nothing about modern technological society, nothing about the investigations of scientists who have changed the face of the earth for good and for ill, nothing about the work of doctors or nurses upon whom modern society is so dependent. That said, the provision made is generous, three Mass-formulas being given for the church, for Christian Unity and for one or two other occasions.

The collects for the church reflect Vatican II quite clearly: the first (A) sees that it is God's will that Christ's kingdom should be spread throughout the world and asks that the church should be the 'sacrament' of salvation to all, the sign of God's love for all men and the means by which the mystery (of Christ) shall be made present among them.

This last point is made very strongly in the prayer (E) for the local church which, united to its pastor, and gathered in the Spirit by the Word of the Gospel and by the eucharist (the combination of the two reflects the Constitution on the Liturgy) is to be the sign and instrument (*instrumentum*) of Christ's presence in the world.

Another prayer (C) sees the church's union as reflecting that of the Father, Son and Holy Spirit and as, consequently, the 'sacrament' of holiness and unity in the world.

In the prayers for the pope there are references to the gospel passages about Peter. Thus in Mass A the collect sees him as the head of the apostles and the one on whom the church is built (Matthew 16:18), and the petition is that he may be the visible source and foundation of unity of faith and communion. This is a thought carried further in prayer B where there is a reminiscence of Luke 22:32 about Peter confirming the brethren, and the prayer asks that the whole church may be in communion with him and that he may be the bond of unity, love and peace. These prayers, it seems to me, have been written in an ecumenical spirit and in the event of restored unity they would still be most appropriate.

There are three (good) Mass-formulas for Christian Unity, the collect of the first asking that those who are (already) made one holy people by the same baptism may share an integral faith and be bound together by the bond of love. The collect of the third Mass is a prayer more specifically for the situation as it is now: may a love of truth grow and by effort and zeal may the perfect unity of Christians be achieved.

After a variety of prayers for the pope, for bishops, priests and other ministers there is a prayer for the laity, again echoing the Council documents. Here we note that it is the 'power of the *gospel*' that is to be the leaven of the world (rather than the church) and the petition is that the laity may restore God's kingdom precisely through their work in the world. The postcommunion prayer asks that they may make the church present and effective in the world.

There is a whole Mass-formula for persecuted Christians, the collect of which states that God has willed his church to be associated with the sufferings of his Son. This reminds us of Pascal's *Jésus sera en agonie jusqu'à la fin du monde*, a sentiment that Leo the Great gave utterance to eleven centuries earlier. In a sermon on the Passion he said: 'The Passion of the Lord is prolonged until the end of the world . . . it is he who suffers in and with all who bear adversity for righteousness'.[19] The petition goes on that those who suffer for God's name may have the spirit of patience and love and be found true and faithful witnesses of his promises.

There are prayers for the nation, for rulers and for the United Nations. This last asks that its representatives may act wisely, seek the good and peace of all and not depart from God's will. In this context there is a long prayer for the Advancement of Peoples (*Populorum progressio*, in the Latin) which unmistakably reflects both the Council document on the Church in the Modern World and the Pope's encyclical of that title. It runs: all peoples have a common origin in God and it is his will that they should be one family. Fill the hearts of all with love, *enkindle in them a desire for just progress.* May the goods (of this earth) that are distributed abundantly (*affluenter*) to all, make for human dignity so that equity and justice may be established in human society.

~

An investigation of the prayers over the offerings and those after communion would be very lengthy. We must content ourselves with two observations. The prayers over the offerings in the old missal (and they come from traditional Roman sources for the most part) were very puzzling. Often they seemed to attribute all sorts of effects, which could only be those of the eucharistic action itself, to the bread and wine lying on the altar. The only way to interpret them was by prolepsis: they were being spoken of *as if* they were already consecrated, and this seems to have been part of the Roman (and, indeed, Byzantine) tradition. The action of the eucharistic prayer, as it were, flowed back on the offerings. It is a mentality that is very different from our own, for if we can see that the whole eucharistic prayer performs the action, we find it difficult to extend its effect outside the prayer. A cursory examination of the new prayers over the offerings seems to show that much that was difficult to understand in this respect has been removed. One example is an illustration of this. It is the prayer for V Sunday of the Year: God has given us these created things for the support of our human nature: may they become for us the *sacramentum*, the efficacious sign of eternal life. It is a prayer that sees very clearly the *symbolism* of the elements used in the eucharist and so what is their function and purpose.

The prayers after communion in the old missal were often monotonous and astonishingly medical in their language. Again and again in the new missal one finds that the prayers are asking for a whole variety of effects, usually within the context of the Mass of which they are a part.

~

This rich anthology of prayers does, however, raise questions. The sources have been investigated, a fine discernment has been shown in the selections made from them, the modern compositions are for the most part worthy to stand by them, the rhythms (*cursus*), so far as I can judge, have been beautifully constructed, and in *Latin* these prayers are going to be very satisfactory to say. But they remain *Latin* prayers and, quite apart from the difficulty of translating them adequately, they have

~

a mentality that is not always that of the modern English-speaking world. It may be true[20] that we need to go to school with the great Roman writers of the past for our liturgical forms. It could indeed be said that we need to *learn* from them how to pray in public and it may be admitted that if this tradition had been ignored the results would have been calamitous. But the question remains, and it may be that we shall have to think of this euchology as a stage on the way to a more native form of prayer. It is not just a question of finding 'modern language' in which to express what we need. There are whole situations which demand a different kind of expression, and this we shall eventually have to find for ourselves. The very form of the collect is the product of a particular culture and indeed of a particular era within that culture. It is highly probable that the Roman collect began to be written in the fifth century. By the ninth century at the latest the art was lost in spite of the fact that there were a few successes later than that time. The collect is the expression of a very hieratic type of worship (the utterance of the president was thought to be *all*-important) and its literary form with its conciseness and brevity makes it a difficult prayer-medium for modern Christians whose minds do not work in that way. It is conceivable that a much looser form of prayer is required which would consist of a series of statements or invitations (rather like the General Intercessions of the Mass) and the responses of the people. Much of the essence of the collects could be preserved in this form, but it would allow of a much greater flexibility, easily admit a greater variety of subjects and provide a greater participation by the people in the prayer. Rome has apparently seen that the present situation is not quite satisfactory, since the rubric in the missal for Good Friday says that local conferences of bishops may insert acclamations for the people between the invitation of the celebrant and the prayer in the great series of intercessions on that day. This form, which is almost certainly the oldest Roman form of prayer, is in itself more acceptable than the usual one, and it is all the more significant that this adaptation has been suggested for this occasion. The whole form, invitation, acclamation (petition, etc.), prayer and final response (Amen) may well provide a model for the sort of prayer that is suitable to modern Christians.

*The prefaces*

If the prayers are derived from the sacramentaries, the distinguishing feature of the many new prefaces is that they echo the scriptures. Homiletically this is of great importance for it means that what has been heard in the scripture readings and expounded in the homily is now echoed in prayer. It is an old device perhaps and the Roman liturgy has done it in a variety of ways (notably in the Divine Office), but too often in the past the Sunday liturgy appeared to be no more than an haphazard miscellany of texts and sometimes was. The preface, as we have observed in speaking of the eucharistic prayer, is *proclamation*, the proclamation of the message of salvation, and may be regarded as the pivot of the ministry of the word. It picks up the themes of the gospel (or other readings) and leads the people into the celebration of the eucharist so that they are able to see that the events of salvation are here and now being actualized. Practically, it means that the people should be able to see the whole Mass-formula as a coherent whole and psychologically, if they hear the scriptures being expounded in the homily and echoed in the preface, they will both understand and remember the message of the day.

The prefaces that have already come into use, for instance, those for Advent and the Sundays of the Year, have already made this point clear. In that for Advent II there is a résumé of all the gospel teaching for the last days of the season: the virgin-mother receives the Word with love beyond all telling into her womb, St John the Baptist proclaims that he is to come, points him out when he does and Christ fills us with joy as we prepare to celebrate the *mysterium nativitatis*, the saving mystery of his birth. Preface I for the Sundays of the Year is a résumé of 1 Peter 2:4–9, II is thoroughly Pauline and Common I puts in prayer-form the teaching of Philippians 2:6–11.

But it is with the Sundays of Lent that we find the closest relationship between the preface and the gospel. Lent I draws out (part of) the meaning of the Temptation in the Wilderness and ends by asking that 'celebrating the paschal mystery (now) we may pass to the celebration of the eternal passover', thus indicating that Lent is orientated to Easter. Lent II reflects the Transfiguration, Lent III the gospel of the Samaritan woman (which may be read every year) and takes its message from the gospel itself. Lent IV (the gospel of the man born blind) refers to baptism:

we, born the slaves of sin, are made children of God by the waters of baptism. The preface of Lent V (the raising of Lazarus) naturally speaks of the new life that will be given to us by the celebration of the *sacra mysteria*. This compendious phrase includes both the celebration of baptism (and confirmation) and the celebration of the 'mysteries of our redemption' in Holy Week.

With Lent VI (Palm Sunday) there is a change. The preface takes up the theme of the Servant Song of Isaiah 52:13–53:12, and in the Latin manages to echo verse 12, *cum sceleratis reputatus est ( pro sceleratis condemnari)*: Jesus was innocent, yet suffered for the guilty and was unjustly condemned for the wicked; his death has wiped away our sins and his resurrection has reconciled us to God.

These prefaces are short, but with Maundy Thursday we get a (new) long preface for the Chrism Mass in which a vast amount–perhaps too much–of teaching is contained. It is, however, interesting for the emphasis it gives on the priestly church and the view it expresses that 'men are chosen out from this priestly community' to serve the rest. It can best be presented by a synopsis:

(a) God anointed his Son high priest of the new and eternal covenant and planned that 'this one priesthood' should continue in the church;

(b) Christ gives this royal priesthood to the people he has made his own;

(c) but he chooses men to share his ministry by the laying on of hands;

(d) in his name they are to renew the sacrifice of redemption, setting before God's family the paschal meal;

(e) they are to nourish them by the word;

(f) strengthen them by the sacraments;

(g) be leaders of the holy people in love;

(h) be ready to give their lives for them;

(i) and they are called to spiritual maturity by growing 'in likeness to Christ'.

In all this we see the influence of the documents of Vatican II, though one feels that this preface is too packed and too didactic to be successful as a prayer.

As we have observed above, a new collect for the Ascension is virtually a passage from St Leo which has been re-worded into the form of a prayer. A new preface for the feast likewise reflects the same writer. This means that collect and preface will be delivering the same message and, with a judicious choice of prefaces for the Sunday of the Year, the same will be true on other occasions also.

There are *eight* prefaces for the Sundays of the Year and if we are to avoid monotony, all of them are necessary and all should be used. As I have indicated above, some selection will be necessary. If we look into their content we find that again they are based on scripture, that they repeat the teaching of the paschal mystery (Sunday is the Day of the Lord, a 'little Easter') but throw different lights on it. A theme that appears here and elsewhere is that of the eschatological issue of the paschal mystery. Thus Sunday Preface VI which is a closely-knit anthology of Pauline doctrine proclaims that since we live, move and have our being in God (Acts 17:28 – an echo of an ancient Greek poet) and are made by him (*ibid.*, v. 26), we have experienced in our lives the effects of his love and mercy and already we have the guarantee of a life that is eternal. Possessing 'the first fruits of the Spirit who raised Jesus from the dead, we hope to possess eternally the paschal mystery'.

We meet again in Sunday Preface VIII one of the underlying themes of Vatican II, that the unity of the church derives from the unity of the Trinity and it is described as the people (of God), the body of Christ and the temple of the Holy Spirit. Perhaps a little too much for one text, but it does bring before us a whole wealth of doctrine about the church which is too easily forgotten.

If we turn to other prefaces prescribed for other occasions and times and look into them for some distinctively modern note we are disappointed. There is a Sunday Preface (V) which is headed 'On creation' which sums up, very skilfully, a good deal of Genesis 1: God has made all the elements of the world and ordered the changing seasons; he formed man to his own likeness, subjected all the wonders (*miracula*) of creation to his power and placed him in charge over them (*vicario munere*) so that he may praise God for all the wonders of his works. The text recognizes that there are wonders of creation (and the use of the word *miracula* is interesting), but it says nothing about *man's* uncovering of the wonders of creation. It goes on to say that man enjoys a certain charge over them; they are to be used by him and, we may gloss, the potentialities God has put into things are to be used (and not abused) by man. But one feels that if the revisers had been in close contact with modern thought and life they would have hardly produced a prayer like this. The impression given to the sharp-minded young is that of a *Weltanschauung* that is no longer credible. 'God made all things'? Yes, but how? In the twinkling of an eye? And if man has a vicarious function in relation to created things, how far does his writ run? Does God interfere? Some may think that this is to suggest a wicked 'demythologization of God'; others that to mistake poetry for prose is just as crass an error.

In connection with prefaces there is one practical device the revisers have used that merits attention. Every preface is headed by a sentence giving the subject of the text and since this is a place where the celebrant may intervene with a brief catechesis, these headings will obviously suggest the content of his remarks. It is a matter that needs handling discreetly – the celebration can be too easily drowned in the verbiage of the celebrant, a danger that is not always avoided – but with certain congregations (e.g. children) a few remarks at this point are necessary. Very neatly the new missal has provided a useful tool.

Since these headings are of some importance and indicate in any case the subject-matter of the prefaces, it will be of interest to give those for the Sundays of the Year:

I On the Paschal Mystery and the People of God.
II On the Mystery of Salvation.
III On the Salvation of Man by Man.
IV On the History of Salvation (a very brief recalling of it).
V On Creation.
VI On the Pledge of the Eternal Passover.
VII Salvation through the Obedience of Christ.
VIII On the Unity of the Church derived from the Unity of the Trinity.


*Introits and communion verses*

One of the most puzzling features of the new missal is the provision it has made for introits and communion verses. For the Proper of Time they are almost exactly the same as those of the old missal. The exceptions I have noted are no more than alternatives for the midnight Mass of Christmas and Whitsunday. There are some *additions* for the Sundays of the Year. This is so extraordinary a situation that one felt it was necessary to seek light on the subject, and it is to be found in the article of Mgr Jounel.[21] It will be best to quote from his article:

The essence of these texts is that they should be said or read and *not sung*. It is in fact wrong to call them 'antiphons'—a more neutral term would have been better. Nor is it a question of preserving in the missal the greater part of the *Graduale Romanum* so that they can be translated into the vernacular. Hence the two books will follow a different course, as in fact they did for centuries. The *Graduale* will constantly be adapted to meet the changes imposed by the new organisation of the Proper of Time, but there has never been any question of composing neo-Gregorian melodies for new texts of the missal. Likewise, there is no point in having these antiphons sung in the vernacular: they were created to make up for the absence of song. A text destined for singing must be conceived on quite other lines.

On the other hand the same writer goes on to say that it was out of the question to jettison altogether this great corpus of texts with their chant and, of course, where they (and the graduals) can be sung, they may continue to be sung.[22]

All this explains why these texts remain and, a smaller detail, why no references to psalms or their verses are given. They are not *meant* to be sung. How, then, are they to be used? I think we can distinguish. If the communion verses were set to music, perhaps even elaborate music, they could be suitable texts to assist the people's prayer during the time of holy communion. Obviously, this would be the work of a choir, which would have to be competent, but it would give them a role which some people say (wrongly, in fact) has been taken away from them and it would mean that the texts sung, instead of being more or less haphazard motets, would be an integral part of the liturgy of the day. This will be all the easier to achieve since on many Sundays (and all the Sundays of the Year) alternative texts are provided from the New Testament. Where they are not sung (and this will be the usual situation), the celebrant will be able to use them to lead the people in their meditation after communion.

It is apparently lawful to use the introit verses in a similar fashion, according to the opinion of Mgr Jounel:[23] 'The purpose of these antiphons is to help the people to enter into the spirit of the day. The manner of executing them will depend on the mentality of different peoples. In France, a brief address from the priest will be more helpful in creating a united and lively assembly than the reading of the text by

a few of the faithful.' Since the *Ordo Missae* provides for such an intervention between the greeting and the act of penitence, the text of the introit
will, quite naturally, supply the matter for such an intervention. We note
in any case that on certain days the text takes this form: 'Let us all rejoice
in the Lord: our Saviour has been born into the world. Today true peace
has descended on us from heaven' (alternative introit for the midnight
Mass of Christmas). This is the sort of interpretation that does not easily
occur to the more prosaic Anglo-Saxon mind and, coming from one who
worked on the subcommission that produced the missal, it has a good
deal of force. He, if anyone, is likely to know 'the mind of the legislator'.
Used in this way, then, these texts can be very helpful not only on
Sundays but also on other days too, such as those in Paschaltide which
are now provided with an extremely interesting series, illustrating almost
every aspect of the paschal mystery. This interpretation, too, releases us
from the agonizing problem of trying to devise musical settings, admit-
ting of the participation of the people, for these texts.

# Notes
~

[1] That is, missals containing not only the prayers but also the choral parts and
eventually the lectionary.
[2] In what follows I am much dependent on P. Jounel, 'Le Missel de Paul VI', *La
Maison-Dieu*, 103 (1970), pp. 16–45. Among other things I take my statistics
from him.
[3] (Vatican Press, 1970).
[4] My only reservation is about the illustrations which presumably purport to be
'modern' but are often at once dull and mannered. It is unpardonable that the
prefaces should be divided from the eucharistic prayers by a full-page illustration of
the crucifixion. For two generations liturgists have been trying to inculcate into the
people that the eucharistic prayer runs from the beginning of the preface to the
doxology, and here this teaching is virtually denied.
[5] The offertory verses have disappeared.
[6] See above, Chapter 8.
[7] See revised **Order of Christian Funerals** (1990).
[8] So Jounel, **art. cit.**, p. 18.
[9] And including those called 'neo-Gallican', drawn up mostly in the eighteenth
century. At least one collect is based on a prayer of the Nîmes Missal.
[10] One has the impression that there have been some very fine Latinists employed in
this work.
[11] It must be confessed that it is going to be a little difficult to translate. The whole of
the foregoing paragraph is dependent on Jounel, **art. cit.**, pp. 37–8. How often
the revisers have had recourse to this device I am unable to say. The examination

of half-a-dozen sacramentaries would be a very lengthy business.

[12] Jounel, *art. cit.*

[13] See A. Dumas, **Notitiae**, 61 (February 1971).

[14] **Sacr. Veron**. (ed. Mohlberg), no. 493. Even so, the heavily legal language of **Veron**. remains in the new (Latin) version: **sacrae legis, constituta, praecepta**, all in four lines! The Romans seem to have had an ineradicable tendency to think of love in terms of law.

[15] It **could** have been changed without great difficulty:

> Deus, qui nobis sub sacramento mirabili
> passionis **Christi Filii tui** memoriam reliquisti,
> tribue quaesumus,
> ita nos Corporis et Sanginis **eius** mysteria venerari,
> ut redemptionis (tuae–om.) fructum in nobis iugiter sentiamus.

> Alternatively it could begin **Domine, Iesu Christe**, which would keep the trinitarian relationships in order. The text as it stands suggests that 'God' 'suffered', which to the second-century church would have suggested Patripassianism!

[16] See Jounel, *art. cit.*

[17] It seems to be inspired by the Verona Sacramentary no. 733, though the last part is quite different and I do not know where it comes from.

[18] Apart from the phrases from the Rule, I do not know the source of the prayer or even whether it has one.

[19] **De Pass**. XIX, PL 54, c. 383: **Passio enim Domini usque ad finem producitur mundi . . . in omnibus qui pro iustitia adversa tolerant ipse compatitur**. Perhaps the revisers could have made use of this passage.

[20] As Jounel suggests, *art. cit.*

[21] *Art. cit.*, pp. 41–4.

[22] If there is a case for singing introits and communion verses, I do not see that there is one for singing the graduals. The ministry of the word is now a closely integrated whole, the psalm is a commentary on the readings, and unless the verbal text of the gradual is such a commentary, it is totally irrelevant to the day's celebration.

[23] *Art. cit.*, p. 41.

# *T E N*
~
# *Celebration*[1]
~~~~~~

COMMUNITY, PARTICIPATION, the importance of the word of God, these constituents of the liturgy have received considerable emphasis in the course of this book. Another word, 'celebration', appears frequently in the new liturgical documents and it needs elucidation. Sometimes, it is true, it is used in a neutral way but at other times it seems to be saying more. Thus, Bible Services are called 'Celebrations of God's Word', the Order of Baptism speaks of 'celebrating' the sacrament and in the Order of the Mass the General Instruction opens with the heading 'The Importance and Dignity of the Celebration of the Eucharist'. What follows is an investigation into its meaning which, it is hoped, will throw light not merely on eucharistic celebration but on the celebration of the whole of the liturgy.

It is arguable, and Harvey Cox in his *Feast of Fools*[2] argues it, that modern people have forgotten how to celebrate and the reason for this he sees in the development of Western culture. The emphasis on the rational, as in medieval scholasticism, the scientific, which it prepared, and on activity, work and production in more recent times, has atrophied the sense of keeping festival and what Harvey Cox calls fantasy, which he associates with festivity and which later he shows is imagination. Proofs immediately spring to mind. The seventeenth-century Puritans banished holidays and they and their descendants worshipped work. In the last fifty years the poet has appeared as a more and more peripheral character and probably no age of European culture has produced so little poetry as our own. Anglo-American society is geared to production, to the production of ever more and more goods, almost regardless of whether anyone needs them or can buy them. As the same writer remarks, we have indeed produced the monumental achievements of Western science and industrial technology but in doing so we have not only done it at the expense of millions of people in the poor nations and of the environment in which we live, but we have damaged the inner experience of man (*ibid.*, p. 12). It is a heavy

~

indictment and I do not think it can be gainsaid.

In all this the liturgy appears as a peripheral activity, without influence on social life, indulged in by 'religious' people who indeed for the most part get little enough joy out of it. The term 'feast-day' has been reduced to a title in a church calendar, and perhaps the most peculiar manifestation of our mentality is the term 'holiday of *obligation*' – obligation completely obscuring the idea of holiday. It is just one more occasion for committing mortal sin, as, technically, so many millions do. In fact the only festivals worthy of the name the church still celebrates are those that the world has secularized, made its own. Christmas is the most notable example and Easter the most striking since its Christian content has almost entirely disappeared. Its symbols are not the Paschal Candle and the blessed water but the new hat and the motor car in which the family departs for the first excursion of the year. Nor is the performance of the liturgy marked by any particular joy, whether it is the old or the new that is in question. As a piece of worship the old low Mass was as dismal a liturgy as you could get and the new still lacks that note of poetry that would carry people beyond the concerns of everyday life. Partly responsible for this is its English, which betrays the typical work-a-day character of an efficient technological civilization. It is indeed a symbol of it and it is this world that has killed the religious vocabulary in which for centuries man has expressed himself in worship. No doubt in time we shall find such a language, and, more optimistically, we shall find music, movement and perhaps occasionally the dance that will express our celebration of the liturgy.

But if we are to understand celebration, we must go a little deeper and here the history of the word has something to offer. 'Celebrate' obviously comes from *celebrare*, a word that at first sight seems somewhat negative. It is in fact quite rich in meaning. The adjective, for instance, suggests the notion of 'crowd' or 'multitude' and a famous place is one that 'contains a multitude of people'. The first meaning of the verb is 'to go in great numbers' to a place for celebration. The first element, then, of celebration is people, a crowd. One cannot celebrate alone. On Christmas Day I may be very happy reading a long and learned history of the Dark Ages, but I am not celebrating. Celebration requires community. On the other hand the Latin writers use the word in a way that is familiar to us: thus Cicero speaks of celebrating *festos dies*, Virgil of celebrating *coniugia*, weddings, and Livy of birthdays (*diem natalem*) and even of funerals (*exequias*). These were variously national, civic and family occasions; communities large and small were involved. For Ovid there were celebrations marked by word (*sermone*) and joy (*laetitia*); he is speaking of a *convivium*, convivial meal, and thinking of the conversation and joy that accompanied it. People, conversation, joy are the elements of celebration that marked 'celebration' as it emerges from this brief historical review of the word.[3] To this may be added, according to the authors, yet another element, that of song, expressing honour and praise.

Roman (pagan) religion was at once intensely national and markedly domestic. The official liturgy was an expression of the life of the state. From Augustus onwards, although already becoming enfeebled, perhaps decadent, it enshrined the genius of the Empire more than any other activity. Roma Dea coupled with the worship of the Emperor was the object of the official celebrations. Whatever we may think of the 'theology' underlying it, worship and life were all but identified. At the same time, Roman religion was very domestic. Every home had its shrine – there were the *lares* and *penates*, the household gods – and, at least in pre-imperial days, it was the focus of family life. Roman religion was the religion of a community whether great or small. Yet, it was sober, perhaps a little grim, lacking the *élan* of the Dionysiac spirit that formed one important element in Greek worship. Roman worship failed to touch the deeper springs of man and that is why the people welcomed with an indiscretion that knew no bounds the Eastern mystery religions that carried them beyond the solemn rituals of state worship and drew them out of themselves into realms where fantasy could range free. Even so, the worship of the Roman Empire seems to have lacked joy and simple gaiety. There were bacchanalia, saturnalia, wild and unrestrained celebrations, there was a desperate seeking for some sort of salvation, a desire that the mystery religions ultimately failed to satisfy, and it was not until we come to the first accounts of Christian worship that we catch the note of a simple and unalloyed joy.

However, the Greek and Roman experience was by no means exceptional. Man has 'celebrated' or kept festival throughout the ages, and it is possible, even empirically, to discern other elements of celebration. There is a wide agreement among scholars that myth celebrated in ritual lies at the heart of celebration and that they are its ultimate source. Huizinga has seen man as *homo ludens* (man as a playing creature) and

Romano Guardini saw the Christian liturgy in at least one aspect as a playing before God.[4] Harvey Cox isolates three elements that he regards as of the essence of festivity or celebration: excess, celebrative affirmation and juxtaposition.[5] By the first he means going beyond our day to day behaviour, taking 'a short vacation from convention' and doing things we do not normally do (wearing funny hats) or in a way that we do not usually do them (e.g. a festive meal). The important feature here, I think, is the breaking away from routine, the willed exclusion of daily concerns and, of course, worries, the desire carried into execution to break through the apparently inevitable round of work, production, getting on, making money and all the rest of the activities that occupy nine-tenths of man's life. In fact he links festivity with fantasy and says that man is the *homo festivus* by nature as well as the *homo fantasis*[6] and by 'excess' he seems to mean precisely this element of the fantastic. In his criticism of modern life, he sees culture dying for want of the spirit of festivity and fantasy, human and immensely necessary values without which man cannot live. They run counter to the values of the economy of production and in the long run, if they can be preserved, should provide the point of departure for a radical criticism of modern life and open the way to an equally radical reform.

'Celebrative affirmation' is best interpreted through Josef Pieper whom he quotes in this context.[7] The latter sees celebration or keeping festival as an affirmation of life, it is to live out 'the universal assent to the world as a whole', it is 'a special time in which we affirm all of life by saying *yes* to part of it'. Birth and marriage are the most ancient moments of celebration, birth obviously for a new life has come into the world and marriage not merely because it is the promise of a new physical life but because it marks the beginning of a new kind of life for a given couple of people. Even death, at least for the Christian, is a moment of celebration, for all the liturgy affirms that the dead have passed from death to life, from the shadows of this world into the light of reality, *ex umbris et imaginibus in veritatem*.[8]

All this may seem pompous and vague. What do the authors mean by 'life'? Is not work, earning one's living, even the rat-race, Life? Is not this in fact life for the vast majority of people on the face of the earth? A clue to their meaning can be gained from another statement of theirs: keeping festival is basically an end in itself, it produces nothing, at least nothing material, and in celebrating, we are saying there are other values in life that are more important because they point us to something beyond ourselves, something beyond the material values of life and, as has been observed, they are *necessary* if man is to remain human. In the circumstances in which we live, the 'secular city', which has become not a place for civilized living as it was for the Greeks but a machine to assist the processes of production (which also are in danger of becoming an end in themselves), threatens the quality of life and perhaps endangers it altogether. But in this criticism of life, there is a danger of Manichaeism, of a flight from the 'city', of a repudiation of the very means that have made life tolerable and easy for millions of people throughout the world. We cannot and should not want to return to 'the acre and a cow' economy but we can ask that the processes of production should themselves be humanized, as indeed they have been to some extent over the hundred and fifty years of the industrial revolution. What is more important and more radical is that we should ask: what is all this production for? Is it just to make money, and often to make more and more money for fewer and fewer people? Or should it not be regarded as a means towards the creation of the Good Life for as many people as possible? If the *purpose* of the present economic system could be changed, then it would be easier to bring into our festival-keeping the celebration of the works of man's hands and minds which are also the work of God. If primitive man celebrated the gathering in of the harvest with a feast, there is no reason why industrialized man should not celebrate the work by which his life is made humanly decent.

It is undeniable, however, that material goods do obsess people, weigh them down and blinker their vision. That is why there must be another element of festival-making. It is the all-important matter of *leisure* which Harvey Cox speaks of as *juxtaposition*. We do need a contrast with our ordinary every-day work; holidays are exceptional, and just as we cannot celebrate alone, so we cannot keep festival all the year round. We need to make a hole in time, to create a space of non-productive activity, we need leisure that is not merely a void, not just not-doing, but a time when we can go out beyond ourselves, become aware of ourselves not as productive agents but as human beings whose potential is by no means exhausted by the business of earning a living. Primitive man knew these moments of creative leisure. After the harvesting or the hunting, there was the feast, a prolonged feast lasting for several days, just as in the Middle Ages there were the Twelve Days of Christmas when the whole of society gave itself up to festivity. The Christian Sunday is an obvious example of the pause in the weekly work, a day of rest that is to be regarded as a day for the re-creation of the human forces so that we can become more fully human as well as better able to take up our work again. It is a time that should be valued as a contribution towards truly human living, and it is to be deplored that in our own country Sunday is becoming ever more filled with daily chores—all that washing hanging out on Sunday mornings—and it was observed in France shortly after the war when religious-sociological enquiries were being made that in households from which no one ever went to Mass, there was a fall in the standard of human living. There was no keeping of festival, Sunday was just like any other day and the gloom of the bitter industrial life was never lifted. Dechristianization went hand in hand with dehumanization.[9]

In the elements of celebration listed above, the most important seems to be leisure, that is, a willed and created intermission from the ordinary tasks of everyday life. Without this you cannot keep festival. You cannot do so if you are hag-ridden with the anxieties of work, weighed down by the responsibilities of decision and organization. With it, the spirit of man can begin to expand, bodily relaxation gives the senses time to open to aspects of life that at other times we give little enough attention to, the imagination will begin to work and we can begin to *enjoy*. The second important element, joy, will emerge from the leisure if there is a *causa laetitiae*, a cause for rejoicing, and traditionally man has found this in the great events of life, birth and marriage, in the cycle of natural processes, seed-time and harvest. But in a special way he has found the cause for rejoicing in the myths he conceived to lie at the heart of his experience of nature. These myths he celebrated with song and dance and prayer and sacrifice. 'Excess' was a normal feature of his celebrations, he and his community, tribe or people, lost themselves in the rejoicing and felt renewed by contact with the god. In fact the whole well-being of the community depended on the celebration of the feast. Life, worship and religion were fused into a single whole and the worship was a symbol which summed up and, in celebration, expressed the deepest things of the life of the people. A whole people could celebrate because they had a common 'theology', a common ritual and a common life, and the ritual celebration which usually required days of leisure was the means by which they broke through the often grinding round of work into the realms of joy, security and peace.

In the vocabulary of Harvey Cox[10] festivity 'helps us to keep alive to time by relating past, present and future to each other'. It is his view that festivity refers principally to the past, though not exclusively so (e.g. a wedding), and fantasy to the future if only because we dream of plans for the future, of what might be, perhaps in a different kind of social order. There is, I think, no need to make this distinction. The celebration of a feast is a nodal point drawing the past into the present and projecting the people into the future because its life lies ahead of it even if it is always being refreshed from the past. It is significant of our society that, if on the one hand it is burdened with historical experience, there is a decreasing sense of the past. There is little sense that what we have now is the fruit of past endeavours, that every society, however modern, has its roots in the past and that man himself has memories of the past that are part of his subconscious and formative of his personality even now. The restoration of 'festivity' or celebration would seem to be a necessity if he is to retain his memory of the past and ultimately his mental health.

It is here that we should be able to see the point of insertion of the Christian liturgy into the life of our time. Liturgy has too often been pursued as if it were a purely church activity. The church calendar has borne less and less relevance to secular life, the style of worship has been determinedly other-worldly in language, gesture and movement and groups of people.

Is it possible to restore the sense of celebration? It will certainly be difficult, for Catholics in particular have looked on Sunday worship rather as a duty than a festival. And we have been very coy about 'enjoying' an act of worship. It seemed to be almost immoral. What is needed is a complete change of mentality and there are signs that more and more people are looking for a style of worship that communicates joy or fellowship or something of the kind. Even a humble parish church where the Sunday liturgy is celebrated with some enthusiasm seems to attract people who do not find it elsewhere. And in spite of the gloomy jeremiads about the current English liturgy, it is possible to celebrate it with liveliness, with song and with a sense that the Good News is being conveyed.

As well as a change of mentality, it is necessary, I think, to exploit the possibilities the new liturgy offers. We will say a word about two matters, music and visual aids.

Music seems to be an indispensable element of festival-making. We lose ourselves, 'make a hole in time', more easily perhaps through singing than in any other way, and although the new Mass can be truly 'celebrated' without it, there is no doubt that it is hardly a festivity. It is interesting to note that the General Instruction (19) speaks of singing as a sign of 'exultation of heart', referring to Acts 2:46. More than anything else it secures the oneness of mind and heart that was characteristic of the apostolic church.

The first question however is: what *should* be sung? The custom of singing four hymns seems to have hardened into a law. There is the entrance hymn, one at the 'offertory', one during the communion and a recessional. Often these are not suitable either to the season of the Liturgical Year or to the place they are sung in the Mass. Moreover there are not enough good and appropriate hymns to go round for the whole year. Traditional hymns, however good in themselves, were not written for the Mass-liturgy and though they should not be banished altogether we need something different. A difference has been sought in the so-called folk hymns, usually accompanied with guitars (not a good accompaniment instrument) and regrettably the quality of the music is usually poor. Some of it lacks that prayer-provoking reverence that good liturgical music has, and often it is self-regarding, more concerned with human beings than with God.

What then is to be done? The first thing to do is to look at the General Instruction to the Roman Missal (19). There we find an order of priority established: 'When deciding what parts of the Mass are actually to be sung *preference should be given to those which are more important*, especially those which the *priest* or one of his assistants is *to sing in alternation with the people*, or *which they are to sing together*'. This covers quite a lot but for simplicity's sake let us say that the primary texts to be sung are those of the Mass itself: the dialogue before the Preface, the *Sanctus*, the acclamation, the great Amen at the end of the eucharistic prayer, and the Lord's prayer. From the ministry of the word we can add the *Gloria*, the responsorial psalm and the Alleluias with verse. If the ministerial chants (those which the celebrant should sing) are regularly sung to the plainsong in the missal (even if it is not entirely satisfactory) this

can do something to lighten an otherwise dull celebration. If in addition
the eucharistic prayer is sung, at least in part, experience shows that it
heightens the attention of the whole assembly. Perhaps it cannot be done
every Sunday but it is very appropriate on the greater festivals.[11] In any
case and whatever the difficulties (real or apparent) these are the texts
that, the Instruction says, should be given first attention. After them
come the chants of the people, the *Gloria*, the *Sanctus*, the *Agnus Dei*
(not to mention them all) and in the last place there are hymns which
if appropriate may be used for entrance, the presentation of the gifts and
the communion procession. The Instruction desires that the Lord's
prayer should be known and at least occasionally sung in Latin, but that
nowadays is hardly possible. What *is* possible is that priest and people
should sing it together in English and for doing so there are several good
musical settings.

The new Order of the Mass opened up new ways of singing the Mass
and suggested that there should be new thinking about the *literary forms*
of the texts to be sung. The first part of the *Gloria* is acclamatory and
lyrical, the middle part supplicatory and the last brief portion returns to
the lyrical. Composers would do well to take note of these facts. The
creed is a statement or series of statements and it seems that by common
consent it is no longer sung but said. The *Sanctus* is a cry of exultation
and demands a song that expresses this and that can be sung with full
voice and joy by the whole assembly. And in this text, as well as in others
like the Alleluias and the acclamations during the eucharistic prayer,
repetitions are called for. 'Hosanna', which in its original form meant
something like 'save', by the time of Christ had become comparable to
'Hurrah'. Musically speaking, if repeated by the assembly it can be very
impressive. These and similar chants can be enriched by parts that can
be sung by the choir while all the time they are supporting the people.

These are but examples taken from the texts that conventionally are
associated with 'the sung Mass'. The new Order opens up many other
possibilities. The entrance chant is no longer tied to a form of words set
down in the missal. It is intended to be a chant that will summon the
congregation to worship and lift them up so that they feel they are
a community. For, this, good hymns, better than many we have got, are
needed, but also different forms are needed. Refrains to be sung by the
people after the verses of hymns would enable composers to devise more
elaborate melodies that could be sung by the choir and which they

would find more interesting. Such a device would also liberate us from the rigid 'four-square' pattern of the Victorian hymn which, good as it was, is now a little stale. For the communion procession such a device is almost a necessity. People do not want to be embarrassed with books as they approach the altar and with the increasing practice of communion in both kinds they need to have their hands free. Again, after the gospel, which is the climax to the ministry of the word, one feels that a musical response is required. This could be a sort of *kontakion*, a text taken from the gospel of the day and set to music which both choir and people could sing. In short, the new Order offers many possibilities of celebration that were formerly excluded and which, if realized, will bring that note of poetry that some complain is so lacking in the new liturgy.[12]

There is another possibility. The place of celebration must speak of festivity—even the room of the Last Supper was 'large, furnished with couches' (Mark 14:15) and, as we know, lighted up. This can be achieved in a variety of ways. On feast days it has long been the custom to decorate the church with flowers, and 'best' vestments and altar-furnishings are used. It is a sound tradition but can be extended. Man does not live only by words and music. He can *see* and his sight needs to be satisfied with light and colour. He can worship through his eyes just as he can through his ears. There are those who say that we have entered an age of new Puritanism, our modern churches are stark, without colour, without statues or pictures. There is some truth in this, though the reason for it is that Catholic churches until recently were such a clutter of miscellaneous objects obscuring the basic liturgical functions of the building that priests and architects have been glad to get rid of them. There should be pictures, there should be statues, but it all depends where you want to put them. The very general regulations of the Constitution (125) indicate that there is a hierarchy of values, there is a 'right order', and in the placing of such objects the people's sense of values must not be distorted. It is generally agreed that pictures and statues should be out of the 'eucharistic room', and the Instruction of 1964 *orders* that side-altars are to be. Undoubtedly the best arrangement is that shrines with statues, pictures, prayer-desks and so on should be in chapels set apart. Here people can pray privately without distraction from movement in the main body of the church.

But, like the Victorians, we have strange notions about the fixity of pictures and such like objects. As Alice Meynell said a very long time ago, if she had enough money she would change her pictures quite frequently; and everyone knows that we do not *see* a picture that is always hanging in the same place. There is need for constant variety and one has long entertained the hope that pictures, plaques, and even statues (why not, with modern materials?) should be mobile and that on great feasts or the feasts of saints they could be put in some prominent position (e.g. in the porch) with some striking text that would both please the eye and instruct the people.

~

Liturgical celebration is in the nature of the case an intra-mural activity and we feel impelled to ask: what, if anything, has it to say to modern society?

In a former and famous book, *The Secular City*,[13] Harvey Cox seemed to be in danger of canonizing the values of Western industrialized—and especially American—civilization. Perhaps that danger was over-emphasized, for in his *Feast of Fools* he makes a radical criticism of it. What is more, he rejects much of ancient and modern theology as being too often but the expression, and in some cases the justification, of the Western dogmas of rationalism, progress, and a somewhat narrow religious experience. He finds 'radical theology' wanting because it is not much more than an 'apotheosis of present experience'.[14] And although he is more sympathetic to the theology of hope (Metz, Moltmann)[15] he rejects it in favour of a theology of juxtaposition which he sketches out.

He began with saying that juxtaposition is an element in keeping festival. It is something that lies alongside ordinary life and supplies a criticism of it by the very fact that it represents a temporary contracting out of production and of all the material values of the world. Harvey Cox is speaking of theology, but I think that we can translate his position into the terms of the church. In the last analysis the church has to stand over against the world, it is discordant with the world, it offers (or woe betide it if it does not) a criticism of the world; there is an inevitable hiatus between its values and those of the world. It is true that the church is traditional, it comes out of the past and cannot annihilate its past; but it must be concerned with the present, otherwise it has ceased to func-tion; it looks on with hope to the consummation, for therein is its final end. So its theology must be at once traditional, radical ('the theology of creative negation') and 'hopeful', that is, eschatological. But 'a theology

~

of juxtaposition plays off the tensions among the three not by neatly balancing them but by maximizing the creative friction among the three. So it focuses precisely on this discomfiting point where memory, hope and experience contradict and challenge each other. It recognizes our estrangement from much of the tradition, but it is also somewhat estranged from the ethos of today. It is unwilling to reconcile itself to either. It delights in this dis-relation.'[16]

It is that word 'dis-relation' (however inelegant) that suggests an attitude in the matter of keeping festival. Harvey Cox indeed makes a plea for the restoration of the jester even in the church – he is sufficiently in the world to know it and out of it so that he can see it in proportion – and perhaps one might add that the church is somewhat in the position of the jester in relation to the world. It sees so much that is transient, relative and unimportant on which men set their hearts and their whole lives, and it is the function of the church, while remaining involved in every human concern and deeply compassionate to those who suffer from the evils of the world, to proclaim that here man has 'no abiding city'. You can do this by the fierce denunciation of the prophet, whether ancient or modern, and this has been tried, not with any great success, in modern times. But you could also do it by 'playing before the Lord', by happily and tranquilly celebrating the feasts of the church. This is not frivolity because we are in touch with the great realities of life and death and we already glimpse, improbably perhaps, the New Testament teaching about the foolishness of God who rejected the wisdom of the wise and the strong things of this world for the folly of the cross (1 Corinthians 1:18–25). One is also irresistibly reminded of St Francis of Assisi, the troubadour of God, who went about singing his songs of the beauty of God, and of the sun and water and fire that he had made. Medieval theologians solemnly debated whether Christ laughed. Perhaps St Francis is the proof that he did.

Whether the world will listen, whether it will learn from us how to celebrate and then what to celebrate are questions that must remain unanswered. If it regards us as 'fools', giving time to such wantonly unproductive activities, we perhaps need the courage to try at least to be 'fools for Christ's sake'.

# *Notes*

~

[1] Part of this chapter appeared in **Life and Worship** (April 1971), and acknowledgements are gratefully made to the Society of St Gregory.

[2] (Harvard University Press, 1969).

[3] The above details are taken from Lewis and Short, **A Latin Dictionary** (1907).

[4] **The Spirit of the Liturgy** (Eng. trans., London, 1930), pp. 171ff.

[5] **Op. cit.**, pp. 22–6.

[6] It seems that he had not the courage to say **homo fantasticus** as the people of the sixteenth century did, meaning precisely that element of excess of which Harvey Cox writes. It is true that they were not thinking of celebration in any ritual sense but they wanted to celebrate Man whom they saw as capable of the wildest dreams and ideas which he might not want to realize in fact but which were the stuff of poetry. This 'fantastic' spirit was excluded from Protestant worship at the time, but do we not catch some echo of it in the exciting and often fantastic churches of the Baroque period? The Baroque artists orchestrated shapes, colour, light and sound into an affirmation of a triumphant faith which was not simply polemical. They exuberated in the possibilities of new-found media or in the new-found ways of manipulating them.

[7] **Op. cit.**, p. 22.

[8] Newman's self-chosen epitaph: from shadows and images into reality.

[9] No doubt things have changed. The greater availability of material goods has been the means of bringing more variety and even joy to such families, and it would seem to be a grudging, clerical attitude that would condemn people because they seek recreation in their cars on Sundays. The much-maligned modern Sunday has in fact meant that whole families take their leisure together and find happiness and relaxation in doing so.

[10] **Op. cit.**, p. 23.

[11] If the eucharistic prayer were sung at concelebrations it would eliminate the unpleasant sound of many male voices trying to speak, all too loudly, together.

[12] One suspects that many who criticize the new rite have never seen it celebrated in full. They are mistaking the libretto for the opera, as Cardinal Schuster said sixty years ago.

[13] (London, 1965).

[14] **Op. cit.**, p. 132: he is thinking of the 'Death of God' theologians.

[15] Radical Theology's mistake was to elevate **present** experience to divine status; the theology of hope comes perilously close to identifying God with the **future. Op. cit.**, p. 130.

[16] **Op. cit.**, p. 133. For a Catholic, acceptance of the proposition 'estranged from much of the tradition' would depend on what is meant by 'tradition'. If it means 'antiquity' it is acceptable. But for Catholics, and, one finds, for many Protestants, tradition is a **living** thing and the 'return to the sources' of recent theology has spelt a renewal, not merely of theology, but of the church.

# Celebration and the New Order of the Mass

~~~~~~~

*I*F, AS WE have tried to show, celebration brings a certain spirit of festivity to an occasion, it is necessary to introduce it into the celebration of Sunday Mass.[1] This is not always an easy task. The very familiarity that everyone has with the rite, the 'ordinariness' of regular Sunday practice, and often enough the necessity to provide a large number of Masses during the day, militate against any sense of celebration. Whatever is to be done about the earlier Sunday Masses, it should be possible to organize at least one during the day where there is a sense of festivity. In countries that are traditionally regarded as Catholic, one has noticed that the people do have a sense of occasion. They foregather before the Mass and after it, meet each other, exchange the time of day and often discuss matters of common interest. Such a custom is at least a pre-condition of celebration. But on the assumption that often enough this is not possible in a large town or city, it means that the celebration begins when the people enter the church. As we have seen, a welcome and an attractive décor have their importance. But much will depend after that on the priest-celebrant, and it is his function that we must now be concerned with.

The General Instruction (10, 60) describes his function clearly enough and there is no doubt that it attributes a great importance to his role as president. Apart from the material details (what he and he alone must do and when), it underlines in a variety of ways that he is leader and that upon him will depend the success or failure of the celebration. Success will come from a proper realization of what he is about. He is there to stimulate and guide a community of people in celebrating the victory of life over death, of holiness over sin, of a life that is triumphant even now. The Mass is essentially *eucharistia* and by whatever circumstances it is conditioned, whether by private or public mourning, it remains thanksgiving. This thanksgiving is made through Jesus Christ who 'by dying destroyed our death and by rising restored our life' and continues to do so. To recall a phrase from the previous chapter, the eucharist is a celebration of life, of divine life that is triumphant in Christ and that day by day is enriching the life of men on this earth. This is the essence of the celebration, which achieves a new dimension when a large number of Christians gather together to profess their faith, to give God thanks through Jesus Christ in joy of heart. The celebrant must be aware of this and if he can communicate *his* sense of occasion to the people, *his* realization that he, with the community, is keeping festival, the Mass will indeed be a 'celebration'. Moreover, *he* has something to communicate to them, he has a word to give them, the word of the gospel, and if he is really interested in that, he will bring to the celebration what one can only call a heightened interest, perhaps an element of excitement, which, if only subdued, will communicate itself to the whole assembly. For this, his first contact with the community in the (brief) address after the formal greeting is crucial. His attitude, conveyed by bearing and voice as well as word, will be apparent to all.

This remains true throughout the service, and the Instruction reminds celebrants, as well as others, that the liturgical texts have different forms, readings, prayers, acclamations, instructions, and that the voice must correspond with these different forms. A certain gravity, enhanced by the previous silence, in the reciting of collects will give them a different tonality from the attitude adopted when reading a narrative. This rule becomes particularly important when the celebrant is leading the people into the eucharistic action through the dialogue and opening passages of the eucharistic prayer. The phrase 'Let us lift up our hearts' is an urgent invitation, and a slight lifting of the voice is demanded by the text and will stimulate the people to respond with vigour. 'Let us give thanks to the Lord our God' is a summary of the whole action and the words should be said with due deliberation and emphasis. So often the familiar phrases, such as these and the noble conclusions of the collects, are rolled off as if they were no more important than a laundry list. Likewise the gospel and the first part of the eucharistic prayer (whether moveable or fixed) are the principal moments of *proclamation* during the Mass, and if the celebrant is aware of this, he will bring that *mental* attitude to them which will result in the right kind of recitation.

But the priest-celebrant is more than a president. He is a producer, he has to organize a 'performance' of the central act of Christian worship and nothing can be left to chance. This is the sense of the Instruction

(GI 313, and compare 10, 60). It speaks of pastoral effectiveness, of the need to *plan* a celebration, of consultation with ministers (if any), with other officials (readers, choir, etc.) and with the people. The president has to co-ordinate and harmonize the activities of all the individuals and groups who are to celebrate the service. In practice this has to be done by training (choir and servers), by discussion (particularly important with the choir), and finally by information so that all concerned know what texts are to be used, what sung, and, of course, who is to undertake the different ministries. At the time of celebration the president must have a clear picture of the whole organization of the service; then *as president* he will be able to guide it effectively towards its desired end.

It may be thought that special gifts are required for this sort of ministry and it is true that qualities of imagination and efficiency will be important. But much will depend on the structure and organization of the parish outside worship. If the clergy and people normally conduct their affairs by consultation, they will do the same quite naturally for their worship. Nor is there any reason to suppose that if a priest has not the necessary qualities he cannot delegate much of the work to others. A choir director or a master of ceremonies who is competent and who has the right attitude towards the worshipping community can relieve him of much of the burden. Even then constant consultation is necessary as the condition of a satisfactory celebration. Experience shows that only constant consultation between all who are concerned in the worship of a given place will ensure its worthy celebration. It is also clear that even if the priest is not musical or is not particularly gifted in organization, his role throughout is the formation of his people, and especially those who take more important parts in the services, in an understanding of the liturgy.

During celebration he has a number of different things to do:

1. The eucharistic prayer, the collect, offertory and postcommunion prayers are presidential and belong to him alone: 'Representing Christ, he addresses them to God in the name of the whole people' (GI 10).

2. He proclaims the gospel and preaches the homily.

3. He may intervene at certain points with brief statements to assist the congregation to renew their desire and intention to participate.

4. He is responsible for a number of significant gestures.

5. There is the question of silences that will be under his control. Of the first group we have already observed that they demand a sense

of their importance and nothing further need be said. But here, as in his function as reader of the gospel and preacher, he has to give an example of clear diction, of unhurried, intelligent reading and of a reverence for the words that are symbols of holy things. This will mean that the texts, both scriptural and liturgical, will need to be studied, prepared and understood. The lectionary in particular demands a competent knowledge of holy scripture and some acquaintance with modern exegesis. Failing this he will be in danger both of misunderstanding the texts and of conveying faulty doctrine to his people.[2]

The third group, what is sometimes called catechesis, is a very delicate instrument to manipulate. On the one hand, there is the danger of an intolerable verbosity that does no more than obscure the pattern of the eucharist (as well as exasperating the people) and on the other, the mistake of using them as occasions for giving mere factual information. They are intended to introduce the people into different parts of the service, help their participation and stimulate their devotion. The Instruction says that the president may intervene at the beginning of the service (of which we have already spoken), before the readings, before the preface and before the dismissal at the end.

The purpose of catechesis before the readings is to help the people to see the connection between them. This is not always clear and needs to be pointed up, but in doing so the celebrant should be able to elucidate any difficult expression or to draw out an allusion. This is often necessary since in the course of a homily lasting about ten minutes he has insufficient time to refer to details. In any case, he has the more important task of conveying the *whole* message of the day to his people. Such catecheses must, of course, be prepared beforehand, preferably written down, and then there would seem to be no reason why the reader should not read them between the announcing of the passage and the reading of the text itself.[3]

In an integrally Catholic congregation it might seem unnecessary to intervene before the eucharistic prayer. Everyone, it is thought, knows what is going to happen. But how many of our congregations nowadays are integrally Catholic? Members of other churches or of none are frequently to be found among us on Sundays and on other occasions and they need help. It *is* a good thing to recall at this moment that the community is now going to do what Christ did at the Last Supper and that the power of his redeeming love is going to be made present among the congregation. For marriages, funerals, for public occasions, for children's Masses, it is certainly necessary. As we have seen in an earlier chapter, the headings to the prefaces are given to guide such catechesis at this point. Where, as on great feasts, the preface is a proclamation of the mystery being celebrated, a 'nuclear' statement at this point will help the people to enter into the eucharistic action with the right sentiments.

The liturgy, as we have seen, is a complexus of symbols and these are more frequently gestures than things. The president has to make the most significant of them and his manner of doing them can enhance or mar the celebration. If he is directed to open his arms to invite the people to pray, as at the 'Lord be with you', it should be a large welcoming gesture, in fact significant.[4] When he is directed to spread his hands over the offerings, he should do so in a generous gesture, stretching out his arms so that people can *see* what he is doing. When he takes the bread, they should be able to see him taking it (it was a gesture of the Lord at the Last Supper which he is re-enacting) and he should hold it before him so that again they can see it. Nowadays, chalices are changing their shapes and he is no longer required to hold the cup in some complicated pattern of fingers. He can take it with both hands and the modern kind demands that he should do so.[5] It goes without saying that gestures like bowing, genuflecting, making the sign of the cross should be made unhurriedly and with dignity.[6]

There is, too, the question of singing and our record in this matter is not impressive. In the old days, when we could use the lovely plainsong recitatives (some of them surely the best in the world), the celebrant's effort was usually the worst in the whole assembly. It would seem to be basic that if the celebrant is to sing texts, he should rehearse them beforehand and with the choir. Even a wrong pitch can throw a whole choir (and congregation) into confusion.[7]

Finally, there is the matter of silence. Very difficult to obtain in a large church (and even in a small one where there are a number of young children), it is an essential element of any satisfactory celebration. But it is not a silence that just happens. It is created and it is created by the celebrant. First, his own bearing, which should be one of recollection (though not abstraction—a different thing altogether) and inner quiet, will induce a sense of recollection in the assembly. Then he will look for the right moments. After the readings, he may say a word and invite the people to reflection. After communion, he will take the words or the sentiment of the communion verse and suggest thoughts and prayers to the people. After the *Sanctus* (especially if it has been a lively one – and why not?) he will make a short pause until the whole assembly has become quiet.[8]

All these details may seem to be matters of no importance and there are many apparently who refuse to give them any attention. They fail to realize that they are all ways of conveying the meaning of the act of worship and ultimately the grace of God. An indifference to them witnesses to another and deeper failure. It is a failure to recognize that we worship God with our bodies or, rather, in the wholeness of our personalities.

There are one or two other matters that usually fall under the control of the clergy. They are concerned with the objects to be used in worship. In all the movement for the betterment of liturgical practice there has been a constant desire for authenticity or genuineness. If rites must be comprehensible and gestures significant, objects must be genuine and not fake. Mercifully, there has been a considerable improvement in recent years, though one still sees vestments that are badly designed, badly made and adorned (if that is the word) with various kinds of metal 'lace'. All that glisters is *not* gold, but some still seem to want it. This is not the place to discourse at length on liturgical art. I will merely remark that an insensitivity to the quality of what is used in worship witnesses to an indifference to the quality of life.

In the new liturgy there are two places where authenticity becomes liturgically important. With the increased number of communicants, with communion in both kinds and the practice of concelebration, a multiplicity of vessels on the altar at the offertory obscures the truth that all are made one in Christ by the taking of the one bread and drinking from a single cup. Ideally, there should be but one communion dish and one cup. Perhaps this will not always be possible, though if the dish is large enough it is always possible to consecrate in it and distribute the hosts into other vessels for the administration of the sacrament. Chalices also need to undergo a radical re-designing. Those in use are, for the most part, based on late medieval or Baroque models when communion in both kinds was unthinkable. On the Continent much larger cups have been made, some of them of great beauty, and whole communities can receive communion from them.

Secondly, there is the rite of fraction. If the symbolism of the New

~

Testament (1 Corinthians 10:17) is to be evident, it is highly desirable that there should be one large altar-bread so that a credible fraction can be made and the people communicated from the one host. Clearly not all can receive from the one bread and there will be special difficulties when there is a very large number of communicants, but the principle should be as far as possible maintained and it would seem desirable that calculations should be made about their optimum size.[9]

A liturgical assembly is a group of people engaged upon the common task of giving glory to God and receiving Christ into their hearts and lives. It is not too much to ask that there should be a certain uniformity of bodily attitudes (GI 21) though it is often resisted. It seems to be regarded as dictatorship on the part of the clergy, leading to a regimentation of the people. Since the General Instruction rationalized this matter, protests have been less and it must be admitted that the pattern suggested is a reasonable one. Catholics had become conditioned by four centuries of custom that required them to kneel almost throughout the Mass and it is not surprising that they should have resisted (resented) the suggestion that it is right to stand for the entrance of the clergy and at their departure as well as at other moments during the rite. Habits were indeed very untidy and there were those who sat while others were kneeling and fell to their knees, if at all, only for the words of consecration. Yet surely the Instruction is right when it says that 'common bodily attitudes are a sign of the community and unity of the assembly'.

Of this unity the 'sign of peace' that is to be exchanged between the people before communion is intended to be the most significant sign. There has been resistance to the notion, precisely because people at worship do not recognize that they are a community. They have not yet caught up with the notion that they are a celebrating community, or in the phrase of Yves Congar, 'the subject of celebration'.[10] No doubt much depends on how the matter is put to them and what gesture is suggested.[11] What above all is important is that they should realize that it is a gesture expressive of the horizontal relationship within the worshipping community through which all can manifest the church as a community of reconciliation. It has taken a long time to persuade people that they should be vocal at Mass, that they are in fact offering it, and it will take more time presumably to help them to see that actions and gestures and words are all so many signs through which they enter into the mystery of Christ and construct the great sign of the church.

~

# *The use of the missal and the lectionary*

As we have seen above, the new missal is rich in content and, as we already know by experience, the same is true of the lectionary. But it is necessary to have a thorough knowledge of both and a willingness to use what is to be found in them if a liturgical celebration is to be what the church intends it to be. The material breaks down into the Mass-formulas of the missal, the readings from the lectionary and the eucharistic prayers. Before considering these in detail, it will be as well to resume briefly the directions of the General Instruction on the principles of selection.

1. Where liberty is given, the celebrant is to remember that he is the servant of the community and that 'he is not to follow his own inclinations but to have a care for the spiritual good of the community' (GI 316). This is particularly important when he departs from the scripture readings of the day, and if he does so the people have a right to know what texts he is going to use and why. Masses for the Dead, for instance, are not to be said frequently, 'for all Masses are offered for the living and the dead' (*ibid.*). It is the church's intention that the people should be nourished by the scriptures which are set out in course so that they can come to a knowledge of the whole Bible.

2. Where several texts are given, notably in the 'Common' of saints, selection should be made in the light of what is known of the saint whose day is being kept. This diversity is *intended* and should be made use of. In the old system nothing was more deadening than the use of the small collection of passages the old missal provided for the saints' feasts that occurred almost every day of the week. The church does not wish to perpetuate that system.

3. A different principle comes into play when Ritual Masses or those for Various Occasions are used. There is a diversity of texts precisely so that the celebration may be adapted to a given congregation. Not all are as familiar with the scriptures as perhaps they should be and certain passages will not only *not* communicate God's word to them but may repel them. Thus, I am not at all sure what would be the impact of the 'Grand Assize' passage from Matthew 25 on an uninstructed audience gathered for a funeral. To take a different situation, experience shows that even the adapted version of Ephesians 5:25–32 is not the best reading for weddings when a number of non-church people are present.

For such occasions the Mass-formula has to be 'composed' (of course from the official books) and it is in such circumstances that the priest's pastoral *savoir-faire* comes into play. Where, on the other hand, practising Christians are celebrating a wedding Mass or a Mass for other occasions, they should be allowed to choose those passages from the missal and the lectionary that they think are most appropriate to the situation. They may need guidance, but usually they readily respond to the invitation.

### Choosing the Mass-formula

When a priest is celebrating Mass with a community of people (the position we adopt here), he must follow the calendar. One or two *modifications* of the rule may be made on certain occasions, as e.g. a wedding on a Sunday when *one* reading from the collection for marriages may replace one of the readings of the day.[12] There is one exception even on days of obligatory commemorations and those of the Advent, Christmas and Easter seasons. If there is 'true necessity or pastoral need' other texts may be chosen. This is a clear example of the church's pastoral sense and evidence of her compassion. Such occasions would be when the local community has suffered, perhaps overnight, a calamity that has plunged everyone into distress. Or, as it seems to me, it might be an occasion of more intimate distress as when a child is 'missing' and the parents are distracted by grief. It is for the parish priest or even the celebrant to make a (pastoral) judgement on the situation and to find texts that will bring consolation (GI 333).

When optional commemorations (*memoriae*) occur, there is a very wide choice: the Mass of the feria, of the saint, or of another saint whose feast occurs the same day or of a saint who is mentioned in the martyrology for the same day. He may do the same when it is a feria (GI 316). On these same occasions, he may use one of the Mass-formulas for various occasions or a votive Mass. For the latter, the rule about serving the people is particularly important: they are not to be deprived of the word of God contained in the daily course. On the other hand, where there is a particular devotion, say, to Our Lady, then the priest should have regard for the people's desires (*ibid.*).

Even where there occurs an obligatory commemoration a certain choice remains (GI 323). The collect must be that of the saint but the prayer over the offerings and that after communion may be either from the Common or from the weekdays of the current season. In Lent the collect of an occurring commemoration may replace that of the day. In view, however, of the importance of the Lenten observance and the fact that the corpus of prayers for Lent has been renewed, one would think that there would have to be a very good reason for substituting the prayer of the day with another.

On 'ordinary' days throughout the year the choice is even wider, and evidently the reason is that there shall be as great a variety as possible so that the Mass shall become really prayerful and adapted to the needs of 'the people, the church and the world' (*ibid.*). As we have seen, there is copious provision for the principal seasons of the year, and for the rest the celebrant may choose either the prayers of the previous Sunday or of any Sunday of the Year or from those provided 'for various occasions'. If this is to be possible, it will be necessary to arrange and print missals so that it can easily be done. The new missal is a bulky volume and if it is published in two parts it will not be possible to use prayers from the 'Various Occasions' section unless this is printed out twice. Naturally, alternative texts will have to be looked up beforehand and could very well form the subject-matter of prayer before Mass. The same of course is true of the readings.

## The use of the lectionary

An adequate treatment of the lectionary would occupy several volumes and here we can give only one or two indications as to its nature and use.

It should be sufficiently known by now (but apparently is not) that in the Sunday lectionary the first reading usually goes with the third, the gospel. Wherever in the Old Testament a text has some parallel with the gospel, this is inserted in the Mass of the day. Recent scripture scholarship has shown how embedded the gospels are in the Old Testament and for any effective treatment of the texts in the homily this fact needs to be known. Almost always the responsorial psalm binds together the Old Testament reading and the gospel and provides a clue to the right interpretation of the readings for the day. The second reading is to all intents and purposes a *lectio continua* of the epistles and non-gospel material of the New Testament, though on the greater feasts and seasons (e.g. Sundays of Lent) all three readings form a pattern. The second reading, then, must be thought of as giving that kind of instruction or as bringing before the people certain aspects of the Christian faith and life that do not need comment. In the homily, it is lawful to use it rather than the other readings, though to do this permanently, or even frequently, would be to frustrate the whole purpose of the lectionary.

Normally all three lessons are to be read and only pastoral reasons and a decree of the local conference of bishops make it permissible to omit one of them (GI 318). The criterion of omission of one of them is neither brevity nor ease of understanding (the homilist is required to do his homework!) but the message intended by the church for the day. In these circumstances it will usually be the first and third (which must always be read) and not the second and third. As the introduction to the lectionary observes (13), the readings form part of the whole presentation of the Liturgical Year and the fundamental purpose of the lectionary is that the people shall be familiarized with the history of salvation (GI 317). For Sundays, for solemnities and the great feasts, there is then no choice and this surely is the best way to have it. Liturgical services are not private celebrations. They are the principal proclamation by the church of the Good News of salvation, and private preconceptions (supposing they are of any value) must give way to the public mission of the church.

The rules governing the use of the lectionary may seem unduly restricting and some would prefer a freer system. To this it must be replied that, left to our own devices, we are all inclined to choose the same parts of the Bible or even the same passages again and again. It needs a vast knowledge of the whole Bible to be able to choose passages at will that are suitable for liturgical celebration. This, quite apart from the fact that most of us are likely to take the line of least resistance and make no very great effort to select. On the other hand, the opinion has been expressed that the pattern of the lectionary is too vague and that it would have been better if the selection had conformed to the theological text-book or catechism so that really 'solid' instruction could be given. In fact, the church has opted for a *biblical* catechesis which is concrete, using a symbolic, poetic kind of language that is now generally agreed to be a better way of communication than the old abstract kind. It was on this, too, that the liturgy was constructed, and it is only this kind of catechesis that is consonant with it. As between freedom and restriction the church has chosen a middle way, giving the preacher all that is necessary for the communication of God's message and leaving him very free in his treatment of it.[13]

In other parts of the missal there is in any case a considerable range of choice, namely for 'Ritual Masses' and for those on 'Various Occasions'.[14] *If* such Masses are to be as rich in scriptural content as they should be, it will be necessary to explore all that is there and to select what is most appropriate for the situation. As a matter of practical pastoral politics, it is very helpful to make up *libelli* or booklets for different occasions in which readings, psalms and prayers will be combined in certain patterns suitable to different situations. Skeletons of these will provide the people with the texts (e.g. responsorial psalms) they need to have.

In principle, the choice of readings during the week is very wide. If there are 'various occasions', particular needs or devotional *desideranda*, these can all be met by a judicious use of the missal and lectionary. But it is the desire of the church that the daily course should normally be used. Where this is interrupted by a greater feast or some other lawful celebration, the priest may combine the omitted readings with those of the day or may use them instead of those of the day (GI 319).

In short, pastoral needs and liturgical suitability are the main criteria for the selection of readings (cf. GI 319).

Although there is a general account of the lectionary above on pp. 86–92, a second edition of it (1981) with its important and much expanded General Introduction calls for some comment. Without going into details one notices that the Introduction again asserts the teaching of Vatican II about the deeper significance of the proclamation of the word of God in the liturgy. God's word is voiced in different ways but 'Always . . . Christ is present in his word; as he carries out the mystery of salvation he sanctifies us and offers to the Father perfect worship' (no. 4 and cf. CL 7). The Introduction takes this teaching a stage further, suggesting a theology of the proclaimed word: 'The working of the Holy Spirit is needed if the word of God is to make what we hear outwardly have its effect inwardly' (no. 9). Indeed, it is the Holy Spirit who 'precedes, accompanies and brings to completion the whole celebration of the liturgy' and it is 'through him that what is proclaimed to the whole assembly is brought home to each member of it'. It is because of this that we can see the whole ministry of the word as a dialogue between God and his people. To his word in which he approaches us through the Holy

Holy
Spirit

Spirit we can respond by song, by prayers, by gesture, all of which are prompted by the Holy Spirit.

While setting out the meaning and importance of the lectionary, the General Introduction does not forget the need for practical guidance which still after so many years seems to be required. Thus (and basically) readers must be audible, clear and read intelligently. This last suggests that they understand what they are reading and the nature of the different texts that they have to read. There is narrative (story), theological statements (St Paul); there is exhortation and rhetoric.

It would be a good thing also if those responsible for the celebration of liturgy realized that certain texts demand song. The *Gloria* is lyrical, a psalm is by definition sung prayer, and Alleluias and other acclamations need to be sung. These are not ornamental extras and if they were sung the ministry of the word would not seem so dull and wordy as some find it.

Finally, the General Introduction emphasizes the need for silences: 'The dialogue between God and his people taking place through the Holy Spirit demands short intervals of silence, suited to the assembly, as an opportunity to take the word of God to heart and to prepare a response to it in prayer' (no. 28). Already recommended by the General Instruction to the Roman Missal (57), silence may be kept after the first two readings and/or after the homily. Experience shows that the latter is the best place. The celebrant can invite the people to a few minutes' silence.

*Choosing the eucharistic prayer*

The use of the four eucharistic prayers is now sufficiently understood and we already have enough experience to know which of them are suitable for different occasions. But perhaps the principle that they are alternatives still needs to be emphasized. Although the General Instruction says that the Roman Canon may always be used (GI 322, a), and especially on Sundays, this, if done, would frustrate their purpose. They have been provided to illustrate the different aspects of the eucharistic mystery and this cannot be done if only one is used on Sundays. In practice EP III seems to be used mostly on Sundays and the Roman Canon is reserved for the greater festivals. EP IV is unfortunately rather long for Sunday worship and although it is a fine prayer, in the English translation it gives an impression of verbosity. EP II can sometimes be used to advantage on Sundays, especially where another sacramental act is inserted into the Mass, e.g. baptism. It *is* shorter, and in spite of severe re-editing it remains a splendid prayer. As I have observed above, it seems a pity, however, to combine it with a proper preface. The first part of it says almost everything that most such prefaces say.

With the eucharistic prayers go the acclamations after the consecration. They do not appear to be tied to any particular prayer and can be used with any of them. *How* they are to be used on Sundays is another question. The people will in any case need to be informed and this can be done either by the provision of texts or by an announcement before the service. Some musical settings have been written and where these are in use, the sung version will be most appropriate to the principal Mass of the day. It would be better not to use the last one (the weakest of the collection) with the Roman Canon as it has no eschatological reference, which is also wanting in the *anamnesis* of that prayer.

## Ritual Masses and Masses for Various Occasions

Of the first group which, among other things, covers Christian Initiation, Holy Orders and Marriage, it is worth pointing out that there are two Mass-formulas for the celebration of baptism and that these may be used (whenever the rubrics allow) for the baptism of infants when this is given during the Mass. The first is a splendid text, with a collect asking that the infant may share in the paschal mystery of Christ's passion and resurrection, a special *Hanc igitur* (that for Eastertime) and other special insertions for the other eucharistic prayers. The Mass for confirmation may be used in similar circumstances, that is, for almost all the Sundays of the year outside Lent, Eastertime and Advent.

There are three formulas for marriage, too, with insertions for the eucharistic prayer, and three for anniversaries, including the twenty-fifth and fiftieth.

It is for Masses such as these that care is needed in selecting readings from the copious provision of the lectionary.

The second group provides, as we have observed, for very many occasions and will be useful when special groups come together for particular purposes, e.g. ecumenism, peace and justice and so on. Here it is simply a matter of knowing what is in the missal and for this some (brief) research is necessary.

With these may be grouped Masses for the Dead. For these a generous provision is made. There are *three* Mass-formulas (one for Eastertime) for funerals and three for anniversaries, as well as prayers for almost every category. These formulas and the readings given in the lectionary must be carefully chosen if the Mass is going to be of that pastoral help to the people the church intends that it should be. There is no longer any excuse for repeating the same texts over and over again.

# Notes

[1] The case for daily Masses is rather different. They are more intimate and when celebrated with a small group in, say, a house the celebratory element will largely be found in the more intimate relationship of the participants.

[2] To take a crude example, if he gave people the impression that the account of the creation of the world in Genesis 1 were a scientific description of what happened in the beginning, he would be positively misleading them. But once he realizes that it is not, then he has got to find out exactly what the text is saying.

[3] There seems to be a tendency for priests to be rooted to the lectern as formerly they were to the altar. There are now three places of celebration: the president's chair, the lectern and the altar. But there would seem to be no reason why the gospel should have to be proclaimed from the lectern. It is meant to be preceded by a procession with lights (and, if desired, incense) and for this reason it will sometimes be better to leave the sanctuary and proclaim the gospel in the midst of the people. The word of Christ is proclaimed to them and for them, the gospel is the climax of the ministry of the word and it would be well to make the point by movement and position.

[4] Actors tell us that a mere turning of the hand on the stage is *in*significant. It does not convey what it is intended to convey and is all but invisible. The **arm** must move.

[5] It is to be hoped that the habit of breathing into the chalice has gone.

[6] As television reveals, most priests move far too quickly. On the other hand Eastern priests seem to be able to move with a natural grace–and sing!

[7] The limitations of the clergy are–at last–recognized. In the directives for Holy Week, we find that the choir can assist the celebrant with the chant for the veneration of the cross and that a layman can sing the **Exsultet**.

[8] It should be hardly necessary to have to say that people need to be given time to move, to sit, to stand and the rest. In a large church it is essential to give them time. But how often, alas, does not the recitation of a text begin while there is all the noise of a large congregation settling down!

[9] In **Nelle Vostre Assemblee** (Brescia, 1970), p. 556, J. Gelineau has calculated that an altar-bread of twenty centimetres diameter and 'a few millimetres thick' can communicate more than a hundred people. He suggests that such breads should be

marked beforehand to make calculation easier.

[10] See Chapter 3.

[11] The handshake or the double-handshake has been found generally acceptable, but other signs of mutual recognition will serve.

[12] On the greatest days of the year (e.g. Easter) this may not be done.

[13] For further considerations on this point see A. Nocent in **Nelle Vostre Assemblee, op. cit.**, p. 236.

[14] As also for special groups. The readings (from the lectionary) may be chosen in the light of special circumstances (GI 319).

# TWELVE
~
# Liturgy and the World

L ITURGY, AS WE have observed often enough in this book, is the sacrament of the church that manifests it to the world. Whatever happens in the church concerns liturgy in one way or another, but it is becoming clearer every day that what happens in the world affects the church. This new situation has been summed up in the phrase 'the world sets the agenda' which, of course, is only a half-truth. The agenda of the church was set by Christ in the beginning and what the phrase indicates is that the saving work of Christ has to be inserted into the world as it is here and now. For that the church has to listen to the world; in the words of Pope John, Christians have to be able to discern the signs of the times, and this has two aspects. The church not only has to discern the signs of the times so as to be able to adapt her mission to men and women at a given time, but also to be able to proclaim the truths of the gospel so that they can hear it.

The church has a prophetic role to play in the world and the ability to say the word, a word the world can understand (even if it rejects it), can come only from a reflection on the course of affairs in the light of the gospel. In the last analysis, the church has nothing but the word of the gospel to utter, but she cannot always understand that word unless and until it is reflected on. God is not locked up in the church, he is at work over the whole range of human activity, and man's search into the secrets of nature, his invention and *his* reflection on reality have in one way or another revealed certain truths that would otherwise never have been known. All who are engaged in the explicitation of natural processes, all who have sought and are seeking to improve the human condition, all who are seeking to establish peace and justice and the good life on earth are fellow-workers with God.

First, then, the church must understand and only after that is she in a position to evaluate. Evaluation in turn is no more than the precondition of the prophetic function which has two aspects:

1. The accusation has been made in recent years that the church's

concern for the well-being of man and especially her involvement in action to improve the lot of man is a betrayal of the gospel which is wholly concerned with other-worldly things. It has been said that certain thinkers and writers are teaching or implying that the end-purpose of the church is merely the well-being of mankind in this world. If this is true, then such people would have been betraying the gospel. It is more likely that they have been misunderstood. If God is at work in history, that history itself is not comprehensible without revelation whose transmission is, as we believe, entrusted to the church. The first part, then, of the church's prophetic function is to reveal, within the limits of her situation at any given time, the meaning of the whole process in which men are involved. Above all, she has to point to the end-purpose of the whole of human history. This is the light she has to hold up to the world, and since the world has not been disposed to listen for a very long time (and perhaps has had reasons for not doing so), it is not surprising that there are many who have developed a philosophy of the absurd.

But, apart from the nucleus of divine teaching, the church has no special knowledge, no special charisma to discern the meaning of things at a given moment. That is why the church has to put herself humbly to school with the world and try and enter into its mind and discover what it is doing and where it is trying to go. Out of this knowledge, which will not be mere information, the church will discover her ability to say the word that is necessary and illuminating to the contemporary situation. The proposition 'God is the final purpose of all things' is useless because it just does not seem true to people. It suggests a short-circuit. Not only will the hearer ask 'How do you know?' but he will go on to expostulate 'How can this and this and that have God for their end?' In a word, we have over-simplified a vast and complicated problem and positively *mis*-led people. Aquinas had a word, 'con-naturality', by which he meant an inner appreciation and understanding of a subject, born of an affinity that suggests the sharing in a common nature. It is this sort of knowledge, this sort of affinity, the church needs if she is to say a credible word to the modern world.

2. With the prophetic function is usually associated the task of judgement. The world (and the church) is under divine judgement and it has often been thought that the denunciations of the prophet are a necessary part of that task. Prophecy is, in fact, a very delicate instrument to wield, and unhappily such prophets, usually self-appointed, have too often

denounced the world as an essentially wicked place from which Christians should withdraw.[1]

'World' in holy scripture is an ambivalent term and means on the one hand the created universe (cosmos) or on the other the world that is still alienated from God by *sin*. Sin alone is at enmity with God and it is this that comes under the judgement. But we ourselves, who are responsible for this world, are only imperfectly redeemed, large parts of our personalities and lives are still alienated from God and the good we do is mixed with evil, sometimes through our fault and sometimes through lack of wisdom. Once again, then, the church needs the gift of discernment and it is only when she can see that certain courses of action are hindering the establishment of the reign of God that she has the right and the duty to point out that they are condemned by the gospel. Whether and how often this is to be done is another matter, as is the way it is to be done. Mere denunciation has long ago been shown to suffer from the law of diminishing returns. The church has to find the moment and the words to intervene and this, too, is part of the reading of the 'signs of the times'. But the prophetic role does not rest only with authority and in the modern world the undramatic witness of ordinary Christians, both clergy and laity by their daily living, to the gospel truths is as effective as any other method.[2]

By nature and vocation the church is, then, the sacrament of God's word, which reveals his purpose for mankind and the sacrament of his love by which 'the scattered children of God may be gathered together until there is one sheepfold and one shepherd' (CL 2). God is present to the world and working in it and the church reveals his presence; she is, as the Second Vatican Council liked to say, 'a sign lifted up among the nations',[3] showing the over-riding purpose of all that man does.

The picture of the church, thus suggested, still bears traces of triumphalism, of the 'two societies' theology which set the church over against the world. The final thought of the Council suggests that the church is concorporate with the world. The church is not separate from human history but is affected by it and works out her own salvation in the world and finds herself involved in the vicissitudes of the historic process. 'The joys and the hopes, the griefs and the anxieties of the men of this age, especially those who are poor or in any way afflicted' are the joys and hopes, the griefs and anxieties of the followers of Christ who are the church.[4] If the church is the sign of salvation, she is also the sign of a salvation gained by suffering and death, the sign of a divine love that still suffers in the sufferings of mankind: *Jésus sera en agonie jusqu'à la fin du monde*. The tragedies of the human race are the tragedies of the church: 'The Council focuses its attention on the world of men, the whole human family along with the sum of those realities in the midst of which the human family lives. It gazes upon the world which is the theatre of man's history, and carries the marks of his energies, his tragedies, and his triumphs; that world which the Christian sees as created and sustained by its Maker's love, fallen indeed into the bondage of sin, yet emancipated now by Christ. He was crucified and rose again to break the stranglehold of personified Evil, so that this world might be fashioned anew according to God's design and reach its fulfilment'.[5]

Underlying this passage and much more of the Constitution on the Church in the Modern World is a theology of what continental theologians have called 'earthly realities'. God is present to the world which is *both* the theatre of God's salvation and the theatre of man's endeavour. There are not two worlds, one sacred and the other profane. In the present order of things there is no such thing as a created world which, *ex hypothesi*, is outside the saving purpose of God. Men are called to be the collaborators with God in the very process of exploring and using the God-given world in which we live. The unfolding of its mysteries, the harnessing of its power and all the investigation of the world and its resources is also the unfolding of God's purpose for man. *All* is under God's saving grace, and the natural and supernatural, the sacred and the profane, existentially are one.[6] They can be distinguished mentally, and for certain purposes it may be necessary to do so, but in fact they are one. The Spirit of God is everywhere, guiding into good the efforts of all men who do not shut their minds and hearts to him: 'Undergoing death itself for us sinners Christ taught us by example that we, too, must shoulder that cross which the world and the flesh inflict upon those who search after peace and justice. Appointed Lord by his resurrection and given plenary power in heaven and on earth, *Christ is now at work in the hearts of men through the energy of his Spirit.* He arouses not only a desire for the age to come, but, by that very fact, he animates, purifies, and strengthens those *noble longings too by which the human family strives to make its life more human* and to render the whole earth submissive to this goal'.[7]

Perhaps the Council document does not quite make the leap from the church to the world and even though showing a deep compassion for men, its outlook is a shade optimistic. If the Council hesitated at the first fence, Professor Karl Rahner takes two or three in his stride. He goes straight to the eucharist and sees this as the sacrament-sign of the world's death and resurrection. Man experiences in the terrestrial process all the agony of suffering, of disease and death, and it is this experience he brings to the celebration of the eucharist which thus becomes the sacrament not merely of his own experience of suffering, but of the tragic experience of the world. He does not move from the sacred to the profane.[8] He is 'profane', part of the profane world, concorporate with it, *its* experience is *his* experience, that of an engraced man who would give himself in all his 'profanity' to God in encounter with Christ through the eucharist. The barriers between 'church' and 'world', between the sacred and the profane, are irrelevant. In this sense they do not exist and the eucharist is the sacrament-sign that God is present in the world, the sign of the tragic situation of the world, but also the means by which the world here and now can, through participation in the passion and death of Christ, overcome that part of the world that is alienated from God by sin and gradually, painfully, shape itself for the purpose God intends. The world is to be conformed to Christ who at the end will be all in all things, but meanwhile the end to be achieved is exerting its dynamic pull in the situation here and now. The whole of creation is straining towards the consummation, the final revelation (Romans 8:19) but that is *now* being realized in the celebration of the eucharist and in the lives of all who do not refuse God's invitation.

For Rahner, the Christian has first (not necessarily in time) an experience of life and it is this that he brings to the eucharist. This he sees as the sacramental expression of that same life now concretized in the re-enactment of the passion, death and resurrection of Christ. It is thus that the eucharist gathers into itself the whole worldly, secular experience of man and draws it into the process of redemption. At this level, there is no distinction between the sacred and the profane: the world of which man is part is brought into the eucharist which both declares the meaning of life and enables the Christian to offer it to God. In the eucharist, the world is achieving its purpose and through the power of Christ present in it is being carried along to the final purpose, the consummation, the *eschaton*, for which it was made.

It is a noble vision, but it assumes an understanding of the immanence of God in the world process that some may shrink from and a realization that this must be balanced by the divine transcendence in which the process finds its meaning and purpose. It assumes, too, a tragic sense of life which will not always be that of the ordinary worshipper. To this it will be said that this is the understanding he *ought* to have and it is one that can be suggested to him by opening his eyes to what is going on around him. What may be questioned is whether the very close association (almost an identity) between the saving work of Christ in death and resurrection and the 'death' and 'resurrection' of the world does not obliterate the analogous relation between the two. *People* die (spiritually) and rise again (spiritually) in baptism and the eucharist, people suffer and in as far as they are 'in Christ', he is suffering in them. But can all this be applied to nations, cultures and civilizations and if it is, are we not using the terms in a highly analogous and perhaps even romantic sense?

~

With these reservations, we may accept the view as valid and then we realize that there are one or two consequences to be drawn from it. The first concerns the mentality that modern people bring to worship and the second the style of liturgy that will express such a view.

1. If people are to bring their world into the eucharist, they need to see it not as a 'magical' world nor yet as a completely secularized world, alienated from God by its very nature and constitution. Not a magical world, the victim of mysterious 'supernatural' forces, which it is the business of religion and worship to placate and manipulate so that they can be bent to the desires of the worshipper. Modern man no longer thinks of God as a celestial tyrant who sends plague, famine and war to punish a disobedient mankind. If there is plague and famine we try to find the bug that causes the one and provide the material resources to end the other. War, alas, which is a moral problem, is more intractable, but we do know that it is no good *merely* praying for peace. We have to work for it. Worship and all prayer are means by which we seek enlightenment about God's purposes and through which we harmonize our wills with his and work along with him to establish his reign. Our world is substantially a rational world, even if it is rifted by tragedy and even if there remains a penumbra of mystery connected with it. We live in a post-Copernican, post-Einsteinian, post-atomic world and it is in *this* world that God, however improbably, is present. It is this world that young Christians bring to their worship and it is the new insights into

~

its nature that must in one way or another be reflected in the liturgical forms that are offered to them for their use.

2. But for the Christian, if this world is a rational world with a real autonomy, it is not a secularized world, a symbol of the *absence* of God. It came from him in the beginning, it is a sign of love, communicated love, and is evidence, or can be, of his wisdom and beauty. Into this complex earthly reality God inserted the whole incarnational and redeeming process of which the church and its liturgy are the continuation and the sacrament. Earthly realities cannot be indifferent to God, as we see in marriage, where the very material union of man and woman is the stuff of the sacrament which it takes up into itself so that the union expresses the creative love of God among men. The eucharist itself begins in the experience of man, in his desire for self-giving, which he expresses in the humble elements of bread and wine. These by the power of Christ become the bearers of the divine, reconciling love by which man is carried into union with God. Earthly and heavenly interpenetrate in a dynamic come-and-go between God and man. Of this meeting the liturgy is the privileged moment (*kairos*) which manifests and makes concrete the unceasing process.

This, it seems to me, is the context in which desacralization ought to be discussed. As we saw in the first chapter of this book, for primitive man the sacred was the *real* and worship, the re-enactment of the myth, was the way in which he got into contact with the real. We have seen, too, that transposed into the Christian scheme of things, this is a valuable insight. But we cannot return to the world of primitive man. If there is talk of desacralization, it is because modern man, and I include the modern Christian, has moved away from that world and has a different understanding of the world and of its relation to God. Desacralization is not iconoclasm, it is not a wanton desire to destroy an ancient heritage. It is a demand, springing out of a new understanding, for a God and a worship of him that is compatible with new insights and that makes both credible to man as he is here and now. The word 'sacred' is indeed polyvalent. It can mean the divine reality that is at the heart of the liturgy, it can mean the world seen as coming from God and consecrated by Christian work and worship, but it can also mean the envelope, heavily conditioned by a particular culture, of the liturgy that modern people are asked to use in this latter half of the twentieth century. Desacralization for many means the stripping off of this envelope and not the vulgarization of public worship.

Much of the Roman liturgy emerged in what is called a 'sacral' civilization. The Roman pagan civilization was originally such a civilization and its language is still discernible in many of the prayers of the Roman rite. Later, during the formative period of the Roman liturgy, which was, of course, pre-Copernican, with little or no understanding of the operation of secondary causes, the sacralization continued. The emperor was a sacred person, *the* sacred person, and at Constantinople there grew up around him a highly elaborate court ceremonial that is best described as a liturgy. He was approached with awe, as were other great personages, and the language used in addressing them seems to us the ultimate in adulation. Some of this 'sacredness' overflowed on to the bishops, who were given senatorial rank, and especially on to the bishop of Rome. It was in the fourth and fifth centuries that the liturgy was ceremonialized and it is not surprising that the language accompanying it was equally affected. If emperors and bishops were sacred persons and had to be addressed in a special kind of language, God, who was the Super-Sacred, had to be addressed in even more impressive language. Although neither Eastern nor Western liturgies ever lost a deep sense of the reality of God present and available to man in Christ, in both there was an obscuring of the fact that God is our Father and not a heavenly potentate made in the image of the emperor.

This sort of sacredness is no more than a contingent adjunct to the liturgy coming from the culture in which it was formed, and there is no reason at all why it should not be replaced with other forms that are more consonant with our age. Pointers in the direction of a radical change in this matter are the procedures of adaptation going forward in the countries like Africa and India which have not been formed, or only very superficially, by Western culture. They are evolving rites and gestures that are expressive of their mentality, rites and gestures that will, incidentally, 'incarnate' the liturgy in their own culture and that will speak to those who are not yet part of the Christian community.[9] Such adaptation leaves intact the inner zone of the sacred which for Christians is the mystery of Christ. Desacralization in these terms seems not so much to be reprehensible as inevitable.

The problem in industrialized countries is greater. As we observed in the first chapter, modern man has been cut off from his origins, he has a disregard for the past and symbols apparently no longer move him. He has a certain harshness of touch, he is direct, abrupt and unfeeling about modes of speech or ways of acting. The church's answer to this in recent years is to aim at simplicity, even austerity, and most modern Christians demand genuineness, authenticity. The danger, which some say we have not avoided, is that we should cultivate a dull philistinism whether in language, music or the visual arts. How far we have fallen into the danger is anyone's guess, and one suspects that those who bring the accusation are generalizing from a somewhat narrow experience. There are modern churches that are good (and I think beautiful), that are good because they are adapted to the celebration of the liturgy as the church now understands it. And there are more good objects– crucifixes, statues, pictures, frescoes, chalices and a dozen other things–in churches now than there ever were forty years ago. One of the most gratifying aspects of our situation is that architects and their clients are commissioning artists of all kinds to decorate and furnish the churches they are designing. There are churches where the 'new' liturgy is celebrated with all the resources of music and (the right kind of) ceremonial, showing that the liturgy can still be an aesthetic experience. But not everything can be achieved all at once and if the new liturgy is often celebrated inadequately, so was the old. The only difference is that the bad celebration of the old was too often taken for granted.

~

Is it possible to say, in the light of the foregoing considerations, what a modern liturgy should be? Should it be made plain, practical and completely functional so that only those things should be said and done that are absolutely necessary for, say, a eucharist? Are we to deceremonialize it to the point where people behave as if they were at a board meeting, wearing the secular clothes of modern secular life? Is the language to be that of a report on the new sewage farm of Little Muddleton-on-the-Ouse? Are we to banish poetry and music and the plastic arts from our worship and leave the worshippers with nothing but a read word and the staccato gestures of a modern business man? Would all this and much more make the liturgy more available and acceptable to modern man? It is more than doubtful and efforts in the past to reduce the celebration of the eucharist to what was thought to be 'primitive' practice have shown their bankruptcy. In any case, even industrialized man is not going to be satisfied with anything as pedestrian as that. Nor is he impressed with desperate efforts to be 'with it'. Even in worship the church exercises a prophetic function. There she is engaged upon expressing, within the limits of what is possible, values that the (alienated) world does not accept. In worship the church is witnessing to the transcendence of God who, if through his Son he has involved himself in it, remains the purpose, outside it, towards which it is destined. Moreover, God is not a scientist nor yet an industrialist. He is the source of beauty, of a beauty that is reflected in the created world and whose meaning is to be discerned in the 'consecration' of the material universe that was initiated by the incarnation.

What is in fact necessary is a liturgy which over the whole range of its words, gestures and symbols makes available to modern man the mystery of Christ. *Anything* that obscures this purpose must be abolished or kept away from it. Music that obscures the words and hinders the people's response to them, archaic and highly ceremonialized gesture, a symbolism that is piled on the basic Christian symbolism of the liturgy and that needs a key to understand it, all these have no place in common public worship.

There would in fact seem to be three areas where it might be useful to discuss desacralization: language, symbolic gestures and liturgical clothing and buildings.

1. How should we address God? The central revelation of the New Testament is that God is our Father and modern man will have nothing to do with the ogre God, the policeman God, the punishing God, or even the manipulating God who is always tinkering with his universe. As Christians we are the redeemed, adopted children of God and we were taught, as we do at every eucharist, to address him as 'Our Father'. Especially in the English translations of the new rites this point is made again and again. Prayers that in Latin begin *Deus*, in the English begin 'Father' and it is to be supposed that the reason for this is not simply that it is almost impossible to begin an English sentence with 'God' but that the translators felt this better expressed the sense of the prayer for modern Christians.[10] We are, it is true, infinitely less than God and we must approach him humbly, but the filial relationship remains and we did not have to wait for a revision of the liturgy to be told that. For centuries the theologians have told us that we must *not* have a servile fear of God but a filial 'fear' which I suppose we should translate as 'reverence'.

For this reason one could wish that a word like 'placate' was banned from our liturgy. It seems to derive from a pre-Christian stratum of prayer and we find it hardly tolerable to say that God was 'placated' by the death of his own Son. 'Propitiation' is also tricky and when it is applied, as in some prayers over the offerings, to a piece of bread, we feel that if it is to be used at all, it should be used in the context of the eucharistic prayer itself. However, an inspection of the new missal indicates that many of such prayers no longer appear.

As to the *style* of prayers, almost all modern Christians demand that they should be direct, simple in structure and unrhetorical. The tone of public speech nowadays is conversational, unemphatic. Rhetoric of the old style suggests insincerity and no longer moves people. Modern written style is for the most part paratactic, one statement is added to another and Latinized forms have almost disappeared. This may seem to some regrettable, it may be indeed that our language is becoming impoverished, but it seems inevitable that the 'secular' style should be used on 'sacred' occasions. Certainly, this is one way, if a small one, that modern liturgy can be made acceptable to modern people who do not want to have to put on a special culture to worship God.

In fact, much of this has been achieved already in the English translations which have been offered to us in recent years. This does not mean that they have always been as good as they might be, even taking into account the convention the translators have adopted. But complete success is too much to ask for all at once and it remains to be proved that any other style is satisfactory. In the early days of turning liturgical Latin into English, the experiments then made were far from happy.

There is, too, the question of the *literary form* of certain prayers, notably the collects and the eucharistic prayers. The former have been much extolled for their concision and brevity. But these are precisely the qualities that provide difficulties. In practice, they are over almost before the people have been able to take in their content. It is true that they are presidential prayers and there is no question here of the validity and appropriateness of the presidential role. But the form does need thinking about and there would seem to be some official evidence that it is not always thought to be as satisfactory as it might be. In the revised liturgy of the Holy Week we learn that local conferences of bishops may *add* acclamations to the General Intercessions on Good Friday. This is a pointer in the right direction. The collect-form needs teasing out and possibly it should approximate to that of the prayer of the faithful in the Mass. That is, it would be perfectly possible to state the main theme of the prayer in an invitation, give time for reflection and then sum up the whole petition in one or two short phrases to which responses for the people could be attached.

As we have observed elsewhere, much the same could be done for the eucharistic prayer. Interventions, in addition to the acclamation after the consecration, could be arranged at other points too, as has in fact been done with the two alternative prayers of blessing in the baptismal rite. Granted that the eucharistic prayer is the supremely presidential prayer, it does not follow that it should be a monologue.

There is another matter related to this. While I would insist that any public liturgy must have a fixed pattern (otherwise all is confusion), it does not follow that you have to have fixed forms.[11] Improvised prayers, especially when there is nothing else in a service, have their dangers that are well known, but our liturgy is still too rigid in this respect. Might there not be room for *extempore* prayer? For instance, the postcommunion prayers often seem remote from the concerns of the local congregation. Why should we always have a fixed text at this point? It is true, as we have observed, that the celebrant may use the communion verse to lead the people to prayer at this point. But then, why have to say a fixed text as well? This is perhaps a small matter, but sometimes our worship seems *over*-hieratic and a little freedom would do much to humanize it.

2. The church has now recognized that gestures may have different meanings in different parts of the world and does not insist that they should always be the same everywhere. It is said that the hand-clasp in the marriage service is unacceptable in certain parts of Africa. It may be replaced by something else. The celebrant no longer has to *kiss* the book after the gospel: he may reverence the book in some other way, by bowing for instance (GI 232). Genuflexions to bishops and such like personages have, mercifully, been abolished (a nice piece of desacralization!) and on the positive side, the Hindu sign of greeting (the closing of the hands before the breast) has now been introduced into the liturgy in India.

These are but indications that there is still much to be done to work out acceptable gestures in the Western world. It will have to be done by experiment for we have lost the art of using our bodies, and it would seem to be a task the church could very usefully perform.

Fundamentally, it means not that someone should devise beautiful gestures but that the Christian community should ask itself: what is the *meaning* of, say, the sign of peace? Why do we stand or kneel for certain parts of the service and are there other ways in which we can express what we discover to be the meaning of these attitudes? Is it quite beyond the bounds of possibility that the congregation should approach the sanctuary and gather round it for the eucharistic action and thus learn the meaning of being together? This in fact happens quite spontaneously in smaller and less formal groups, so it *is* natural. What stands in its way are the large amorphous congregations that have been forced on us by circumstances and which now have come to be regarded as normal. Whatever can be done about that situation, it is interesting to observe that the smaller community finds the postures and gestures that are appropriate to the occasion. Again, it is worth emphasizing that these gestures are found in a natural 'secular' situation and the members of the community bring into their worship certain 'worldly' attitudes.

When we come to the clothing of the liturgy we have to apply a rather different set of criteria. Special clothes are part of 'celebration', part of the décor that we saw was a necessary part of celebration. There is, then, nothing particularly 'sacred' about putting on such clothes. On the other hand, if we are to judge by what is now being designed and made, there is considerable dissatisfaction with the style of liturgical clothes, even those of better quality, that has been common in recent centuries. The trend has definitely set towards flowing simplicity and austerity of decoration. Yet, such clothes are 'unworldly' and we have to ask whether they are necessary.

The question must be asked first of the president. In recent years, some priests have been seen to celebrate in the more intimate assembly in their ordinary clothes upon which, frequently, they have laid a stole. A piece of ecclesiastical embroidery added to jacket and trousers was so incongruous as to be risible, and one wonders what mystical significance the former added to the latter.

It may be said, I think, that all liturgical celebrations have a focal point. For the building it is the altar;[12] of the whole service it is the president. That does not mean that he should or even may absorb all the ministerial functions of the rite but he has to direct them and should be visibly in control of them. He has a special relationship to Christ the Priest and a special relationship to the people he is there to serve. Just as the former is externalized by a sacrament, so the latter may fittingly be marked by a special dress. The necessity is first psychological and secondly, in the broad sense, sacramental. At the same time, what is required in one kind of assembly, as, for instance, in a large church where his role needs to be emphasized, is not necessarily right for another. One can but regret that the Instruction on House Masses[13] rigidly insisted that the celebrant should wear everything he does in church. In fact, a certain simplification of liturgical vesture is already apparent. One garment, with a stole worn outside it, is becoming common and this, one would have thought, was sufficient for celebration wherever it takes place.

If it be said that this is to sacralize a perfectly normal function, it can only be replied that just as with the notion of community, as with the need to find suitable gestures for worship, so here, it may very well be the task of the church to discover appropriate signs for a liturgy which cannot do without them. In so doing, she may well teach the 'world' a lesson about old, far-off, forgotten things which are only old and far-off because the world has forgotten that they enshrined certain human values.[14]

Should other members of the assembly be vested? This is more problematical and the consensus seems to be that readers should not. They come from the assembly and should visibly remain members of it even when performing their function. If, however, one of them carries the Book of the Gospels in a procession whose participants are vested, it would seem better that he were also. The vesting of others, servers and choir, seems to be a matter of aesthetics. A collection of bejeaned or short-trousered males on the sanctuary is usually not a pretty sight and their sartorial idiosyncrasies are better disguised. But there is no case at all for dressing them up as 'little clergymen'.[15] A single, well-made garment is both more practical and better to look at.

There are those who will say that all this is unnecessary. Perhaps so, but I wish I could be persuaded that modern dress is beautiful. Objectively it is quite bizarre. However, much will depend on the mood of the assembly, on its intimacy or otherwise, and on the very building in which it meets.

3. In recent years there has been a vast debate, which continues, about, first, the kind of building that is needed for the celebration of the liturgy and then, whether there should be church-buildings

at all, set apart exclusively for worship.[16]

As to the first, the guide-lines were laid down in the Instruction *Inter Oecumenici* of 1964[17] and repeated in the General Instruction now included in the *Missale Romanum* of 1970. There are three principles: the shape of the church must be such as to allow the people to act as the celebrating community, the altar is the focal point of the whole building and all other elements, side-altars, shrines, statues and the rest must be subordinated to the first two. Most newly-built churches have conformed with some degree of success to these principles, but there remain the vast numbers of traditional churches throughout the world. Adaptation has sometimes been possible, though not always. In any case, there is the continuing problem of providing for the needs of great numbers of people of the vast industrial parishes and the consequence, that in these circumstances anything like a community cannot be established. The main solution to this has been the search for and animation of sub-groups within the parish which can be brought together for what one must call celebration with a human dimension. But, where the church does by its shape suggest community, where the hard and fast divisions made by screens and receding sanctuaries no longer exist, where it is possible to establish a real *rapport* between president and people, some sense of community, at least during the time of worship, can be fostered. In this *ambiance* attitudes, gestures, vestments can play their part without ever turning the worship into a hieratic performance.

The second question is much more complex and differing points of view are hotly contested.

One view is that to set up churches, sacred buildings that are never used for anything except worship, is to take religion, worship and so the people, *away* from secular life. It is to suggest to them that 'world' and 'church' are opposites, that the world is not merely secular but secularized, that God is absent from it and can only be found 'in church'. It may be so, though much will depend on the mentality people bring with them to church. Buildings as such, and divorced from community, can do very little, and the promoters of the 'secular' church may themselves be suffering from a certain historically conditioned hang-over. In the nineteenth century, churches appear to have been purposely disfunctional; they were a protest or even a defiance of a style of worship and by implication of the religion and society that supported it. There was much of this in Pugin's attitude. But most modern churches no longer point a finger of defiance to the world. They settle into its background and visibly emerge from its culture – for good and for ill! The important question is whether even modern churches are expressions of a community or merely religious service-stations for a number of people who happen to live near it. In other words, the crucial test is the quality of the service that the community the building is supposed to express is giving to the wider community which surrounds it. To this matter we shall return.

The difficulties on a practical level are greater and more important. A conventional church-building is used for a single purpose and for a limited number of hours per week. The cost of such buildings is enormous and their maintenance in heating, lighting and other necessary services is considerable. The question is pressed whether Christians are justified in this sort of expenditure in a world that suffers want on a very considerable scale. Are not such buildings not so much the sign of the serving church as its contradiction? Is it a good thing for the pilgrim church to weigh itself down with property? Should we give the impression that Christians are very well installed in this world order, and will not its witness to unworldly values be obscured? Then there are the needs of the Christian people, whether they may be described as a community or not, needs that go far beyond worship. Should not the parish buildings be such that they can foster a spirit of community, perhaps even create community where otherwise it does not exist? If they can, then buildings do become important, and so we are brought to the question of the multi-purpose church.

This is being strongly urged but it is necessary to insist that there is no inherent virtue in a building of whatever sort. The question that has to be asked – and answered – is whether a multi-purpose building is going to serve a community already existing or that can be brought into existence. If around the church-complex there is a natural community – and such still exist – with sufficient provision to enable people to meet, to know each other and to engage in the activities that people normally seek, there would seem to be very little case for the multi-purpose church. But where there is nothing but a church-building, where you have new areas and people are alienated from their surroundings, which they have not chosen, and where many if not most have only the most tenuous attachment to any kind of church, there is a very strong case for the multi-purpose building.

The first thing necessary is that these people should be able to make a *human* contact with the Christian community and this the right kind of building can very powerfully assist. It will be a place into which flow the normal activities of human life, at least in its leisure moments. Ideally it will be placed at the centre of local life, easily accessible to people who come to shop, to conduct whatever business they have with the local authorities, where in fact they naturally meet. Where a new community is forming the church may be able to offer certain facilities to the public authorities who have not yet set up their organizations. In any case, there will be other needs that are not officially catered for at all: the care of the old, nursery provision for children of pre-school age and facilities for youth. If at the heart of this complex there is a 'worship room' which is known and preferably visible and if the clergy or laity are known to be available to people whatever their needs, the building will help in the work that waits to be done and it will be justified by the work it makes possible. But all depends on the *people*, both those who are trying to serve and those who come seeking various kinds of service.

To this extent, but to this extent only, a building can be said to be 'missionary'. It is positive, turned towards the world instead of away from it, it is welcoming rather than repelling, it *can* become a centre of ordinary life and through the ministry of its servants it can do something to reach out to those to whom the gospel is to be proclaimed. For it needs to be emphasized that 'the church' is people and as we have learned from Vatican II, the church is by nature missionary and the whole people bear the responsibility and burden of mission. Buildings can help or hinder, but if the most perfect multi-purpose church ever thought up were run as a conventional church, if the community were concerned with no more than its own worship and its own affairs, it would be no more missionary than a neo-Gothic structure beautifully arranged for medieval usage.

Nor should it be thought that such a building is without its difficulties. Anyone who has had to preside over a parish where the only building was a parish hall will know the daunting tasks that present themselves. There are those who argue that the 'worship room' should be used for secular activities to emphasize (such is the argument) that there are no divisions between the sacred and the secular. But, in practice, such activities are likely to take place on Saturday evening, may go on to a late hour, and then who is going to clear up the mess?

How can the building be ventilated and prepared for worship the next day? There are other problems of supervision and maintenance which may be even greater. There is a case for the multi-purpose building and in many areas it is a strong one, but it is probable that experience will show that if it is to serve the Christian mission successfully, the 'worship room' will have to be reserved for worship.

The discussion could be continued and whatever may be decided in detail, there is one over-riding consideration. The Christian community exists to serve others and it should be as close to them as possible, showing a solidarity with them in their needs, their sufferings and their joys. It is then that the 'others' will discover that 'church' can be part of ordinary life and may become part of theirs. If the buildings can become in some way the sign of this concern, they will be an authentic expression of the church's mission.

~

The purpose of the foregoing considerations is to show that the liturgy, without detriment to its essential structure, can be made more accessible to modern people, that it can be brought closer to their mentality and meet their needs more effectively. The result of such a mild desacralization is that the life of our society could more easily flow into and affect the celebration of the liturgy, making it visibly the expression of people of this generation. The young in particular would not feel alienated and it would be much more possible to celebrate life (in the sense of Rahner), the life of the world as we know it and experience it. At present the gap between worship and world is too wide. Liturgy still looks too much like the cultic preoccupation of a minority grouping, and although it has been transformed beyond the dreams of even the most progressive in five years, it still bears too many marks of its past.

We should be clear, however, that liturgy is not a missionary device and attempts to make the liturgy more accessible to people of our time should not be mistaken for propaganda efforts to 'bring them in', to capture the unbelieving multitudes. There is indeed a regrettable tendency to expose the eucharist to those without Christian faith. The eucharist is the sign of the believing, Christian community and whenever the faith of the community is diluted the credibility of the sign is diminished.[18] Once again, it is for the members of the community to take the gospel to others who must be prepared for participation in the worship of the community.

~

But the liturgy, and in a particular way the eucharist, remains the sign of the missionary, pilgrim church, and if we are to take the Constitution on the Church in the Modern World seriously, the liturgy of the church must be relevant to the world, must be accessible to the world, if it is to become the authentic sign of both the church and the world. But it must become more than sign. It must be the means by which this world can be lifted up to God, drawn into his continuing creative purpose so that in the end it can be transfigured, bearing the image of the Risen Christ who triumphed over sin, evil, pain, suffering and death.

This is the final message of the Second Vatican Council. The pilgrim church is moving towards the consummation and it and the whole world are destined to be transformed so that there will be a new heaven and a new earth: 'We do not know the time of the consummation of the earth and all humanity. Nor do we know how all things will be transformed. . . . But we are taught that God is preparing a new dwelling place and a new earth where justice will abide and whose blessedness will answer and surpass all the longings for peace which spring up in the human heart.' But the end is now, is being realized in the processes of human history: 'For here grows the body of a new human family, a body which even now is able to give some kind of foreshadowing of the new age.' It is through the liturgy, 'the source of all the church's power', that this is being achieved now—or can be, if men can bring to it the whole of their living. Earth and heaven co-inhere, the 'sacred' and the 'profane' find their point of juncture in the worship that Christian people offer to God and 'if earthly progress must be carefully distinguished from the growth of God's kingdom', it is nevertheless true that 'the former can contribute to the better ordering of human society' and is consequently a matter of vital concern to the Christian church.

But this human society which is now being painfully shaped towards God's purpose, is destined to be transformed: 'After we have obeyed the Lord, and in his Spirit nurtured on earth the values of human dignity, brotherhood and freedom, and indeed all the good fruits of our nature and enterprise, *we will find them again*, but freed of stain, burnished and *transfigured*. This will be so when Christ hands over to the Father "a kingdom eternal and universal: a kingdom of truth and life, of holiness and grace, of justice, love and peace".[19] On this earth *that kingdom is already present in mystery*. When the Lord returns, it will be brought to full flower' (Church in Modern World, 39).

This teaching suggests the final importance of a liturgy that will welcome and embrace all earthly values. For it is this liturgy that lies at the heart of the process by which men and things are being slowly transformed until they bear the image of Christ. In the eucharist there is that same power of reconciliation, union and restoration that was present in the redeeming work of Christ on the cross and this power is made available to mankind now. It is God's intention that all things should be brought under Christ as head and that all things should be offered through him, should be purified, renewed, and their hidden potentialities revealed. But the daily offering of the world is but a preparation for the final eucharist when Christ, the Second Adam and the High Priest of the human race, will offer all things to his Father, handing them over to him so that he may be all in all.[20]

# Notes
~

[1] Such an impression might have been gathered from some of the prayers in the missal and it is interesting to observe that they have been corrected. Cf. II Advent, postcommunion, where we ask that we may set a right value on earthly things (**sapienter perpendere**) instead of 'despising' (**despicere**) them.

[2] And sometimes it is a very dramatic witness. Mother Teresa probably reveals God's love to people far more effectively than all the speeches of popes and bishops.

[3] Isaiah 11:12 (perhaps in a slightly accommodated sense).

[4] Constitution on the Church in the Modern World, introduction.

[5] **Ibid.**

[6] Karl Rahner, **Mission and Grace** (London, 1963), pp. 71-85.

[7] Constitution on the Church on the Modern World, p. 236.

[8] See Karl Rahner, 'Secular Life and the Sacraments', **The Tablet** (13 March 1971), pp. 267-8.

[9] It is said, too, that in some parts of Africa, **Eastern** liturgies are proving to be more acceptable to the various peoples there rather than even an adapted Roman liturgy.

[10] If it is said that they were doing a spot of demythologizing on the side, it can be answered that the New Testament did a fairly extensive job of demythologizing the Old.

[11] For further discussion, see J. D. Crichton, 'Liturgical Forms', **The Way**, Supplement (Autumn 1970).

[12] See the Instruction, **Inter Oecumenici**, of 1964, 91.

[13] 15 May 1969: **Notitiae**, 51 (February 1970), pp. 50-5.

[14] The young at any rate are abandoning the dull 'business-like' dress of their elders and are indulging in the fantastic. Perhaps they do not succeed very well, but they **are** trying to 'celebrate'.

[15] The Italian word **chierichetti** is a bit of a give-away.

[16] See, *inter alia*, the many publications of the Institute for Liturgy and Architecture, Birmingham University.

[17] For commentary, see J. D. Crichton in **Changes in the Liturgy** (London, 1965), pp. 86–104.

[18] I am thinking of certain weddings and funerals where the congregation may largely be made up of non-believers. Are we right in exposing the 'sacred mysteries' to them? With funerals certainly the Mass can take place either beforehand or at some other time altogether.

[19] Preface of the Feast of Christ the King.

[20] Ephesians 1:10; 1 Corinthians 15:25–28.

# Name Index

Names which appear in the main text have been indexed. Those appearing only in the end-notes have been included if quoted extensively in the text.

# Subject Index

Major references within a sequence are indicated by **bold type**.